THE MASTER KEY SYSTEM

Other Books in the Study Guide Series

Narrative of the Life of Frederick Douglass
The Art of War with Study Guide
The Magic of Believing with Study Guide
The Prince with Study Guide
The Richest Man In Babylon with Study Guide
The Science of Getting Rich with Study Guide
The Secret of the Ages with Study Guide
Think and Grow Rich with Study Guide

THE MASTER KEY SYSTEM

with Study Guide
by Theresa Puskar

CHARLES F. HAANEL

Published 2022 by Gildan Media LLC
aka G&D Media
www.GandDmedia.com

THE MASTER KEY SYSTEM WITH STUDY GUIDE. Copyright © 2022 by G&D Media. Afterword copyright © 2022 by Joe Vitale. All rights reserved.

No part of this book may be reproduced or transmitted in any form, by any means, (electronic, photocopying, recording, or otherwise) without the prior written permission of the author. No liability is assumed with respect to the use of the information contained within. Although every precaution has been taken, the author and publisher assume no liability for errors or omissions. Neither is any liability assumed for damages resulting from the use of the information contained herein.

Front Cover design by David Rheinhardt of Pyrographx

Interior design by Meghan Day Healey of Story Horse, LLC

Library of Congress Cataloging-in-Publication Data is available upon request

ISBN: 978-1-7225-0524-0

10 9 8 7 6 5 4 3 2 1

Contents

Note from the Study Guide Author 7

Foreword 11

Introduction 13

Part One 59

Part Two 72

Part Three 86

Part Four 100

Part Five 113

Part Six 125

Part Seven 138

Part Eight 152

Part Nine 166

Part Ten 181

Part Eleven 194

Part Twelve 208

Part Thirteen 220

Part Fourteen 233

Part Fifteen 246

Part Sixteen 259

Part Seventeen 274

Part Eighteen 288

Part Nineteen 301

Part Twenty 313

Part Twenty-One 327

Part Twenty-Two 341

Part Twenty-Three 355

Part Twenty-Four 368

Afterword 382

Glossary 384

Questions and Answers 394

Note

from the Study Guide Author

"Those who will give no attention to the world without;
will seek only to ascertain the truth..."
—CHARLES F. HAANEL

Charles F. Haanel wrote the first edition of *The Master Key System* in 1912. This was twenty-five years before Napoleon Hill created his masterpiece, *Think and Grow Rich*. He truly was a pioneer bringing the wisdom of the Law of Attraction to the masses. In disseminating the wisdom of this powerful book over a century later, I am amazed at how universal and timeless its message is. Now more than ever, as chaos, misinformation, fear and anxiety continue to mount in the world, as Haanel so clearly articulates, you would be wise to seek your power from the True Source within you, and he shows you why and how.

This brilliant and pioneering book takes you on a very specific and concise journey towards moving from a place of lack conscious into a world of possibilities and potentialities. While there have been many books written on this subject, what I like about this book is that Haanel provides you will specific, direct, and intentionally paced steps that support movement from the external world in which you suffer, into an internal world of vast knowing and great peace. In my own journey of personal development, I have recently learned that seeking that which I desire from a place of desperation, obsession and suffering does not work. The Universe merely matches our suffering state with more of it! However, when we ask from a peaceful place of joy, flow and harmony that we can find within us, the Universe energetically joins us in our inner sanctuary, and benevolently responds.

A word of caution: At times the verbiage in this book can be dense and difficult to comprehend. If you have ever been privileged enough to sit with an enlightened master, you may have experienced the same. If you stay the course, you will find great wisdom and the potential to experience massive shifts within your psyche, and ultimately within your life experiences.

To assist you in further understanding the teachings, I have formulated corresponding Comprehension Surveys for each of the 24 Parts. Each survey statement I created, corresponds with the same number in Haanel's chapters. They are reflections of his original message that are directed towards your own personal experience. You will respond to each statement, rating your understanding of it on a scale from 1 to 10. For example, Part 15, #20: Haanel writes, *"We know that the Universal Thought has for its goal the creation of form, and we know that the individual thought is likewise forever attempting to express itself in form, and we know that the word is a thought form, and a sentence is a combination of thought forms, therefore, if we wish our ideal to be beautiful or strong, we must see that the words out; of which this temple will eventually be created are exact, that they are put together carefully, because accuracy in building words and sentences is the highest form of architecture in civilization and is a passport to success."* The corresponding Comprehension Survey question I created: "You and Universal Thought have a joint goal to create. In order to create a temple of beauty and strength, you must take care and build with accuracy and highest intentions (you would then rate yourself on the scale). At the end of the segment, you will tally your score, and uncover your overall comprehension of the material.

You may find it more effective to read each of Haanel's statements, and then do the corresponding Comprehension Survey question immediately upon reading it. Doing so will immediately reinforce your understanding. You may choose to read through each of Haanel's chapters, and then do the corresponding survey. Whatever you choose, I encourage you to do the surveys. They will assist in propelling you into action, as opposed to merely reading another book.

While you may be tempted to highly rate your knowledge in response to each question, take time to sit with each survey statement, allowing it to reverberate throughout your mind and body. Have you experienced it as truth, or are you citing what you have heard but not really experienced? Do an honest and candid inventory with yourself. If you have read a lot of self-development books, you may "know" the principles in your intellect, but have not fully integrated them into your experiences. Taking the time to reflect on the questions and respond accordingly, will allow them to move from your conscious to your subconscious mind. When you mindfully take each of the 24 surveys, you shift from reading basic theory into committed integration. After each Comprehension Survey, I encourage you to reflect on your results. Ideally, have a journal in hand and be ready to write any insights you gain in both your waking and sleeping states.

One of the greatest strengths of this book are the experiential exercises that Charles Haanel very intentionally and methodically asks you to do each of the 24 weeks that are required to reach this book. I would also encourage you to stop and do his exercises, along with the Comprehension Surveys. Promising yourself that you will go back and do them will not work. As Haanel states throughout the book, knowing without applying is futile. You will likely activate the saboteur within you, keeping you from taking the necessary action steps to shift your life.

As Charles Haanel asserts throughout this wonderful book, dream big and know that nothing is impossible in the Limitless Creative Field provided by Universal Source Intelligence.

Theresa Puskar
Study Guide Author

Foreword

Nature compels us all to move through life. We could not remain stationary however much we wished. Every right-thinking person wants not merely to move through life like a sound-producing, perambulating plant, but to develop—to improve—and to continue the development mentally to the close of physical life.

This development can occur only through the improvement of the quality of individual thought and the ideals, actions and conditions that arise as a consequence. Hence a study of the creative processes of thought and how to apply them is of supreme importance to each one of us. This knowledge is the means whereby the evolution of human life on earth may be hastened and uplifted in the process.

Humanity ardently seeks "The Truth" and explores every avenue to it. In this process it has produced a special literature, which ranges the whole gamut of thought from the trivial to the sublime—up from Divination, through all the Philosophies, to the final lofty Truth of "The Master Key."

The "Master Key" is here given to the world as a means of tapping the great Cosmic Intelligence and attracting from it that which corresponds to the ambitions, and aspirations of each reader.

Every thing and institution we see around us, created by human agency, had first to exist as a thought in some human mind. Thought therefore is constructive. Human thought is the spiritual power of the cosmos operating through its creature man. "The Master Key" instructs the reader how to use that power, and use it both constructively and creatively. The things and conditions we desire to become realities we must first create in thought. "The Master Key" explains and guides the process.

"The Master Key" teaching has hitherto been published in the form of a Correspondence Course of 24 lessons, delivered to students one per week for 24 weeks. The reader, who now receives the whole 24 parts at one time, is warned not to attempt to read the book like a novel, but to treat it as a course of study and conscientiously to imbibe the meaning of each part—reading and re-reading one part only per week before proceeding to the next. Otherwise the later parts will tend to be misunderstood and the reader's time and money will be wasted.

Used as thus instructed "The Master Key" will make of the reader a greater, better personality, and equipped with a new power to achieve any worthy personal purpose and a new ability to enjoy life's beauty and wonder.

F.H. BURGESS

Introduction

Before any environment, successful or otherwise, can be created, action of some kind is necessary, and before any action is possible, there must be thought of some kind, either conscious or unconscious, and as thought is a product of mind, it becomes evident that Mind is the creative center from which all activities proceed.

It is not expected that any of the inherent laws which govern the modern business world as it is at present constituted can be suspended or repealed by any force on the same plane, but it is axiomatic that a higher law may overcome a lower one. Tree life causes the sap to ascend, not by repealing the law of gravity but by surmounting it.

To control circumstances a knowledge of certain scientific principles of mind-action is required. Such knowledge is a most valuable asset. It may be gained by degrees and put into practice as fast as learned. Power over circumstances is one of its fruits; health, harmony and prosperity are assets upon its balance sheet. It costs only the labor of harvesting its great resources.

The naturalist who spends much of his time in observing visible phenomena is constantly creating power in that portion of his brain set apart for observation. The result is that he becomes very much more expert and skillful in knowing what he sees, and grasping an infinite number of details at a glance, than does his unobserving friend. He has reached this facility by exercise of his brain. He deliberately chose to enlarge his brain power in the line of observation, so he deliberately exercised that special faculty, over and over, with increasing attention and concentration. Now we have the result a man learned in the lore of observation far above his fellows. Or, on the other hand, one can, by stolid inaction, allow the delicate brain matter to harden and ossify until his whole life is barren and fruitless.

Every thought tends to become a material thing. Our desires are seed thoughts that have a tendency to sprout and grow and blossom and bear fruit. We are sowing these seeds every day. What shall the harvest be? Each of us today is the result of his past thinking. Later we shall be the result of what we are now thinking. We create our own character, personality and environment by the thought which we originate, or entertain. Thought seeks its own. The law of mental attraction is an exact parallel to the law of atomic affinity. Mental currents are as real as electric, magnetic or heat currents. We attract the currents with which we are in harmony—are we selecting those which will be conducive to our success? This is the important question.

Lines of least resistance are formed by the constant action of the mind. The activity of the brain reacts upon the particular faculty of the brain employed. The latent power of the mind is developed by constant exercise. Each form of its activity becomes more perfect by practice. Exercises for the development of the mind present a variety of motives for consideration. They involve the development of the perceptive faculties, the cultivation of the emotions, the quickening of the imagination, the symmetrical unfoldment of the intuitive faculty, which without being able to give a reason frequently impels or prohibits choice, and finally the power of the mind may be cultivated by the development of the moral character.

"The greatest man," said Seneca, "is he who chooses right with invincible determination." The greatest power of the mind, then, depends upon its exercise in moral channels, and therefore requires that every conscious mental effort should involve a moral end. A developed moral consciousness modifies consideration of motives, and increases the force and continuity of actions; consequently the well developed symmetrical character necessitates good physical, mental and moral health, and this combination creates initiative, power, resistless force, and necessarily success.

It will be found that Nature is constantly seeking to express Harmony in all things, is for ever trying to bring about an harmonious adjustment, for every discord, every wound, every difficulty; therefore when thought is harmonious, nature begins to create the material conditions, the possession of which is necessary in order to make up an harmonious environment.

When we understand that mind is the great creative power, what does not become possible? With Desire as the great creative energy, can we not see why Desire should be cultivated, controlled and directed in our lives and destinies? Men and women of strong mentality, who dominate those around them, and often those far removed from them, really emanate currents charged with power which, coming in contact with the minds of others, causes the desires of the latter to be in accord with the mind of the strong individuality. Great masters of men possess this power to a marked degree. Their influence is felt far and near, and they secure compliance with their wishes by making others "want" to act in accord with them. In this way men of strong Desire and Imagination may and do exert powerful influence over the minds of others, leading the latter in the way desired. The magnetic persons attract, allure and draw. They are emotional, and capture the will of others.

No man is ever created without the inherent power in himself to help himself. The personality that understands its own intellectual and moral power of conquest will certainly assert itself. It is this truth which an enfamined world craves today.

The possibility of asserting a slumbering intellectual courage that clearly discerns, and a moral courage that grandly undertakes is open to all. There is a divine potency in every human being.

We speak of the sun as "rising" and "setting," though we know that this is simply an appearance of motion. To our senses the earth is apparently standing still, and yet we know it is revolving rapidly. We speak of a bell as a "sounding body," yet we know that all that the bell can do is to produce vibrations in the air. When these vibrations come at the rate of sixteen a second they cause a sound to be heard in the mind. It is possible for the mind to hear vibrations up to the rate of 38,000 a second. When the number increases beyond this all is silence again; so that we know that the sound is not in the bell; it is in our own mind.

We speak and even think of the sun as "giving light," yet we know it is simply giving forth energy which produces vibrations in the ether at the rate of four hundred trillion a second, causing what are termed light waves, so that we know that what we call light is simply a mode of motion, and the only light that there is, is the sensation caused in the mind by the motion of these waves. When the number of vibrations increases, the light changes in color, each change in color being caused by shorter and more rapid vibrations; so that although we speak of the rose as being red, the grass as being green, or the sky as being blue, we know that these colors exist only in our minds, and are the sensation experienced by us as the result of the vibrations of light. When the vibrations are reduced below four hundred trillion a second, they no longer affect us as light but we experience the sensation of heat.

So we have come to know that appearances exist for us only in our consciousness. Even time and space become annihilated, time being only the experience of succession, there being no past or future except as a thought relation to the present. In the last analysis, therefore, we know that one principle governs and controls all there is. Every atom is for ever conserved; whatever is parted with must inevitably be received somewhere. It cannot perish and it only exists for use. It can go only where it is attracted, and therefore required. We can receive only what we give, and we may give only to those who can receive; and it remains with us to determine our rate of growth and the degree of harmony that we shall express.

The laws under which we live are designed solely for our advantage. These laws are immutable and we cannot escape from their operation. All the great eternal forces act in solemn silence, but it is in our power to place ourselves in harmony with them and thus express a life of comparative peace and happiness.

Difficulties, inharmonies, obstacles, indicate that we are either refusing to give out what we no longer need, or refusing to accept what we require. Growth is attained through an exchange of the old for the new, of the good for the better; it is a conditional or reciprocal action, for each of us is a complete thought entity and the completeness makes it possible for us to receive only as we give. We cannot obtain what we lack if we tenaciously cling to what we have.

The Principle of Attraction operates to bring to us only what may be to our advantage. We are able consciously to control our conditions as we come to sense the purpose of what we attract, and are able to extract from each experience only what we require for our further growth. Our ability to do this determines the degree of harmony or happiness we attain.

The ability to appropriate what we require for our growth continually increases as we reach higher planes and broader visions, and the greater our ability to know what we require, the more certain we shall be to discern its presence, to attract it and to absorb it. Nothing may reach us except what is necessary for our growth. All conditions and experiences that come to us do so for our benefit. Difficulties and obstacles will continue to come until we absorb their wisdom and gather from them the essentials of further growth. That we reap what we sow, is mathematically exact. We gain permanent strength exactly to the extent of the effort required to overcome our difficulties.

The inexorable requirements of growth demand that we exert the greatest degree of attraction for what is perfectly in accord with us. Our highest happiness will be best attained through our understanding of and conscious co-operation with natural laws.

Our mind-forces are often bound by the paralyzing suggestions that come to us from the crude thinking of the race, and which are accepted and acted upon without question. Impressions of fear, of worry, of disability and of inferiority are given us daily. These are sufficient reasons in themselves why men achieve so little—why the lives of multitudes are so barren of results, when all the time there are possibilities within them which need only the liberating touch of appreciation and wholesome ambition to expand into real greatness.

Women, perhaps even more than men, have been subject to these conditions. This is true because of their finer susceptibilities making them more open to thought-vibrations from other minds, and because the flood of negative and repressive thoughts has been aimed more especially at them.

But it is being overcome. Florence Nightingale overcame it when she rose in the Crimea to heights of tender sympathy and executive ability before unknown among women. Clara Barton, the head of the Red Cross, overcame it when she wrought a similar work in the armies of the Union. Jenny Lind overcame it when she showed her ability to command enormous financial rewards while at the same time gratifying the passionate desire of her nature and reaching the front rank of her day in musical art. And there is a long list of women singers, philanthropists, writers and actresses who have proved themselves capable of reaching the greatest literary, dramatic, artistic and sociological achievement.

Women as well as men are beginning to do their own thinking. They have awakened to some conception of their possibilities. They demand that if life holds any secrets, these shall be disclosed. At no previous time has the influence and potency of thought received such careful and discriminating investigation. While a few seers have grasped the great fact that mind is the universal substance, the basis of all things, never before has this vital truth penetrated the more general consciousness. Many minds are now striving to give this wonderful truth definite utterance. Modern science has taught us that light and sound are simply different intensities of motion, and this may lead to discoveries of forces within man that could not have been conceived of until this revelation was made.

A new era has dawned, and now, standing in its light, man sees something of the vastness of the meaning of life—something of its grandeur. Within that life is the germ of infinite potencies. One feels convinced that man's possibility of attainment cannot be measured, that boundary lines to his onward march are unthinkable. Standing on this height he finds that he can draw new power to himself from the infinite energy of which he is a part.

Some men seem to attract success, power, wealth, attainment, with very little conscious effort; others conquer with great difficulty; still others fail altogether to reach their ambitions, desires and ideals. Why is this so? Why should some men realize their ambitions easily, others with difficulty, and still others not at all? The cause cannot be physical, else the most perfect men, physically, would be the most successful. The difference, therefore, must be mental—must be in the mind; hence mind must be the creative force, must constitute the sole difference between men. It is mind, therefore, which overcomes environment and every other obstacle in the path of men.

It is the actualizing of interior quality through the creative power of thought which has given us great leaders like Alexander, Napoleon, Cromwell, Marlborough and Washington; captains of industry like Carnegie, Morgan, Rockefeller and Leverhulme; inventors like Stephenson, Morse, Marconi, Edison, Tesla, and hosts of others. If, then, the only difference between men lies in their ability to think, to use and control their thought, to develop it—if the secret of all success, all power, all attainment is the creative power of mind, the force of thought—surely the ability of think correctly should become the paramount object of every man.

When the creative power of thought is fully understood, its effect will be seen to be marvelous. But such results cannot be secured without proper application, diligence and concentration. The student will find that the laws governing in the mental and spiritual world are as fixed and infallible as in the material world. To secure the desired results, then, it is necessary to know the law and to comply with it. A proper compliance with the law will be found to produce the desired result with invariable exactitude. The student who learns that power comes from within, that he is weak only because he has depended on help from outside, and who unhesitatingly throws himself on his own thought, instantly rights himself, stands erect, assumes a dominant attitude, and works miracles.

Scientists tell us that we live in the universal ether. This is formless, of itself, but it is pliable, and forms about us, in us and around us, according to our thought and word. We set it into activity by that which we think. Then that which manifests to us objectively is that we have thought or said.

Thought is governed by law. The reason we have not manifested more faith is because of lack of understanding. We have not understood that everything works in exact accordance with definite law. The law of thought is as definite as the law of mathematics, or the law of chemistry, or the law of electricity, or the law of gravitation. When we begin to understand that happiness, health, success, prosperity and every other condition or environment are results, and that these results are created by right thinking, either consciously or unconsciously, we shall realize the importance of a working knowledge of the laws governing thought.

Those coming into a conscious realization of the power of thought find themselves in possession of the best that life can give; substantial things of a higher order become theirs, and these sublime realities are so constituted that they can be made tangible parts of daily personal life. They realize a world of higher power, and keep that power constantly working. This power is inexhaustible, limitless, and they are therefore carried forward from victory to victory. Obstacles that seem insurmountable are overcome. Enemies are changed to friends, conditions are overcome, elements transformed, fate is conquered.

The supply of good is inexhaustible, and the demand can be made along whatever lines we may desire. This is the mental law of demand and supply.

Our circumstances and environment are formed by our thoughts, We have, perhaps, been creating these conditions unconsciously. If they are unsatisfactory, the remedy is to consciously alter our mental attitude and see our circumstances adjust themselves to the new mental condition. There is nothing strange or supernatural about this; it is simply the Law of Being. The thoughts which take root in the mind will certainly produce fruit after their kind. The greatest schemer cannot "gather grapes of thorns, or figs of thistles." To improve our conditions we must first improve ourselves. Our thoughts and desires will be the first to show improvement.

To be in ignorance of the laws governing in the mental world is to be like a child playing with fire, or a man manipulating powerful chemicals without a knowledge of their nature and relations. This is universally true, because Mind is the one great cause which produces all conditions in the lives of men and women.

Admitting that you agree with everything that has been stated, thus far, and most persons will take no exception to anything that has been said, it still remains to make a practical application of the law.

In order to take advantage of this law, and put ourselves into harmonious relationship with it, so that the benefit may be made manifest in our lives, it is necessary to see that the conditions are all met for its proper operation. We may know the laws governing electricity, we may have all the proper mechanism, the lamps, the wires, the switches, and we may even know how to generate the power, but if the connections are not properly made, we can work the switch till doomsday and no light will appear; so with the law of attraction—it is in operation all the time, everywhere, something is constantly being created, something is appearing, everything is continually changing, but to take advantage of this process, it is just as necessary to comply with the law as it is in the case of electricity or gravitation.

Mind is creative and operates through the law of attraction. We are not to try to influence any to do what we think they should do. Each individual has a right to choose for himself, but aside from this we would be operating under the law of force, which is destructive in its nature and just the opposite of the law of attraction. A little reflection will convince you that all of the great laws of nature operate in silence and that the underlying principle is the law of attraction. It is only destructive processes such as earthquakes and catastrophes, that employ force. Nothing good is ever accomplished in that way.

To be successful, attention must invariably be directed to the creative plane; it must never seek to deprive. You do not wish to take anything away from any one else, you want to create something for yourself, and what you want for yourself you are perfectly willing that everyone else should have.

You know that it is not necessary to take from one to give to another, but that the supply for all is abundant. Nature's storehouse of wealth is inexhaustible and if there seems to be a lack of supply anywhere it is only because the channels of distribution are as yet imperfect.

Abundance is a natural law of the universe. The evidence of this law is conclusive; we see it on every hand. Everywhere Nature is lavish—wasteful, extravagant. Nowhere is economy observed in any created thing. Profusion is manifested in everything. The millions and millions of trees and flowers and plants and animals and the vast scheme of reproduction where the process of creating and recreating is for ever going on, all indicates the lavishness with which Nature has made provision for man. That there is an abundance for everyone is evident, but that many seem to have been separated from this supply is also evident; they have not yet come into a realization of the Universality of all substance, and that mind is the active principle which starts causes in motion whereby we are related to the things we desire.

It is evident, therefore, that he who fails to fully investigate and take advantage of the wonderful progress which is being made, in this last and greatest science, will soon be as far behind as the man who would refuse to acknowledge and accept the benefits which have accrued to mankind through an understanding of the laws of electricity.

Of course, mind creates negative conditions just as readily as favorable conditions, and when we consciously or unconsciously visualize every kind of lack, limitation and discord, we create these conditions; this is what many are unconsciously doing all the time.

This law as well as every other law is no respecter of persons, but is in constant operation and is relentlessly bringing to each individual exactly what he has created; in other words, "Whatsoever a man soweth that shall he also reap."

Abundance, therefore, depends upon a recognition of the laws of Abundance, and the fact that Mind is not only the creator, but the only creator of all there is. Certainly nothing can be created, before we know that it can be created and then make the proper effort. There is no more Electricity in the world today than there was fifty years ago, but until someone recognized the law by which it could be made of service, we received no benefit; now that the law is understood, practically the whole world is lit by it. So with the law of Abundance; it is only those who recognize the law and place themselves in harmony with it, who share in its benefits.

A recognition of the law of abundance develops certain mental and moral qualities, among which are Courage, Loyalty, Tact, Sagacity, Individuality and Constructiveness. These are all modes of thought, and as all thought is creative, they manifest in objective conditions corresponding with the mental condition. This is necessarily true because the ability of the individual to think is his ability to act upon the Universal mind and bring it into manifestation, it is the process whereby the individual becomes a channel for the differentiation of the Universal. Every thought is a cause and every condition an effect.

This principle endows the individual with seemingly transcendental possibilities, among which is the mastery of conditions through the creation and recognition of opportunities. This creation of opportunity implies the existence or creation of the necessary qualities or talents which are thought forces and which result in a consciousness of power which future events cannot disturb. It is this organization of victory or success within the mind, this consciousness of power within which constitutes the responsive harmonious action whereby we are related to the objects and purposes which we seek. This is the law of attraction in action; this law being the common property of all, can be exercised by any one having sufficient knowledge of its operation.

Courage is that power of the mind which manifests in the love of mental conflict; it is a noble and lofty sentiment, it is equally fitted to command or obey. Both require courage. It often has a tendency to conceal itself. There are men and women, too, who apparently exist only to do what is pleasing to others, but when the time comes and the latent will is revealed, we find under the velvet glove an iron hand—and no mistake about it. True courage is cool, calm and collected, and is never foolhardy, quarrelsome, ill-natured or contentious.

Accumulation is the power to reserve and preserve a part of the supply which we are constantly receiving, so as to be in position to take advantage of the larger opportunities which will come as soon as we are ready for them. Has it not been said, "To him that hath shall be given." All successful business men have this quality well developed. James J. Hill, who recently died leaving an estate of over fifty-two million dollars, said: "If you want to know whether you are destined to be a success or a failure in life, you can easily find out. The test is simple and it is infallible: Are you able to save money? If not, drop out. You will lose. You may think not, but you will lose as sure as you live. The seed of success is not in you." This is very good so far as it goes, but any one who knows the biography of James J. Hill, knows that he acquired his fifty million dollars by following the exact methods we have given. In the first place, he started with nothing; he had to use his imagination to idealize the vast railroad which he projected across the western prairies. He then had to come into a recognition of the law of abundance in order to provide the ways and means for materializing it; unless he had followed out this program he would never have had anything to save.

Accumulativeness acquires momentum; the more you accumulate the more you desire and the more you desire the more you accumulate, so that it is but a short time until the action and reaction acquire a momentum that cannot be stopped. It must, however, never be confounded with selfishness, miserliness or penuriousness; they are perversions and will make any true progress impossible.

Constructiveness is the creative instinct of the mind. It will be readily seen that every successful business man must be able to plan, develop or construct. In the business world it is usually referred to as initiative. It is not enough to go along in the beaten path. New ideas must be developed, new ways of doing things. It manifests in building, designing, planning, inventing, discovering, improving. It is a most valuable quality and must be constantly encouraged and developed. Every individual possesses it in some degree, because he is a center of consciousness in that Infinite and Eternal Energy from which all things proceed.

Water manifests on three planes, as ice, as water and as steam; it is all the same compound, the only difference is the temperature, but no one would try to drive an engine with ice; convert it into steam and it easily takes up the load. So with your energy; if you want it to act on the creative plane, you will have to begin by melting the ice with the fire of imagination, and you will find that the stronger the fire, and the more ice you melt, the more powerful your thought will become, and the easier it will be for you to materialize your desire.

Sagacity is the ability to perceive and cooperate with Natural Law. True Sagacity avoids trickery and deceit as it would the leprosy; it is the product of that deep insight which enables one to penetrate into the heart of things and understand how to set causes in motion which will inevitably create successful conditions.

Tact is a very subtle and at the same time a very important factor in business success. It is very similar to intuition. To possess tact one must have a fine feeling, must instinctively know what to say or what to do. In order to be tactful one must possess Sympathy and Understanding, that understanding which is so rare, for all men see and hear and feel, but how desperately few "understand." Tact enables one to foresee what is about to happen and calculate the result of actions. Tact enables us to feel when we are in the presence of physical, mental and moral cleanliness, for these are today invariably demanded as the price of success.

Loyalty is one of the strongest links which bind men of strength and character. It is one which can never be broken with impunity. The man who would lose his right hand rather than betray a friend will never lack friends. The man who will stand in silent guard, until death, if need be, beside the shrine of confidence or friendship of those who have allowed him to enter will find himself linked with a current of cosmic power which will attract desirable conditions only. It is inconceivable that such a one should ever meet with lack of any kind.

Individuality is the power to unfold our own latent possibilities, to be a law unto ourselves, to be interested in the race rather than the goal. Strong men care nothing for the flock of imitators who trot complacently behind them. They derive no satisfaction in the mere leading of large numbers, or the plaudits of the mob. This pleases only petty natures and inferior minds. Individuality glories more in the unfolding of the power within than in the servility of the weakling.

Individuality is a real power inherent in all and the development and consequent expression of this power enables one to assume the responsibility of directing his own footsteps rather than stampeding after some self-assertive bellwether.

Truth is the imperative condition of all wellbeing. To be sure, to know the truth and to stand confidently on it is a satisfaction beside which no other is comparable. Truth is the underlying verity, the condition precedent to every business or social relation. Truth is the only solid ground in a world of conflict, doubt and danger.

Every act not in harmony with Truth, whether through ignorance or design, cuts the ground from under our feet, leads to discord, inevitable loss, and confusion, for while the humblest mind can accurately foretell the result of ever correct action, the greatest, most profound and penetrating mind loses its way hopelessly and can form no conception of the results due to a departure from correct principles.

Those who establish within themselves the requisite elements of true success have established confidence, organized victory, and it only remains for them to take such steps from time to time as the newly-awakened thought force will direct, and herein rests the magical secret of all power.

Less than ten percent of our mental processes is conscious, the other ninety percent is subconscious and unconscious, so that he who would depend upon his conscious thought alone for results is less than ten percent efficient. Those who are accomplishing anything worth while are those who are enabled to take advantage of this greater storehouse of mental wealth. It is in the vast domain of the subconscious mind that great truths are hidden, and it is here that thought finds its creative power, its power to correlate with its object, to bring out of the unseen the seen.

Those familiar with the laws of Electricity understand the principle that electricity must always pass from a higher to a lower potentiality and can therefore make whatever application of the power they desire. Those not familiar with this law can effect nothing; and so with the law governing in the Mental World, those who understand that Mind penetrates all things, is Omnipresent and is responsive to every demand, can make use of the law and can control conditions, circumstances and environment; the uninformed cannot use it because they do not know it.

The fruit of this knowledge is, as it were, a gift of the Gods; it is the "truth" that makes men free, not only free from every lack and limitation, but free from sorrow, worry and care, and is it not wonderful to realize that this law is no respecter of persons, that it makes no difference what your habit of thought may be the way has been prepared.

With the realization that this mental power controls and directs every other power which exists, that it can be cultivated and developed, that no limitation can be placed upon its activity, it will become apparent that it is the greatest fact in the world, the remedy for every ill, the solution for every difficulty, the gratification of every desire, in fact, that it is the Creator's magnificent provision for human emancipation.

The scientific spirit now dominates every field of effort, relations of cause and effect are no longer ignored.

The discovery of a reign of law marked an epoch in human progress. It eliminated the element of uncertainty and caprice from men's lives, and substituted law, reason and certitude.

Men now understand that for every result there is an adequate and definite cause, so that when a given result is desired, they seek the condition by which alone this result may be attained.

The basis upon which all law rests was discovered by inductive reasoning which consists of comparing a number of separate instances with one another until the common factor which gives rise to them all is seen.

It is this method of study to which the civilized nations owe the greater part of their prosperity and the more valuable part of their knowledge; it has lengthened life, it has mitigated pain, it has spanned rivers, it has brightened night with the splendor of day, extended the range of vision, accelerated motion, annihilated distance, facilitated intercourse, and enabled men to descend into the sea and to soar in the air, what wonder then that men soon endeavored to extend the blessings of this system of study to their method of thinking, so that when it became plainly evident that certain results followed a particular method of thinking it only remained to classify these results.

This method is scientific and it is the only method by which we shall be permitted to retain, that degree of liberty and freedom which we have been accustomed to look upon as an inalienable right, because a people is safe at home and in the world only if national preparedness means such things as growing surplus of health, accumulated efficiency in public and private business of whatever sort, continuous advance in the science and art of acting together, and the increasingly dominant endeavor to make all of these and all other aspects of national development center and revolve about ascending life, single and collective, for which science, art and ethics furnish guidance and controlling motives.

The Master Key is based on absolute scientific truth and will unfold the possibilities that lie dormant in the individual, and teach how they may be brought into powerful action, to increase the person's effective capacity, bringing added energy, discernment, vigor and mental elasticity. The student who gains an understanding of the mental laws which are unfolded will come into the possession of an ability to secure results hitherto undreamed of, and which has rewards hardly to be expressed in words.

It explains the correct use of both the receptive and active elements of the mental nature, and instructs the student in the recognition of opportunity; it strengthens the will and reasoning powers, and teaches the cultivation and best uses of imagination, desire, the emotions and the intuitional faculty. It gives initiative, tenacity of purpose, wisdom of choice, intelligent sympathy and a thorough enjoyment of life on its higher planes.

The Master Key teaches the use of Mind Power, true Mind Power, not any of the substitutes and perversions; it has nothing to do with Hypnotism, Magic or any of the more or less fascinating deceptions by which many are led to think that something can be had for nothing.

The Master Key cultivates and develops the understanding which will enable you to control the body and thereby the health. It improves and strengthens the Memory. It develops Insight, the kind of Insight which is so rare, the kind which is the distinguishing characteristic of every successful business man, the kind which enables men to see the possibilities as well as the difficulties in every situation, the kind which enables men to discern opportunity close at hand, for thousands fail to see opportunities almost within their grasp while they are industriously working with situations which under no possibility can be made to realize any substantial return.

The Master Key develops Mental Power which means that others instinctively recognize that you are a person of force, of character—that they want to do what you want them to do; it means that you attract men and things to you; that you are what some people call "lucky," that "things" come your way; that you have come into an understanding of the fundamental laws of Nature, and have put yourself in harmony with them; that you are in tune with the Infinite; that you understand the law of attraction, the Natural laws of growth, and the Psychological laws on which all advantages in the social and business world rest.

Mental Power is creative power, it gives you the ability to create for yourself; it does not mean the ability to take something away from some one else. Nature never does things that way. Nature makes two blades of grass grow where one grew before, and Mind Power enables men to do the same thing.

The Master Key develops insight and sagacity, increased independence, the ability and disposition to be helpful; it destroys distrust, depression, fear, melancholia, and every form of lack, limitation and weakness, including pain and disease;

it awakens buried talents, supplies initiative, force, energy, vitality—it awakens an appreciation of the beautiful in Art, Literature and Science.

It has changed the lives of thousands of men and women, by substituting definite principles for uncertain and hazy methods—and principles are the foundation upon which every system of efficiency must rest.

Elbert Gary, the chairman of the United States Steel Corporation, said: "The services of advisors, instructors, efficiency experts in successful management are indispensable to most business enterprises of magnitude, but I deem the recognition and adoption of right principles of vastly more importance." The Master Key teaches right principles, and suggests methods for making a practical application of the principles; in that it differs from every other course of study. It teaches that the only possible value which can attach to any principle is in its application. Many read books, take home study courses, attend lectures all their lives without ever making any progress in demonstrating the value of the principles involved. The Master Key suggests methods by which the value of the principles taught may be demonstrated and put in actual practice in the daily experience.

There is a change in the thought of the world. This change is silently transpiring in our midst, and is more important than any which the world has undergone since the downfall of Paganism.

The present revolution in the opinions of all classes of men, the highest and most cultured of men as well as those of the laboring class, stands unparalleled in the history of the world.

Science has of late made such vast discoveries, has revealed such an infinity of resources, has unveiled such enormous possibilities and such unsuspected forces, that scientific men more and more hesitate to affirm certain theories as established and indubitable or to deny certain other theories as absurd or impossible, and so a new civilization is being born; customs, creeds, and cruelty are passing; vision, faith and service are taking their place. The fetters of tradition are being melted off from humanity, and as the dross of materialism is being consumed, thought is being liberated and truth is rising full orbed before an astonished multitude.

The whole world is on the eve of a new consciousness, a new power and a new realization of the resources within the self. The last century saw the most magnificent material progress in history. The present century will produce the greatest progress in mental and spiritual power.

Physical Science has resolved matter into molecules, molecules into atoms, atoms into energy, and it has remained for Sir Ambrose Fleming, in an address before the Royal Institution, to resolve this energy into mind. He says: "In its ultimate essence, energy may be incomprehensible by us except as an exhibition of the direct operation of that which we call Mind or Will."

Let us see what are the most powerful forces in Nature. In the mineral world everything is solid and fixed. In the animal and vegetable kingdom it is in a state of flux, forever changing, always being created and recreated. In the atmosphere we find heat, light and energy. Each realm becomes finer and more spiritual as we pass from the visible to the invisible, from the coarse to the fine, from the low potentiality to high potentiality. When we reach the invisible we find energy in its purest and most volatile state.

And as the most powerful forces of Nature are the invisible forces, so we find that the most powerful forces of man are his invisible forces, his spiritual force, and the only way in which the spiritual force can manifest is through the process of thinking. Thinking is the only activity which the spirit possesses, and thought is the only product of thinking.

Addition and subtraction are therefore spiritual transactions; reasoning is a spiritual process; ideas are spiritual conceptions; questions are spiritual searchlights and logic, argument and philosophy is spiritual machinery.

Every thought brings into action certain physical tissue, parts of the brain, nerve or muscle. This produces an actual physical change in the construction of the tissue. Therefore it is only necessary to have a certain number of thoughts on a given subject in order to bring about a complete change in the physical organization of a man.

This is the process by which failure is changed to success. Thoughts of courage, power, inspiration, harmony, are substituted for thoughts of failure, despair, lack, limitation and discord, and as these thoughts take root, the physical tissue is changed and the individual sees life in a new light, old things have actually passed away, all things have become new, he is born again, this time born of the spirit, life has a new meaning for him, he is reconstructed and is filled with joy, confidence, hope, energy. He sees opportunities for success to which he was heretofore blind. He recognizes possibilities which before had no meaning for him. The thoughts of success with which he has been impregnated are radiated to those around him, and they in turn help him onward and upward; he attracts to him new and successful associates, and this in turn changes his environment; so that by this simple exercise of thought, a man changes not only himself, but his environment, circumstances and conditions.

You will see, you must see, that we are at the dawn of a new day; that the possibilities are so wonderful, so fascinating, so limitless as to be almost bewildering. A century ago any man with an airplane or even a Gatling gun could have annihilated a whole army equipped with the implements of warfare then in use. So it is at present. Any man with a knowledge of the possibilities contained in the Master Key has an inconceivable advantage over the multitude.

Part One

Tells upon what possession is based, explains the cause of all gain, explains the cause of loss as well as all other experiences in life. It explains how power is secured. It tells of a world within and how this world is governed. It explains how the solution for every problem in life may be found. It tells how practical men and women find the courage, power, hope, enthusiasm and confidence by which they are given the intelligence and wisdom to make their dreams come true. It tells how more efficiency is obtained and retained, and how our future may be placed under our own control instead of being at the mercy of any capricious or uncertain external power. It explains the cause of every condition, the reason for every experience, the origin of all power, and why all power is absolutely under our own control.

Part Two

Tells how and why the operations of the mind are carried on by two parallel modes of activity, the one conscious and the other subconscious. It explains why the thought processes of the subconscious are the theatre of the most important mental phenomena, why ease and perfection depend entirely upon the degree in which we cease to depend upon the consciousness. It explains the origin of all great, noble, brilliant thoughts and ideas, why we find ourselves sometimes endowed with tact, instinct, courage, sagacity and inspiration. In fact, it tells of a vast mental storehouse in which ninety percent of our thought processes originate it explains also how this vast mental storehouse may be placed under the supervision and in the keeping of the conscious mind. It tells why those who are familiar with the laws governing in this larger mental domain are enabled to accomplish, to achieve, to become writers, authors, artists, ministers, captains of industry, and why all others must necessarily remain less than ten percent efficient.

Part Three

Tells why the necessary action and interaction of the conscious and subconscious minds requires two corresponding systems of nerves. It explains how the connection is made between these two systems of nerves. It explains and tells of a central point in the body for the distribution of energy. How this energy is distributed. How the distribution of this energy gives the individual pleasant sensations, how the interruption of this distribution brings discord, inharmony and lack and limitation of every kind. It tells of an arch enemy which must be destroyed, and tells how to destroy it. It tells what determines the experiences in life with which we are to meet, and why these experiences are under our own control. One enthusiastic reader says of this Part: "This document in my opinion is the greatest single document beneficial to mankind ever written in the history of the world; it is the first time that I have come into a true understanding of the Silent Powers that dominate and determine one's success."

Part Four

This Part tells what it is which controls that which you call yourself. "You" are not your body; the body is simply the physical instrument which the ego uses to carry out its purpose. "You" are not your mind; this is simply another instrument which the ego uses to think, reason and plan. When you say "'I' go" you tell the body where to go, when you say "'I' think" you tell the mind what to think. When you come into a realization of the true nature of the "I" you will enjoy a sense of power which nothing else can give, because you will come to know what you are, who you are, what you want, and how to get it.

Part Five

This Part tells how the subconscious processes are continually at work, and it tells how we may consciously direct this work instead of being mere passive recipients of its activity. It tells how we may have a vision of the destination to be reached, the dangers and pitfalls to be avoided. It tells how "the word has become flesh," how we are constantly creating and re-creating ourselves. It tells of a mental home which each of us is building for ourselves, the importance of this home, where the material is secured, the character of the furnishing, how and why many of us need a mental housecleaning in case we wish to realize our ideas. It tells of the conditions by which we may come into an inheritance of health, harmony and prosperity, and the condition is one which demands no sacrifice except the loss of our limitations, our servitudes and our weaknesses, and costs only the labor of harvesting its great resources.

Part Six

Tells of the unlimited possibilities of the Universal Mind, which is the life principle of every atom in existence, and explains how this mind is differentiated in form. It tells of the most marvelous piece of mechanism which has ever been constructed, and tells how the effect which will be produced depends entirely upon the "mechanism to which it is attached." It tells why we should all become familiar with the mechanism so as to secure the effects which we desire. The power to which it can be attached is unlimited, and we can accordingly secure any effect we desire when we become familiar with the mechanism, and understand how to make the proper connections. An understanding of this part will enable you to plan courageously and execute fearlessly, because you will have come into a knowledge of the source of all power and this will determine your course in life, bringing you into contact with all that is strongest and best and most desirable.

Part Seven

This Part tells of a method by which you may construct the mold or model from which your future will emerge. It tells how you may make it grand and beautiful; it explains that you are not limited as to cost or material, that no one can place any limitation on it but yourself. It explains that in the construction of this model, there is much work to be done, that no one can do the work but yourself, but it tells you what to do and how to do it, it suggests methods and plans which if faithfully and persistently carried out will result in conditions exactly in accordance with the purpose and thought. It tells of millions of faithful helpers which will come to your aid if you are faithful in your work, and it tells why some who are apparently faithfully endeavoring to realize their ideal seem to fail. It is sometimes just as important to know what not to do as what to do.

Part Eight

This Part tells of the creative principle of the Universe, what it is, how it takes form and how it is brought into manifestation. This principle being the underlying principle of all existence must necessarily be governed by an immutable law. It tells how the character, health and circumstances of the individual are formed, and suggests methods whereby desirable conditions and circumstances may be created. It tells how and why and when the material from which your future is to emerge is secured. It suggests methods and exercises by which you may secure complete control of the power which governs in this mighty field of action. Mighty because it is the most important work which any individual can undertake. We are making our future now, to-day, when it comes we shall have to accept what is given, it will be too late to change it, but we can dominate it, control it, make it what we want it to be, and this Part explains how.

Part Nine

This Part tells of the fundamental principle, the imperative condition, the immutable law underlying every successful business relation or social condition. It tells of the law by which you may make yourself irresistible, by which you may sweep away every form of discord, inharmony and doubt. It tells the secret of the solution to every problem. It explains that there are only three things which all mankind requires for complete happiness and development. It tells what they are and how they may be had.

Part Ten

This Part tells of the Law of Abundance. It shows that Nature has provided an abundance for all, and why some seem to be separated from this supply. It tells of a connecting link between the individual and the supply, explains the Law of Attraction, the law by which your "own" is brought to you. It tells why every experience in life is the result of this law. It tells why and how you attract the things to you which make up the sum total of your existence. It tells how you may place yourself in harmony with this law and thereby assist in bringing about desirable conditions in your health, environment, or finances. It shows that this Law of Attraction is fundamental and eternal and that there is no escape from the result of its operation. A knowledge of this Law is absolutely essential to those desiring to make permanent progress.

Part Eleven

This Part tells of the means by which we have discovered that the infinitely small as well as the infinitely large is in the last analysis nothing but force, motion, life and mind. It tells of the process by which we have become familiar with the vast organization by which we are identified with the complex operations of Nature. It gives concise directions for making use of the creative power of the Universe, the power by which all things are brought into existence. It shows how this marvelous power may be utilized, directed and made available for the solution of every human problem.

Part Twelve

This Part tells of numerous counterfeits and perversions by which many are led to think that something can be had for nothing. There is no royal road to success, we must give before we can get; if we cannot give money, we must give service, we must give time and thought, the Law of Compensation demands an eye for an eye. It tells how we may create the implements by which we may put into operation the laws by which we can gain access to the unlimited resources of Nature.

Part Thirteen

This Part explains why certain forms of thought often result in disaster and frequently sweep away the result of a lifetime of effort. It explains the modern method of thinking and shows how actual, tangible results are thereby secured, and how conditions must change in order to meet the requirements of a changed consciousness. It explains the process by which this change is brought about and how we may hasten it.

Part Fourteen

This Part explains the source of all Power, Wisdom and Intelligence, and how we may bring it into harmonious relations in our affairs. It shows that those who understand the principle get results in exact accordance with their understanding and their ability to make the proper application. This opens up possibilities hitherto undreamed of and by an orderly sequence of law. It explains the source of all energy and all substance and the method by which this Universal Substance is differentiated into form. It explains the nature of electrons and of cells upon which the maintenance of health and life depend; it explains how we may bring about radical changes in our life and what the result of such changes must necessarily be.

Part Fifteen

This Part explains the Law of Growth, and explains why we cannot obtain if we tenaciously cling to what we have, and that difficulties, inharmonies and obstacles indicate that we are either refusing to give up what we no longer need, or refusing to accept what we require; we are holding on to worn-out and useless material, or we are allowing a deficiency to exist and are not obtaining the material necessary for our growth. It explains how the ability to appropriate what we require for our growth is secured. It explains how vitality is important to thought, and what determines the importance of words the vessels in which thought is carried. How abundance may be secured and why we must be prepared to assume the responsibility for every thought and action. It explains the necessity of Insight, its value in examining facts and conditions at long range and in turning our attention to profitable channels instead of working with problems which contain no possibility of any kind.

Part Sixteen

This Part explains the nature of Wealth, it shows how it is created and upon what it depends. It shows why success is contingent upon an ideal higher than the mere accumulation of riches, it shows that success depends upon creative ability and explains the necessary condition for attainment. It explains why premature wealth is but the forerunner of humiliation and disaster. It explains the methods by which we may take our fate out of the hands of chance, and consciously make for ourselves the conditions which we desire, it tells how we may compel success by the utilization of scientific and exact methods, and it explains that while we have the ability to create harmonious and constructive conditions we also have the ability to create inharmonious and destructive conditions, and unfortunately, through ignorance of the law, this is what many are doing.

Part Seventeen

This Part tells of the Law of Vibration and why the highest principle necessarily determines the circumstances, aspects and relations of everything with which it comes in contact. It tells why and how a knowledge of these higher forces makes all physical force sink into insignificance. It explains the nature of concentration; it tells something of the practice of concentration, tells something of the results of concentration. It tells how the mind may become a magnet, how it may irresistibly attract the conditions which it desires; it tells why it is necessary "to be" in order "to have." It tells how to unfasten the prison bars of weakness, impotence and self-belittlement and realize the joy of overcoming obstacles. It tells how the intuitive power is set in operation and how this inevitably leads to success. It tells of the difference between real power and the symbols of power, and why the symbols turn to ashes just as we overtake them.

Part Eighteen

This Part tells of a change in the thought of men, a change which is silently transpiring in our midst and which is unparalleled in the history of the world. The fetters of tradition are being melted off from humanity and truth is rising full orbed before an astonished multitude. It tells how the individual is enabled to control every form of intelligence which has not yet reached this level of self-recognition. It tells when and how the creative power originates, it tells how the Universal produces the various combinations which result in the formation of phenomena, it explains the principle of attraction by which things are brought together, which is the sole means by which existence is carried into effect. It explains the real source of wealth of the individual. It explains the method by which attention and concentration may be developed and shows why the power of attention is the distinguishing characteristic of every man of ability.

Part Nineteen

This Part tells of the search for truth, which is another name for ultimate cause. If we can find the truth we shall have found the cause for every effect, and having found the cause we shall be in a position to control the effect. It explains that all things are finally resolvable into one thing, and that as they are thus translatable they must ever be in relation and can never be in opposition to one another. It explains that a knowledge of this primary substance is power; it explains that a knowledge of cause and effect is power, that wealth is the offspring of power, that events and conditions are significant only as they effect power, and finally that all things represent certain forms and decrees of power. It tells of a certain form of power which can control every other power, why it is superior and how we may make use of this superior power.

Part Twenty

This Part tells what the true business of life is and the result. It shows that we can obtain no results as long as we remain oblivious to the only power there is, an understanding of the principles, forces, methods and combinations of mind and its relation to the Universal mind. It explains that the Universal can act only through the Individual; it shows that we are the channel for its activity, that it is within us, that we are it. We can, of course, fail to recognize it and so exclude it from our consciousness, but it will nevertheless be the basic fact of all existence. It tells of inspiration, the art of adjusting the individual mind to that of the Universal, the art of becoming a channel for the flow of Infinite Wisdom.

Part Twenty-One

This Part explains how we may come into possession of power sufficient to meet every situation which may arise in life. It explains that the ability to eliminate imperfect conditions depends upon mental action. It explains that great ideas have a tendency to eliminate smaller ideas, so that it is well to hold ideas which are large enough to counteract and destroy all small or undesirable tendencies. This is one of the secrets of success, one of the accomplishments of the Master Mind. It explains that the creative energy finds no more difficulty in handling a large situation than a small one. It explains how conditions are produced in our lives by the predominant thoughts which we entertain. It explains how you may set causes in motion which will create an irresistible magnetic power which will bring the things you require to you. It explains the issue between the old regime and the new, it explains the crux of the social problem, it explains the true secret of health, wealth and power.

Part Twenty-Two

This Part explains the cause of our present character, our present environment, our present ability, our present physical condition, and tells how we can make our future what we wish it to be. It explains how the vast panorama of Nature is being constantly changed by simply changing the rate of vibration. It tells how the rate of vibration is being constantly changed in our bodies, usually unconsciously and often with detrimental and disastrous results. It tells how we may effect this change consciously and thus bring about only harmonious and salutary conditions. It explains that the Law of Health is based on the law of vibration, and that with a proper knowledge of the law we may externalize health conditions. It explains the operation of this law and how it is being more generally understood and appreciated, and how many physicians are now giving the matter their earnest attention.

Part Twenty-Three

This Part tells of the money consciousness and the power which sets the current in motion which produces the attractive force which opens the doors to the arteries of commerce. It tells how the current is stopped or completely reversed and turned away from us. It tells how money is woven into the outer fabric of our existence. Why it engages the best thought of the best minds. How we make money. How to recognize opportunity. How to make a money magnet of yourself. How to get the necessary insight to perceive and utilize opportunities. How to recognize values. It tells how to convert an idea into an income, how to make a direct connection with the Universal Mind, how to secure practical results; in fact, it tells what the only really practical thing is.

Part Twenty-Four

This Part explains the entire theory and practice of every system of Metaphysics; it tells how to express harmony, how to express health, how to express abundance. It explains the nature of all conditions, and how they may be changed or removed. It explains how every difficulty, no matter what it is or where it is, can be removed or dissolved, and it explains the only way in which this is ever done or can be done. It also tells of a Master Key by which those who are wise enough to understand, broad enough to weigh the evidence, firm enough to follow their own judgment, and strong enough to make the sacrifice exacted, may enter and partake.

STUDY GUIDE

Summary

This Part explains the entire theory and practice of every system of Metaphysics; it tells how to express harmony, how to express health, how to express abundance. It explains the nature of all conditions, and how they may be changed or removed. It explains how every difficulty, no matter what it is or where it is, can be removed or dissolved, and it explains the only way in which this is ever done or can be done. It also tells of a Master Key by which those who are wise enough to understand, broad enough to weigh the evidence, firm enough to follow their own judgment, and strong enough to make the sacrifice exacted, may enter and partake.

Foreword

1. Charles Haanel opens this book by stating that "every right-thinking person wants not merely to move through life . . . but to improve—and to continue the development mentally to the close of physical life." Are your passions rooted in mental development? In your journal, write two columns. On the top of the left column, write "Mental Opportunity" and at the top of the right column write, "Examples of Mental Development." Then provide specific examples of how you have mentally developed through the years. For example:

MENTAL OPPORTUNITY	EXAMPLE OF MENTAL DEVELOPMENT
1986: I was filled with road rage	2020: I have 50% less anger when driving

2. You are encouraged to pace yourself and only complete one chapter each week for a complete duration of 24 weeks of lessons. Track your progress by putting a √ in each of the boxes below as you complete each chapter.

    ☐ Week 1—Completed Chapter 1
    ☐ Week 2—Completed Chapter 2
    ☐ Week 3—Completed Chapter 3
    ☐ Week 4—Completed Chapter 4
    ☐ Week 5—Completed Chapter 5
    ☐ Week 6—Completed Chapter 6
    ☐ Week 7—Completed Chapter 7
    ☐ Week 8—Completed Chapter 8

- ☐ Week 9—Completed Chapter 9
- ☐ Week 10—Completed Chapter 10
- ☐ Week 11—Completed Chapter 11
- ☐ Week 12—Completed Chapter 12
- ☐ Week 13—Completed Chapter 13
- ☐ Week 14—Completed Chapter 14
- ☐ Week 15—Completed Chapter 15
- ☐ Week 16—Completed Chapter 16
- ☐ Week 17—Completed Chapter 17
- ☐ Week 18—Completed Chapter 18
- ☐ Week 19—Completed Chapter 19
- ☐ Week 20—Completed Chapter 20
- ☐ Week 21—Completed Chapter 21
- ☐ Week 22—Completed Chapter 22
- ☐ Week 23—Completed Chapter 23
- ☐ Week 24—Completed Chapter 24

1. The "Master Key" taps into the great Cosmic Intelligence and attracts your life's desires from that source. Do you believe that there is an intelligence that hears you and responds to the messages that you share? Please explain.

2. Start Date: _____
   Projected Completion Date (24 weeks later): _____

Introduction

1. You could see the chain of manifesting as being a basic formula: Thought + Action = Environment. Everything begins with a thought. If this is the case, what do you believe precipitated the first thought?

2. Charles Haanel asserts that "tree life causes the sap to ascend, not by repealing the law of gravity but by surmounting it." Provide an example of how you have "surmounted" the gravity of potential negativity in your life.

3. Health, harmony and prosperity are listed as three aspects of your life that can be enhanced once you understand the Master Key System. Describe in specific detail the ways in which each of these areas in your life can be improved upon, as you continue your journey towards mastery.

4. The author uses the analogy of the naturalist becoming proficient at observing nature, as they enlarge the part of the brain that involves observation. What are the three key areas in which you are currently focusing your attention?

5. Are these areas ideal to support your further growth? If not, what currents can you attract to further support greater success in your life?

6. Haanel lists several areas of the mind that you should "exercise" to develop your faculties. Reflect on each to establish which you are cultivating and which need further attention:

   • The development of the perceptive faculties

   • The cultivation of the emotions

   • The quickening of the imagination

   • The symmetrical unfoldment of the intuitive faculty (impels or prohibits choice)

   • The development of the moral character.

7. "Every conscious effort should involve a moral end." Are there any areas of your life in which you are not in moral integrity? If so, list them and describe how you plan to right the moral wrong you are following.

8. Harmony is key to growth and success. Make two lists. In one, write all of the areas in which you experiencing harmony in your life. In the second, list the areas in which you are experiencing disharmony in your life. What "inner" steps can you take to increase the "outer" harmony in your life?

9. Those who possess a strong sense of desire and imagination exert a powerful influence over others. On a scale from one to ten, rate how magnetic and influential you believe yourself to be (1 being "not at all" and 10 being "a great deal").
   1 —— 2 —— 3 —— 4 —— 5 —— 6 —— 7 —— 8 —— 9 —— 10

10. Colors are described as sensations that are experienced by us as a result of the vibrations of light. Do you have a passion for a certain color? What does that color mean to you and how does it make you feel?

11. "Growth is attained through an exchange of the old for the new." Are you holding onto any "old" thoughts or feelings that you need to replace with new ones? If so, list them.

12. Haanel asserts that "all conditions and experiences that come to us do so for our benefit. Difficulties and obstacles will continue to come

until we absorb their wisdom and gather from them the essentials of further growth." Reflect on and write about one obstacle you overcame in your life and how that obstacles supported your growth.

13. "Impressions of fear, of worry, of disability and of inferiority are given us daily." What impressions of each of these four areas are currently being cast in the world, and perhaps in your life?

14. The author asserts that because of their "finer susceptibilities," women are more open to thought-vibrations for other minds. Do you believe this to be true? Why or why not?

15. Several women who overcame negativity and repression are listed. Write about a woman you know who has overcome adversity and negativity.

16. "The student who learns that power comes from within, that he is weak only because he has depended on help from outside, and who unhesitatingly throws himself on his own thought, instantly rights himself, stands erect, assumes a dominant attitude, and works miracles." Are you such a student? Why or why not?

17. The author asserts that the reason we have not manifested more faith is because we lack understanding. Do you struggle with faith? Do you understand that laws outlined in this book thus far?

18. Describe the Law of Being as you know it.

19. It is one thing to know the laws of attraction, but it is another thing to experience it. Do you experience this law in your life, or is it still a principle in your mind? Please explain, using specific examples.

20. There is no lack in nature's storehouse of wealth. Do you believe this to be true. Share examples of it in your life.

21. A recognition of the law of abundance develops the following mental and moral qualities: Courage, Loyalty, Tact, Sagacity, Individuality and Constructiveness. Rate your current development within each system (1 being "not at all" and 10 being "a great deal").

    COURAGE:

    1 —— 2 —— 3 —— 4 —— 5 —— 6 —— 7 —— 8 —— 9 —— 10

    LOYALTY:

    1 —— 2 —— 3 —— 4 —— 5 —— 6 —— 7 —— 8 —— 9 —— 10

    TACT:

    1 —— 2 —— 3 —— 4 —— 5 —— 6 —— 7 —— 8 —— 9 —— 10

SAGACITY (FORESIGHT OR DISCERNMENT):

1 — 2 — 3 — 4 — 5 — 6 — 7 — 8 — 9 — 10

INDIVIDUALITY:

1 — 2 — 3 — 4 — 5 — 6 — 7 — 8 — 9 — 10

CONSTRUCTIVENESS:

1 — 2 — 3 — 4 — 5 — 6 — 7 — 8 — 9 — 10

22. According to Haanel, civilized nations owe a great part of their prosperity to inductive reasoning (comparing a number of separate instances with one another until the common factor which gives rise to them all is seen). Do you believe this to be true? Where do you currently see examples of it in the world?

23. The Master Key is "based on absolute scientific truth and will unfold the possibilities that lie dormant in the individual." Once you understand the laws, your life will change. Do you believe that you already understand these laws? If so, what you do you believe is getting in the way of greater success in your life?

24. The Master Key System is said to improve your memory. Rate your memory on a scale from 1 to 10 (1 being "not at all" and 10 being "a great deal"):

1 — 2 — 3 — 4 — 5 — 6 — 7 — 8 — 9 — 10

25. According to Haanel, "the whole world is on the eve of a new consciousness." He wrote this book over a century ago, however, the world is constantly growing and changing. Do you see this statement to hold true today? Why or why not?

26. "Addition and subtraction are . . . spiritual transactions." In your own words, explain how the author describes them as being so.

27. The author ends the Introduction by providing you with an overview of each of the book's chapters. Put a (√) beside any of the Parts that you find of particular interest.

Part One

Tells upon what possession is based, explains the cause of all gain, explains the cause of loss as well as all other experiences in life. It explains how power is secured. It tells of a world within and how this world is governed. It explains how the solution for every problem in life may be found. It tells how practical men and women find the courage, power, hope, enthusiasm and confidence by which they are given the intelligence and wisdom to make their dreams come true. It tells how more efficiency is obtained and retained, and how our future may be placed under our own control instead of being at the mercy of any capricious or uncertain external power. It explains the cause of every condition, the reason for every experience, the origin of all power, and why all power is absolutely under our own control.

Part Two

Tells how and why the operations of the mind are carried on by two parallel modes of activity, the one conscious and the other subconscious. It explains why the thought processes of the subconscious are the theatre of the most important mental phenomena, why ease and perfection depend entirely upon the degree in which we cease to depend upon the consciousness. It explains the origin of all great, noble, brilliant thoughts and ideas, why we find ourselves sometimes endowed with tact, instinct, courage, sagacity and inspiration. In fact, it tells of a vast mental storehouse in which ninety percent of our thought processes originate it explains also how this vast mental storehouse may be placed under the supervision and in the keeping of the conscious mind. It tells why those who are familiar with the laws governing in this larger mental domain are enabled to accomplish, to achieve, to become writers, authors, artists, ministers, captains of industry, and why all others must necessarily remain less than ten percent efficient.

Part Three

Tells why the necessary action and interaction of the conscious and subconscious minds requires two corresponding systems of nerves. It explains how the connection is made between these two systems of nerves. It explains and tells of a central point in the body for the distribution of energy. How this energy is distributed. How the distribution of this energy gives the individual pleasant sensations, how the interruption of this distribution brings discord, inharmony and lack and limitation of every kind. It tells of an arch enemy which must be destroyed, and tells how to destroy it. It tells what determines the experiences in life with which we are to meet, and why these experiences are under our own control. One enthusiastic reader says of this Part: "This document in my opinion is the greatest single document beneficial to mankind ever written in the history of the world; it is the first time that I have come into a true understanding of the Silent Powers that dominate and determine one's success."

Part Four

This Part tells what it is which controls that which you call yourself. "You" are not your body; the body is simply the physical instrument which the ego uses to carry out its purpose. "You" are not your mind; this is simply another instrument which the ego uses to think, reason and plan. When you say "'I' go" you tell the body where to go, when you say "'I' think" you tell the mind what to think. When you come into a realization of the true nature of the "I" you will enjoy a sense of power which nothing else can give, because you will come to know what you are, who you are, what you want, and how to get it.

Part Five

This Part tells how the subconscious processes are continually at work, and it tells how we may consciously direct this work instead of being mere passive recipients of its activity. It tells how we may have a vision of the destination to be reached, the dangers and pitfalls to be avoided. It tells how "the word has become flesh," how we are constantly creating and recreating ourselves. It tells of a mental home which each of us is building for ourselves, the importance of this home, where the material is secured, the character of the furnishing, how and why many of us need a mental housecleaning in case we wish to realize our ideas. It tells of the conditions by which we may come into an inheritance of health, harmony and prosperity, and the condition is one which demands no sacrifice except the loss of our limitations, our servitudes and our weaknesses, and costs only the labor of harvesting its great resources.

Part Six

Tells of the unlimited possibilities of the Universal Mind, which is the life principle of every atom in existence, and explains how this mind is differentiated in form. It tells of the most marvelous piece of mechanism which has ever been constructed, and tells how the effect which will be produced depends entirely upon the "mechanism to which it is attached." It tells why we should all become familiar with the mechanism so as to secure the effects which we desire. The power to which it can be attached is unlimited, and we can accordingly secure any effect we desire when we become familiar with the mechanism, and understand how to make the proper connections. An understanding of this part will enable you to plan courageously and execute fearlessly, because you will have come into a knowledge of the source of all power and this will determine your course in life, bringing you into contact with all that is strongest and best and most desirable.

Part Seven

This Part tells of a method by which you may construct the mold or model from which your future will emerge. It tells how you may make it grand and beautiful; it explains that you are not limited as to cost or material, that no one can place any limitation on it but yourself. It explains that in the construction of this model, there is much work to be done, that no one can do the work but yourself, but it tells you what to do and how to do it, it suggests methods and plans which if faithfully and persistently carried out will result in conditions exactly in accordance with the purpose and thought. It tells of millions of faithful helpers which will come to your aid if you are faithful in your work, and it tells why some who are apparently faithfully endeavoring to realize their ideal seem to fail. It is sometimes just as important to know what not to do as what to do.

Part Eight

This Part tells of the creative principle of the Universe, what it is, how it takes form and how it is brought into manifestation. This principle being the underlying principle of all existence must necessarily be governed by an immutable law. It tells how the character, health and circumstances of the individual are formed, and suggests methods whereby desirable conditions and circumstances may be created. It tells how and why and when the material from which your future is to emerge is secured. It suggests methods and exercises by which you may secure complete control of the power which governs in this mighty field of action. Mighty because it is the most important work which any individual can undertake. We are making our future now, today, when it comes we shall have to accept what is given, it will be too late to change it, but we can dominate it, control it, make it what we want it to be, and this Part explains how.

Part Nine

This Part tells of the fundamental principle, the imperative condition, the immutable law underlying every successful business relation or social condition. It tells of the law by which you may make yourself irresistible, by which you may sweep away every form of discord, inharmony and doubt. It tells the secret of the solution to every problem. It explains that there are only three things which all mankind requires for complete happiness and development. It tells what they are and how they may be had.

Part Ten

This Part tells of the Law of Abundance. It shows that Nature has provided an abundance for all, and why some seem to be separated from this supply. It tells of a connecting link between the individual and the supply, explains the Law of Attraction, the law by which your "own" is brought to you. It tells why every experience in life is the result of this law. It tells why and how you attract the things to you which make up the sum total of your existence. It tells how you may place yourself in harmony with this law and thereby assist in bringing about desirable conditions in your health, environment, or finances. It shows that this Law of Attraction is fundamental and eternal and that there is no escape from the result of its operation. A knowledge of this Law is absolutely essential to those desiring to make permanent progress.

Part Eleven

This Part tells of the means by which we have discovered that the infinitely small as well as the infinitely large is in the last analysis nothing but force, motion, life and mind. It tells of the process by which we have become familiar with the vast organization by which we are identified with the complex operations of Nature. It gives concise directions for making use of the creative power of the Universe, the power by which all things are brought into existence. It shows how this marvelous power may be utilized, directed and made available for the solution of every human problem.

Part Twelve

This Part tells of numerous counterfeits and perversions by which many are led to think that something can be had for nothing. There is no royal road to success, we must give before we can get; if we cannot give money, we must give service, we must give time and thought, the Law of Compensation demands an eye for an eye. It tells how we may create the implements by which we may put into operation the laws by which we can gain access to the unlimited resources of Nature.

Part Thirteen

This Part explains why certain forms of thought often result in disaster and frequently sweep away the result of a lifetime of effort. It explains the modern method of thinking and shows how actual, tangible results are thereby secured, and how conditions must change in order to meet the requirements of a changed consciousness. It explains the process by which this change is brought about and how we may hasten it.

Part Fourteen

This Part explains the source of all Power, Wisdom and Intelligence, and how we may bring it into harmonious relations in our affairs. It shows that those who understand the principle get results in exact accordance with their understanding and their ability to make the proper application. This opens up possibilities hitherto undreamed of and by an orderly sequence of law. It explains the source of all energy and all substance and the method by which this Universal Substance is differentiated into form. It explains the nature of electrons and of cells upon which the maintenance of health and life depend; it explains how we may bring about radical changes in our life and what the result of such changes must necessarily be.

Part Fifteen

This Part explains the Law of Growth, and explains why we cannot obtain if we tenaciously cling to what we have, and that difficulties, inharmonies and obstacles indicate that we are either refusing to give up what we no longer need, or refusing to accept what we require; we are holding on to worn-out and useless material, or we are allowing a deficiency to exist and are not obtaining the material necessary for our growth. It explains how the ability to appropriate what we require for our growth is secured. It explains how vitality is important to thought, and what determines the importance of words the vessels in which thought is carried. How abundance may be secured and why we must be prepared to assume the responsibility for every thought and action. It explains the necessity of Insight, its value in examining facts and conditions at long range and in turning our attention to profitable channels instead of working with problems which contain no possibility of any kind.

Part Sixteen

This Part explains the nature of Wealth, it shows how it is created and upon what it depends. It shows why success is contingent upon an ideal higher than the mere accumulation of riches, it shows that success depends upon creative ability and explains the necessary condition for attainment. It explains why premature wealth is but the forerunner of humiliation and disaster. It explains the methods by which we may take our fate out of the hands of chance, and consciously make for ourselves the conditions which we desire, it tells how we may compel success by the utilization of scientific and exact methods, and it explains that while we have the ability to create harmonious and constructive conditions we also have the ability to create inharmonious and destructive conditions, and unfortunately, through ignorance of the law, this is what many are doing.

Part Seventeen

This Part tells of the Law of Vibration and why the highest principle necessarily determines the circumstances, aspects and relations of everything with which it comes in contact. It tells why and how a knowledge of these higher forces makes all physical force sink into insignificance. It explains the nature of concentration; it tells something of the practice of concentration, tells something of the results of concentration. It tells how the mind may become a magnet, how it may irresistibly attract the conditions which it desires; it tells why it is necessary "to be" in order "to have." It tells how to unfasten the prison bars of weakness, impotence and self-belittlement and realize the joy of overcoming obstacles. It tells how the intuitive power is set in operation and how this inevitably leads to success. It tells of the difference between real power and the symbols of power, and why the symbols turn to ashes just as we overtake them.

Part Eighteen

This Part tells of a change in the thought of men, a change which is silently transpiring in our midst and which is unparalleled in the history of the world. The fetters of tradition are being melted off from humanity and truth is rising full orbed before an astonished multitude. It tells how the individual is enabled to control every form of intelligence which has not yet reached this level of self-recognition. It tells when and how the creative power originates, it tells how the Universal produces the various combinations which result in the formation of phenomena, it explains the principle of attraction by which things are brought together, which is the sole means by which existence is carried into effect. It explains the real source of wealth of the individual. It explains the method by which attention and concentration may be developed and shows why the power of attention is the distinguishing characteristic of every man of ability.

Part Nineteen

This Part tells of the search for truth, which is another name for ultimate cause. If we can find the truth we shall have found the cause for every effect, and having found the cause we shall be in a position to control the effect. It explains that all things are finally resolvable into one thing, and that as they are thus translatable they must ever be in relation and can never be in opposition to one another. It explains that a knowledge of this primary substance is power; it explains that a knowledge of cause and effect is power, that wealth is the offspring of power, that events and conditions are significant only as they effect power, and finally that all things represent certain forms and decrees of power. It tells of a certain form of power which can control every other power, why it is superior and how we may make use of this superior power.

Part Twenty

This Part tells what the true business of life is and the result. It shows that we can obtain no results as long as we remain oblivious to the only power there is, an understanding of the principles, forces, methods and combinations of mind and its relation to the Universal mind. It explains that the Universal can act only through the Individual; it shows that we are the channel for its activity, that it is within us, that we are it. We can, of course, fail to recognize it and so exclude it from our consciousness, but it will nevertheless be the basic fact of all existence. It tells of inspiration, the art of adjusting the individual mind to that of the Universal, the art of becoming a channel for the flow of Infinite Wisdom.

Part Twenty-One

This Part explains how we may come into possession of power sufficient to meet every situation which may arise in life. It explains that the ability to eliminate imperfect conditions depends upon mental action. It explains that great ideas have a tendency to eliminate smaller ideas, so that it is well to hold ideas which are large enough to counteract and destroy all small or undesirable tendencies. This is one of the secrets of success, one of the accomplishments of the Master Mind. It explains that the creative energy finds no more difficulty in handling a large situation than a small one. It explains how conditions are produced in our lives by the predominant thoughts which we entertain. It explains how you may set causes in motion which will create an irresistible magnetic power which will bring the things you require to you. It explains the issue between the old regime and the new, it explains the crux of the social problem, it explains the true secret of health, wealth and power.

Part Twenty-Two

This Part explains the cause of our present character, our present environment, our present ability, our present physical condition, and tells how we can make our future what we wish it to be. It explains how the vast panorama of Nature is being constantly changed by simply changing the rate of vibration. It tells how the rate of vibration is being constantly changed in our bodies, usually unconsciously and often with detrimental and disastrous results. It tells how we may effect this change consciously and thus bring about only harmonious and salutary conditions. It explains that the Law of Health is based on the law of vibration, and that with a proper knowledge of the law we may externalize health conditions. It explains the operation of this law and how it is being more generally understood and appreciated, and how many physicians are now giving the matter their earnest attention.

Part Twenty-Three

This Part tells of the money consciousness and the power which sets the current in motion which produces the attractive force which opens the doors to the arteries of commerce. It tells how the current is stopped or completely reversed and turned away from us. It tells how money is woven into the outer fabric of our existence. Why it engages the best thought of the best minds. How we make money. How to recognize opportunity. How to make a money magnet of yourself. How to get the necessary insight to perceive and utilize opportunities. How to recognize values. It tells how to convert an idea into an income, how to make a direct connection with the Universal Mind, how to secure practical results; in fact, it s tell what the only really practical thing is.

Part Twenty-Four

This Part explains the entire theory and practice of every system of Metaphysics; it tells how to express harmony, how to express health, how to express abundance. It explains the nature of all conditions, and how they may be changed or removed. It explains how every difficulty, no matter what it is or where it is, can be removed or dissolved, and it explains the only way in which this is ever done or can be done. It also tells of a Master Key by which those who are wise enough to understand, broad enough to weigh the evidence, firm enough to follow their own judgment, and strong enough to make the sacrifice exacted, may enter and partake.

Part One

INTRODUCTION

Would you bring into your life more power? Get the power consciousness. More health? Get the health consciousness. More happiness? Get the happiness consciousness. Live the spirit of these things until they become yours by right. It will then become impossible to keep them from you. The things of the world are fluid to a power within man by which he rules them.

You need not acquire this power. You already have it. But you want to understand it; you want to use it; you want to control it; you want to impregnate yourself with it, so that you can go forward and carry the world before you.

Day by day, as you go on and on, as you gain momentum, as your inspiration deepens, as your plans crystallize, as you gain understanding, you will come to realize that this world is no dead pile of stones and timber, but that it is a living thing! It is made up of the beating hearts of humanity. It is a thing of life and beauty.

It is evident that it requires understanding to work with material of this description, but those who come into this understanding are inspired by a new light, a new force, they gain confidence and greater power each day, they realize their hopes and their dreams come true, life has a deeper, fuller, clearer meaning than before.

1. All possession is based on consciousness. All gain is the result of an accumulative consciousness. All loss is the result of a scattering consciousness. That much gathers more is true on every plane of existence and that loss leads to greater loss is equally true.
2. Mind is creative, and conditions, environment and all experiences in life are the result of our habitual or predominant mental attitude.
3. The attitude of mind necessarily depends upon what we think. Therefore, the secret of all power, all achievement and all possession depends upon our method of thinking.
4. This is true because we must "be" before we can "do," and we can "do" only to the extent which we "are," and what we "are" depends upon what we "think."
5. We cannot express powers which we do not possess, and the only way to secure possession of power is to become conscious of power, and we can never become conscious of power until we learn that all power is from within.
6. There is a world within; a world of thought and feeling and power; of light and life and beauty; and although invisible, its forces are mighty.
7. The world within is governed by mind. When we discover this world we shall find the solution for every problem, the cause for every effect; and since the world within is subject to our control, all laws, of power and possession are also within our control.
8. The world without is a reflection of the world within. What appears without is what has been found within. In the world within may be found infinite Wisdom, infinite Power, infinite Supply of all that is necessary, waiting for unfoldment, development and expression. If we recognize these potentialities in the world within they will take form in the world without.
9. Harmony in the world within will be reflected in the world without by harmonious conditions, agreeable surround-

ings, the best of everything—It is the foundation of health, and a necessary essential to all greatness, all power, all attainment, all achievement and all success.
10. Harmony in the world within means the ability to control our thoughts, to determine for ourselves how any experience is to affect us.
11. Harmony in the world within results in optimism and affluence; affluence within results in affluence without.
12. The world without reflects the circumstances and the conditions of the consciousness within.
13. If we find wisdom in the world within, we shall have the understanding to discern the marvelous possibilities which are latent in this world within, and we shall be given the power to make these possibilities manifest in the world without.
14. As we become conscious of the wisdom in the world within, we mentally take possession of this wisdom, and by taking mental possession we come into actual possession of the power and wisdom necessary to bring into manifestation the essentials necessary for our most complete and harmonious development.
15. The world within is the practical world in which the men and women of power generate courage, hope, enthusiasm, confidence, trust and faith, by which they are given the fine intelligence to see the vision and the practical skill to make the vision real.
16. Life is an enfoldment, not accretion; what comes to us in the world without is what we already possess in the world within.
17. Mental efficiency is contingent upon harmony; discord means confusion; therefore, he who would acquire power must be in harmony with the law of his being.
18. We are related to the world without by the objective mind, the brain is the organ of this mind, and the cerebro-spinal system of nerves puts us in conscious communi-

cation with every part of the body. This system of nerves responds to every sensation of light, heat, odor, sound and taste.

19. When this mind thinks correctly, when it understands the truth, when the thoughts sent through the cerebro-spinal nervous system to the body are constructive, these sensations are pleasant, harmonious.

20. The result are constructive; we build strength, vitality and all constructive forces into our body, but it is through this same organ of the objective mind that all distress, sickness, lack, limitation and every form of discord and inharmony is admitted to our lives. It is therefore through the objective mind, or by wrong thinking, that we are related to all destructive forces.

21. We are related to the world within by the subconscious mind; the Solar Plexus is the organ of this mind; the sympathetic system of nerves presides over all subjective sensations, such as joy, fear, love, emotion, respiration, imagination and all other subconscious phenomena. It is through the subconscious that we are connected with the Universal Mind and brought into relation with the Infinite constructive forces of the universe.

22. It is through the Solar Plexus, the organ of the subconscious mind, that we are related to the world within.

23. It is the equalization of these two centers of our being, and the understanding of their functions, which is the great secret of life. With this knowledge we can bring the objective and subjective minds into conscious co-operation and thus coordinate the finite and the Infinite. Our future is entirely under our own control! It is not at the mercy of any capricious or uncertain external power.

24. All agree that there is but one Principle or Consciousness pervading the entire Universe, occupying all space, and being essentially the same in kind at every point of its

presence. It is Omnipotent, Omniscient and Omnipresent. All thoughts arid things are within Itself. It is all in all.

25. There is but one consciousness in the universe able to think and when it thinks its thoughts become objective things to it. As this Consciousness is omnipresent it must be present within every individual; each individual must be a manifestation of that Omnipotent, Omniscient and Omnipresent Consciousness.

26. As there is only one Consciousness in the Universe which is able to think, it necessarily follows that your consciousness is identical with the Universal Consciousness, or, in other words, all mind is one mind. There is no dodging this conclusion.

27. The consciousness which focuses in your brain cells is the same consciousness which focuses in the brain cells of every other individual. Each individual is but the individualization of the Universal, the Cosmic Mind.

28. The Universal Mind is static or potential energy; it simply is; it can manifest only through the individual, and the individual can manifest only through the Universal. They are one.

29. The ability of the individual to think is his ability to act on the Universal and bring it into manifestation. Human consciousness consists only in the ability of man to think. Thought is the vibratory force formed by converting static mind into dynamic mind.

30. As the sum of all attributes is contained in the Universal Mind; which is Omnipotent, Omniscient and Omnipresent, these attributes must be present at all times in their potential form in every individual. Therefore, when the individual thinks, the thought is compelled by its nature to embody itself in an objectivity or condition which will correspond with its origin.

31. Every thought is therefore a cause and every condition an effect; for this reason it is absolutely essential that you

control your thoughts so as to bring forth only desirable conditions.

32. All power is from within, and is absolutely under your control; it comes through exact knowledge and by the voluntary exercise of exact principles.

33. It should be plain that when you get a thorough understanding of this law, and are able to control your thought processes, you can apply it to any condition; in other words, you will have come into conscious co-operetion with Omnipotent law which is the fundamental basis of all things.

34. The Universal Mind is the life principle of every atom which is in existence; all are continually striving to manifest more life, all are intelligent, and all are seeking to carry out the purpose for which they were created.

35. A majority of mankind lives in the world without; few have found the world within, and yet it is the world within which makes the world without. The world within is one with the Universal, the world in which "we live and move and have our being," the great creative principle of the Universe; it is therefore creative and everything which you find in your world without has been created by you in the world within.

36. This system will bring you into a a realization of the power which will be yours when you understand this relation between the world without and the world within. The world within is the cause, the world without the effect; to change the effect you must change the cause.

37. You will at once see that this is a radically new and different idea; most men try to change effects by working with effects; they fail to see that this is simply changing one form of distress for another. To remove discord, we must remove the cause, and this cause can only be found in the world within.

38. The world within is the Universal Fountain of supply, and the world without is the outlet to the stream. Our ability

to receive depends upon our recognition of this Universal Fountain, this Infinite Energy of which each individual is an outlet, and so is one with every other individual.

39. All growth is from within. This is evident in all nature. Every plant, every animal, every human is a living testimony to this great law, and the error of the ages is in looking for strength or power from without.

40. A practical understanding of this law will substitute abundance for poverty, wisdom for ignorance, harmony for discord and freedom for tyranny, and certainly there can be no greater blessings than these from a material and social standpoint.

41. The three steps necessary to bring desire into realization are Idealization, Visualization and Manifestation. The first step then is to sow the seed; this should be done in the Silence, but few of us know what the Silence is. It is a physical stillness. The time required is from fifteen minutes to half an hour daily. Select a room where you can be alone and undisturbed; sit erect, comfortably, but do not lounge; let your thoughts roam where they will but be perfectly still; continue this for three or four days or for a week until you secure full control of your physical being.

42. Many will find this extremely difficult, other will conquer with ease, but it is absolutely essential to secure complete control of the body before you are ready to progress. Next week you will receive instructions for the next step; in the meantime you must have mastered this one.

Mind in itself is believed to be a subtle form of static energy, from which arises the activities called "thought," which is the dynamic phase of mind. Mind is static energy, thought is dynamic energy—the two phases of the same thing.
—WALKER.

STUDY GUIDE

Part One

Summary

Tells upon what possession is based, explains the cause of all gain, explains the cause of loss as well as all other experiences in life. It explains how power is secured. It tells of a world within and how this world is governed. It explains how the solution for every problem in life may be found. It tells how practical men and women find the courage, power, hope, enthusiasm and confidence by which they are given the intelligence and wisdom to make their dreams come true. It tells how more efficiency is obtained and retained, and how our future may be placed under our own control instead of being at the mercy of any capricious or uncertain external power. It explains the cause of every condition, the reason for every experience, the origin of all power, and why all power is absolutely under our own control.

1. Into which areas of your life would you like to bring more power? Health? Happiness? Career? Relationships? Finances?

2. You are encouraged to "live the spirit of these things until they become yours by right." What do you think the author means by this statement?

3. Haanel asserts that you already have the power and that you need not acquire anything you desire. All you need do is understand, use and control it. Do you believe this to be so? If so, what has prevented you from accessing it? If not, are you open to exploring this principle?

4. As you gain momentum, you will experience all of this world as a "thing of life and beauty." How do you currently experience this beauty in the world? What inspires you the most?

Comprehension Survey

At the beginning of this book, the author, Charles F. Haanel asserts that there is a process that affects how to successfully you move forward in your life. He states, "before any action is possible, there must be thought of some kind." This Comprehension Survey is based on the steps he outlines in Part One of the Master Key System. Once you have completed it, you will get a better sense of how much you are thriving from a place of positivity, or struggling with negativity dominating your life. For each of the principles below, choose the number that is most closely aligns to your beliefs (1 being "not at all" and 10 being "a great deal").

1. All you possess is based on your state of consciousness. Your losses are a result of your scattering consciousness, and your gains are a result of your accumulative consciousness or abundance mindset.
   1 —— 2 —— 3 —— 4 —— 5 —— 6 —— 7 —— 8 —— 9 —— 10

2. Your mind is a creative force that responds to your thought patterns and attitude.
   1 —— 2 —— 3 —— 4 —— 5 —— 6 —— 7 —— 8 —— 9 —— 10

3. The greatest secret of all power lies in your mental attitude or how you think.
   1 —— 2 —— 3 —— 4 —— 5 —— 6 —— 7 —— 8 —— 9 —— 10

4. Who you are depends upon what you "think" and precipitates what you "do."
   1 —— 2 —— 3 —— 4 —— 5 —— 6 —— 7 —— 8 —— 9 —— 10

5. In order to be powerful, you must realize that all power comes from within.
   1 —— 2 —— 3 —— 4 —— 5 —— 6 —— 7 —— 8 —— 9 —— 10

6. The forces that lie within you are invisible, but mighty.
   1 —— 2 —— 3 —— 4 —— 5 —— 6 —— 7 —— 8 —— 9 —— 10

7. When you discover your inner world, you can find the solution to any problem.
   1 —— 2 —— 3 —— 4 —— 5 —— 6 —— 7 —— 8 —— 9 —— 10

8. The outer world you experience is a reflection of your inner world.
   1 —— 2 —— 3 —— 4 —— 5 —— 6 —— 7 —— 8 —— 9 —— 10

9. All goodness in your life is based on your inner harmony.
   1 —— 2 —— 3 —— 4 —— 5 —— 6 —— 7 —— 8 —— 9 —— 10

10. The harmony you experience is related to how you choose to control your thoughts.
    1 —— 2 —— 3 —— 4 —— 5 —— 6 —— 7 —— 8 —— 9 —— 10

11. The degree to which you experience inner harmonious affluence and optimism, will ultimately affect your experiences in the world.
    1 —— 2 —— 3 —— 4 —— 5 —— 6 —— 7 —— 8 —— 9 —— 10

12. Your inner circumstances and conditions are reflected in the world without.

    1 — 2 — 3 — 4 — 5 — 6 — 7 — 8 — 9 — 10

13. When you find your inner wisdom, you awaken latent possibilities that you can then manifest in the world.

    1 — 2 — 3 — 4 — 5 — 6 — 7 — 8 — 9 — 10

14. When you become conscious of inner wisdom, you can take mental possession of it and bring it into actual manifestation in the world.

    1 — 2 — 3 — 4 — 5 — 6 — 7 — 8 — 9 — 10

15. Courage, hope, enthusiasm, confidence, trust and faith are practical traits of your inner world that will make your visions real in the outer world.

    1 — 2 — 3 — 4 — 5 — 6 — 7 — 8 — 9 — 10

16. Life experiences enfold based on that which you possess in your inner world.

    1 — 2 — 3 — 4 — 5 — 6 — 7 — 8 — 9 — 10

17. In order to be mentally effective, you must experience inner harmony.

    1 — 2 — 3 — 4 — 5 — 6 — 7 — 8 — 9 — 10

18. Your nervous system keeps you in constant communication with your body; it responds of light, heat, odor, sound and taste.

    1 — 2 — 3 — 4 — 5 — 6 — 7 — 8 — 9 — 10

19. When you mind thinks correctly, your nervous system experiences pleasant and harmonious sensations.

    1 — 2 — 3 — 4 — 5 — 6 — 7 — 8 — 9 — 10

20. Wrongful thinking by your objective mind is the cause of all destructive forces in your life.

    1 — 2 — 3 — 4 — 5 — 6 — 7 — 8 — 9 — 10

21. Your subconscious mind connects you to the Universal Mind and is seated in your solar plexus.

    1 — 2 — 3 — 4 — 5 — 6 — 7 — 8 — 9 — 10

22. You are related to the world within you through your Solar Plexus, with is the organ of your subconscious mind.

    1 — 2 — 3 — 4 — 5 — 6 — 7 — 8 — 9 — 10

23. When you can bring your conscious and subconscious minds into conscious cooperation, you coordinate the finite with the Infinite and can control your future.
   1 — 2 — 3 — 4 — 5 — 6 — 7 — 8 — 9 — 10

24. The entire Universe is based on an Omnipresence that exists in everything.
   1 — 2 — 3 — 4 — 5 — 6 — 7 — 8 — 9 — 10

25. Each individual is an expression of the Omnipresent Consciousness.
   1 — 2 — 3 — 4 — 5 — 6 — 7 — 8 — 9 — 10

26. There is only one mind, one consciousness in the Universe; all mind is one mind.
   1 — 2 — 3 — 4 — 5 — 6 — 7 — 8 — 9 — 10

27. We are all the individualization of the Universal or Cosmic Mind.
   1 — 2 — 3 — 4 — 5 — 6 — 7 — 8 — 9 — 10

28. The Universal Mind is energy that can only be manifest through you, and you through it.
   1 — 2 — 3 — 4 — 5 — 6 — 7 — 8 — 9 — 10

29. Your ability to think allows you to act on the Universal and manifest it into being.
   1 — 2 — 3 — 4 — 5 — 6 — 7 — 8 — 9 — 10

30. The sum of all attributes is contained in the Omnipresent Universal Mind. So, when you think, your thoughts are compelled by their innate nature.
   1 — 2 — 3 — 4 — 5 — 6 — 7 — 8 — 9 — 10

31. Each of your thoughts is a cause, and each condition is an effect of those thoughts. Thus you must control your thoughts.
   1 — 2 — 3 — 4 — 5 — 6 — 7 — 8 — 9 — 10

32. You control all of your power. It comes from within you.
   1 — 2 — 3 — 4 — 5 — 6 — 7 — 8 — 9 — 10

33. When you understand this law, you will come into alignment with the Omnipotent law, which is the basis of all things.
   1 — 2 — 3 — 4 — 5 — 6 — 7 — 8 — 9 — 10

34. All of life, every atom is intelligent and strives to manifest more life.
   1 — 2 — 3 — 4 — 5 — 6 — 7 — 8 — 9 — 10

35. Most live in the outer world and few have found the world within, which creates everything you experience in your outer world.

1 — 2 — 3 — 4 — 5 — 6 — 7 — 8 — 9 — 10

36. Your inner world is the cause that affects your outer world. You must change your inner world to transform the world around you.

1 — 2 — 3 — 4 — 5 — 6 — 7 — 8 — 9 — 10

37. Most people try to change effects by working with effects, when, in fact, they need to remove the cause from within in order to make any changes.

1 — 2 — 3 — 4 — 5 — 6 — 7 — 8 — 9 — 10

38. Your ability to receive depends upon your recognition of the Universal Fountain of supply that rests within you.

1 — 2 — 3 — 4 — 5 — 6 — 7 — 8 — 9 — 10

39. The growth of every being on this earth comes from within. Most err in believing that it is based on strength of power from without.

1 — 2 — 3 — 4 — 5 — 6 — 7 — 8 — 9 — 10

40. A practical understanding of this law will transform all aspects of your material and social experiences.

1 — 2 — 3 — 4 — 5 — 6 — 7 — 8 — 9 — 10

41. There are three steps to bringing your desires into realization: Idealization, Visualization and Manifestation. To initiate the process, you must sit still in silence until you are able to secure full control of your physical being.

1 — 2 — 3 — 4 — 5 — 6 — 7 — 8 — 9 — 10

42. While it is extremely difficult, you must master complete control of your body before you are ready to progress into manifesting that which you desire in your life.

1 — 2 — 3 — 4 — 5 — 6 — 7 — 8 — 9 — 10

Tally your total score by adding the number you allocated for yourself in each of the 42 principles above. Your score will range from 42 to 420.

If you scored between 280 and 420, already know a great deal about how your inner world masters your outer experiences. This book will serve to reinforce your knowledge and provide you with the tools to further transform knowledge into the wisdom that comes with experience. Be sure to journal about any new insights you gain, and even more so, be sure to document and experience you gain in relation to the knowledge that you receive in this book.

If you scored between 141 and 279, you have started taking steps towards gaining further clarity on how your inner world affects the world that you experience around you. Trust that by reading this book, you are making great strides in further developing your understanding of the mechanics of mind control. Be sure to document any new insights or experiences that you gain as you read this book. Doing so, turns static energy into more dynamic energy, and you will find that your experiences of the teaching will grow exponentially.

If you scored between 42 and 140, while you may have taken some steps towards mastering your inner world, you have a great deal more that you can learn that will assist you in creating greater joy, ease and harmony in your life. Be sure to read and re-read the teachings in this book, and keep a journal to make note of the new insights and practices you implement in order to further turn knowledge into wisdom, and theories into practical life applications.

Introspection:

1. What did you learn about yourself after completing the Comprehension Survey?
2. Was your score what you expected it to be? Why or why not?
3. What areas of the segment of the book have you mastered?
4. What are the areas in this segment of the book that you need to focus on?
5. What three "takeaways" from this segment would you share with others and why?

Exercise

The three steps necessary to bring desire into realization are Idealization, Visualization and Manifestation. The first step then is to sow the seed; this should be done in the Silence, but few of us know what the Silence is. It is a physical stillness. The time required is from fifteen minutes to half an hour daily. Select a room where you can be alone and undisturbed; sit erect, comfortably, but do not lounge; let your thoughts roam where they will but be perfectly still; continue this for three or four days or for a week until you secure full control of your physical being.

NOTES IN RESPONSE TO PERFORMING THIS EXERCISE
Be sure to journal about any findings or experiences you have as you continue to do this exercise as outlined.

Part Two

INTRODUCTION

Our difficulties are largely due to confused ideas and ignorance of our true interests. The great task is to discover the laws of Nature to which we are to adjust ourselves. Clear thinking and moral insight are, therefore, of incalculable value. All processes, even those of thought, rest on solid foundations.

The keener the sensibilities, the more acute the judgment, the more delicate the taste, the more refined the moral feelings, the more subtle the intelligence, the loftier the aspiration—the purer and more intense are the gratifications which existence yields. Hence it is that the study of the best that has been thought in the world gives supreme pleasure.

The powers, uses and possibilities of the mind under the new interpretations are incomparably more wonderful than the most extravagant accomplishment, or even dreams of material progress. Thought is energy. Active thought is active energy; concentrated thought is concentrated energy. Thought concentrated on a definite purpose becomes power. This is the power which is being used by those who do not believe in the virtue of poverty, or the beauty of self-denial. They perceive that this is the talk of weaklings.

The ability to receive and manifest this power depends upon the ability to recognize the Infinite Energy ever dwelling in man, constantly creating and re-creating his body and mind, and ready at any moment to manifest through him in any needful manner. In exact proportion to the recognition of this truth will be the manifestation in the outer life of the individual.

Part Two explains the method by which this is accomplished.

---

1. The operations of the mind are produced by two parallel modes of activity, the one conscious, and the other subconscious. Prof. Davidson says: "He who thinks to illuminate the whole range of mental action by the light of his own consciousness is not unlike one who should go about to illuminate the universe with a rushlight."
2. The subconscious, logical processes are carried on with a certainty and regularity which would be impossible if there existed the possibility of error. Our mind is so designed that it prepares for us the most important foundations of cognition, whilst we have not the slightest apprehension of the modus operandi.
3. The subconscious soul, like a benevolent stranger, works and makes provision for our benefit, pouring only the mature fruit into our lap; thus ultimate analysis of thought processes show that the subconscious is the theatre of the most important mental phenomena.
4. It is through the subconscious that Shakespeare must have perceived, without effort, great truths which are hidden from the conscious mind of the student; that Phidias fashioned marble and bronze; that Raphael painted Madonnas and Beethoven composed symphonies.
5. Ease and perfection depend entirely upon the degree in which we cease to depend upon the consciousness; playing the piano, skating, operating the typewriter, the skilled trades, depend for their perfect execution on the process of

the subconscious mind. The marvel of playing a brilliant piece on the piano, while at the same time conducting a vigorous conversation, shows the greatness of our subconscious powers.

6. We are all aware how dependent we are upon the subconscious, and the greater, the nobler, the more brilliant our thoughts are, the more it is obvious to ourselves that the origin lies beyond our ken. We find ourselves endowed with tact, instinct, sense of the beautiful in art, music, etc., of whose origin or dwelling place we are wholly unconscious.

7. The value of the subconscious is enormous; it inspires us; it warns us; it furnishes us with names, facts and scenes from the storehouse of memory. It directs our thoughts, tastes, and accomplishes tasks so intricate that no conscious mind, even if it had the power, has the capacity for.

8. We can walk at will; we can raise the arm whenever we choose to do so; we can give our attention through eye or ear to any subject at pleasure. On the other hand, we cannot stop our heartbeats nor the circulation of the blood, nor the growth of stature, nor the formation of nerve and muscle tissue, nor the building of the bones, nor many other important vital processes.

9. If we compare these two sets of action, the one decreed by the will of the moment, and the other proceeding in majestic, rhythmic course, subject to no vascillation, but constant at every moment, we stand in awe of the latter, and ask to have the mystery explained. We see at once that these are the vital processes of our physical life, and we can not avoid the inference that these all-important functions are designedly withdrawn from the domain of our outward will with its variations and transitions, and placed under the direction of a permanent and dependable power within us.

10. Of these two powers, the outward and changeable has been termed the "Conscious Mind," or the "Objective Mind"

(dealing with outward objects). The interior power is called the "Subconscious Mind," or the "Subjective Mind," and besides its work on the mental plane it controls the regular functions which make physical life possible.

11. It is necessary to have a clear understanding of their respective functions on the mental plane, as well as of certain other basic principles. Perceiving and operating through the five physical senses, the conscious mind deals with the impressions and objects of the outward life.

12. It has the faculty of discrimination, carrying with it the responsibility of choice. It has the power of reasoning whether inductive, deductive, analytical or syllogistic, and this power may be developed to a high degree. It is the seat of the will with all the energies that flow therefrom.

13. Not only can it impress other minds, but it can direct the subconscious mind. In this way the conscious mind become the responsible ruler and guardian of the subconscious mind. It is this high function which can completely reverse conditions in your life.

14. It is often true that conditions of fear, worry, poverty, disease, inharmony and evils of all kinds dominate us by reason of false suggestions accepted by the unguarded subconscious mind. All this the trained conscious mind can entirely prevent by its vigilant protective action. It may properly be called "the watchman at the gate" of the great subconscious domain.

15. One write has expressed the chief distinction between the two phases of mind thus:

    "Conscious mind is reasoning will. Subconscious mind is instinctive desire, the result of past reasoning will."

16. The subconscious mind draws just and accurate inferences from premises furnished from outside sources. Where the premise is true, the subconscious mind reaches a faultless conclusion, but, where the premise or suggestion is an error,

the whole structure falls. The subconscious mind does not engage in the process of proving. It relies upon the conscious mind, "the watchman at the gate," to guard it from mistaken impressions.

17. Receiving any suggestions as true, the subconscious mind at once proceeds to act thereon in the whole domain of its tremendous field of work. The conscious, mind can suggest either truth or error. If the latter, it is at the cost of wide-reaching peril to the whole being.

18. The conscious mind ought to be on duty during every waking hour. When the "watchman" is "off guard," or when its calm judgment is suspended, under a variety of circumstances, then the subconscious mind is unguarded and left open to suggestion from all sources. During the wild excitement of panic, or during the height of anger, or the impulses of the irresponsible mob, or at any other time of unrestrained passion, the conditions are most dangerous. The subconscious mind is then open to the suggestion of fear, hatred, selfishness, greed, self-depreciation and other negative forces, derived from surrounding persons or circumstances. The result is usually unwholesome in the extreme, with effects that may endure to distress it for a long time. Hence, the great importance of guarding the subconscious mind from false impressions.

19. The subconscious mind perceives by intuition. Hence, its processes are rapid. It does not wait for the slow methods of conscious reasoning. In fact, it can not employ them.

20. The subconscious mind never sleeps, never rests, any more than does your heart, or your blood. It has been found that by plainly stating to the subconscious mind certain specific things to be accomplished, forces are set in operation that lead to the result desired. Here, then, is a source of power which places us in touch with Omnipotence. Herein is a deep principle which is well worth our most earnest study.

21. The operation of this law is interesting. Those who put it into operation find that when they go out to meet the person with whom they anticipate a difficult interview, lo! something has been there before them and dissolved the supposed differences; everything is changed; all is harmonious; they find that when some difficult business problem presents itself they can afford to make delay and something suggests the proper solution; everything is properly arranged; in fact, those who have learned to trust the subconscious find that they have infinite resources at their command.

22. The subconscious mind is the seat of our principles and our aspirations. It is the fount of our artistic and altruistic ideals. These instincts can only be overthrown by an elaborate and gradual process of undermining the innate principles.

23. The subconscious mind can not argue controversially. Hence, if it has accepted wrong suggestions, the sure method of overcoming them is by the use of a strong counter suggestion, frequently repeated, which the mind must accept, thus eventually forming new and healthy habits of thought and life, for the subconscious mind is the seat of Habit. That which we do over and over becomes mechanical; it is no longer an act of judgment, but has worn its deep grooves in the subconscious mind. This is favorable for us if the habit be wholesome and right. If it be harmful and wrong, the remedy is to recognize the omnipotence of the subconscious mind and suggest present actual freedom. The subconscious being creative and one with our divine source will at once create the freedom suggested.

24. To sum up: The normal functions of the subconscious on the physical side have to do with the regular and vital processes, with the preservation of life and the restoration of health; with the care of offspring, which includes an

instinctive desire to preserve all life and improve conditions generally.

25. On the mental side, it is the storehouse of memory; it harbors the wonderful thought messengers, who work, unhampered by time or space; it is the fountain of the practical initiative and constructive forces of life: It is the seat of habit.

26. On the spiritual side, it is the source of ideals, of aspiration, of the imagination, and is the channel through which we recognize our Divine Source, and in proportion as we recognize this divinity do we come into an understanding of the source of power.

27. Some one may ask: "How can the subconscious change conditions?" The reply is, because the subconscious is a part of the Universal Mind and a part must be the same in kind and quality as the whole; the only difference is one of degree. The whole, as we know, is creative, in fact, it is the only creator there is, consequently, we find that mind is creative, and as thought is the only activity which the mind possesses thought must necessarily be creative also.

28. But we shall find that there is a vast difference between simply thinking, and directing our thought consciously, systematically and constructively; when we do this we place our mind in harmony with the Universal Mind, we come in tune with the Infinite, we set in operation the mightiest force in existence, the creative power of the Universal Mind. This, as everything else, is governed by natural law, and this law is the "Law of attraction," which is that Mind is creative, and will automatically correlate with its object and bring it into manifestation.

29. Last week I gave you an exercise for the purpose of securing control of the physical body; if you have accomplished this you are ready to advance. This time you will begin to control your thought. Always take the same room, the same chair, and the same position, if possible. In some cases it is

not convenient to take the same room, in this case simply make the best use of such conditions as may be available. Now be perfectly still as before, but inhibit all thought; this will give you control over all thoughts of care, worry and fear, and will enable you to entertain only the kind of thoughts you desire. Continue this exercise until you gain complete mastery.

30. You will not be able to do this for more than a few moments at a time, but the exercise is valuable, because it will be a very practical demonstration of the great number of thoughts which are constantly trying to gain access to your mental world.

31. Next week you will receive instructions for an exercise which may be a little more interesting, but it is necessary that you master this one first.

Cause and effect is as absolute and undeviating in the hidden realm of thought as in the world of visible and material things. Mind is the master weaver, both of the interior garment of character and the outer garment of circumstance.
—JAMES ALLEN.

STUDY GUIDE

Part Two

Summary

Tells how and why the operations of the mind are carried on by two parallel modes of activity, the one conscious and the other subconscious. It explains why the thought processes of the subconscious are the theatre of the most important mental phenomena, why ease and perfection depend entirely upon the degree in which we cease to depend upon the consciousness. It explains the origin of all great, noble, brilliant thoughts and ideas, why we find ourselves sometimes endowed with tact, instinct, courage, sagacity and inspiration. In fact, it tells of a vast mental storehouse in which ninety percent of our thought processes originate it explains also how this vast mental storehouse may be placed under the supervision and in the keeping of the conscious mind. It tells why those who are familiar with the laws governing in this larger mental domain are enabled to accomplish, to achieve, to become writers, authors, artists, ministers, captains of industry, and why all others must necessarily remain less than ten percent efficient.

1. Charles Haanel states that our difficulties are "largely due to confused ideas and ignorance of our true interest." Do you believe this to be true? What evidence do you have of this in your life?

2. Your greatest task is the "discover the laws of Nature—clear thinking and moral insight."

   Rate your ability to think clearly on a scale from 1 to 10 (1 being "not at all" and 10 being "a great deal"):

   1 —— 2 —— 3 —— 4 —— 5 —— 6 —— 7 —— 8 —— 9 —— 10

   Rate your moral insight on a scale from 1 to 10 (1 being "not at all" and 10 being "a great deal"):

   1 —— 2 —— 3 —— 4 —— 5 —— 6 —— 7 —— 8 —— 9 —— 10

3. "The powers, uses and possibilities of the mind . . . are incomparably more wonderful than the most extravagant accomplishment, or even dreams of material progress." Have you experienced this in your life? If so, how?

4. Does any part of you believe in "the virtue of poverty, or the beautify of self-denial"? Please explain.

5. Do you believe that you have access to Infinite Energy, and that you are creating and recreating your body and mind?

Comprehension Survey

In Part Two, Charles Haanel provides you with an overview of the dynamics between the two parallel modes of activity of the mind: the conscious and the subconscious. This Comprehension Survey will give you an indication of your knowledge of these dynamics and how they engage in your life. For each of the principles below, choose the number that is most closely aligns to your beliefs (1 being "not at all" and 10 being "a great deal").

1. Your mind operates with both conscious and subconscious activity. When you shed light on your consciousness, you illuminate the universe with that light.
   1 — 2 — 3 — 4 — 5 — 6 — 7 — 8 — 9 — 10

2. While you may not know the reasons why you think the thoughts you do, the workings of your subconscious mind are in perfect alignment with your life's necessary lessons.
   1 — 2 — 3 — 4 — 5 — 6 — 7 — 8 — 9 — 10

3. Your subconscious mind consciously and compassionately respond to our soul's needs in a perfect and powerful way.
   1 — 2 — 3 — 4 — 5 — 6 — 7 — 8 — 9 — 10

4. Your subconscious mind holds creative genius that, when accessed, effortlessly expose the world to great masterpieces.
   1 — 2 — 3 — 4 — 5 — 6 — 7 — 8 — 9 — 10

5. Creative skills manifest when you let go of your conscious mind, and allow your subconscious mind to take over.
   1 — 2 — 3 — 4 — 5 — 6 — 7 — 8 — 9 — 10

6. The more brilliant you become, the more you realize that your brilliance responds wholly to your subconscious mind.
   1 — 2 — 3 — 4 — 5 — 6 — 7 — 8 — 9 — 10

7. Your subconscious mind is massive; your conscious mind is nowhere near as powerful.
   1 — 2 — 3 — 4 — 5 — 6 — 7 — 8 — 9 — 10

8. While you can consciously master some of your physical mechanics, a great deal of your bodily functions work without your conscious intentions or interventions.

   1 —— 2 —— 3 —— 4 —— 5 —— 6 —— 7 —— 8 —— 9 —— 10

9. Your core bodily functions function without any interferences from your conscious mind or intentions.

   1 —— 2 —— 3 —— 4 —— 5 —— 6 —— 7 —— 8 —— 9 —— 10

10. Your conscious or objective mind deals with outward objects, whereas, your subconscious or subjective mind reigns over your interior plane of existence.

    1 —— 2 —— 3 —— 4 —— 5 —— 6 —— 7 —— 8 —— 9 —— 10

11. It is important that you are clear that your conscious mind deals with the impressions and objects of your outward life.

    1 —— 2 —— 3 —— 4 —— 5 —— 6 —— 7 —— 8 —— 9 —— 10

12. Your conscious mind is the seat of your will and has choice.

    1 —— 2 —— 3 —— 4 —— 5 —— 6 —— 7 —— 8 —— 9 —— 10

13. Your conscious mind can affect others and is the guardian of your subconscious mind.

    1 —— 2 —— 3 —— 4 —— 5 —— 6 —— 7 —— 8 —— 9 —— 10

14. "Negative" conditions creep into your subconscious mind when unguarded by your conscious mind.

    1 —— 2 —— 3 —— 4 —— 5 —— 6 —— 7 —— 8 —— 9 —— 10

15. Your conscious mind is reasoning will, and your subconscious mind is instinctive desire, the result of your past consciousness.

    1 —— 2 —— 3 —— 4 —— 5 —— 6 —— 7 —— 8 —— 9 —— 10

16. The subconscious mind responds to all impressions by the outside world that are distilled through your conscious mind. As the gatekeeper, it is the discerner to outer influences.

    1 —— 2 —— 3 —— 4 —— 5 —— 6 —— 7 —— 8 —— 9 —— 10

17. Your subconscious mind responds to all stimuli. If your conscious mind mistakenly suggests in error, the outcome can be extremely detrimental.

    1 —— 2 —— 3 —— 4 —— 5 —— 6 —— 7 —— 8 —— 9 —— 10

18. If your conscious mind does not diligently guard your subconscious mind from negative input, you can suffer from fear, hatred, selfishness, greed, self-depreciation and other negative forces that can have a long-term negative effect on you.

    1 —— 2 —— 3 —— 4 —— 5 —— 6 —— 7 —— 8 —— 9 —— 10

19. Your subconscious mind responds quickly through intuition, and cannot respond through the slow process of conscious reasoning.

    1 —— 2 —— 3 —— 4 —— 5 —— 6 —— 7 —— 8 —— 9 —— 10

20. Your subconscious mind never turns off, and is constantly responding and connected to Omnipotence.

    1 —— 2 —— 3 —— 4 —— 5 —— 6 —— 7 —— 8 —— 9 —— 10

21. When you trust the directives of your subconscious mind, life will unfold in your favor.

    1 —— 2 —— 3 —— 4 —— 5 —— 6 —— 7 —— 8 —— 9 —— 10

22. Your subconscious mind is the seat of your principles and ideals, and is the root upon which your artistic and altruistic ideals are founded.

    1 —— 2 —— 3 —— 4 —— 5 —— 6 —— 7 —— 8 —— 9 —— 10

23. Your subconscious mind is the seat of Habit, and to heal incorrect input, you must see its complete loving innocence; that it is Omnipotent and at one with divine source.

    1 —— 2 —— 3 —— 4 —— 5 —— 6 —— 7 —— 8 —— 9 —— 10

24. Your subconscious is responsible for your life functions, including the restoration of your life. It is instinctively committed to preserving all of life and improving conditions.

    1 —— 2 —— 3 —— 4 —— 5 —— 6 —— 7 —— 8 —— 9 —— 10

25. Your subconscious stores your memory, is intuitive and is the seat of your habits.

    1 —— 2 —— 3 —— 4 —— 5 —— 6 —— 7 —— 8 —— 9 —— 10

26. The more you connect to your Divine, the more powerful your understanding of its power, and the more powerful you become.

    1 —— 2 —— 3 —— 4 —— 5 —— 6 —— 7 —— 8 —— 9 —— 10

27. Your subconscious mind is a part of the Universal Mind, and in being so, has the same power to change conditions.

    1 —— 2 —— 3 —— 4 —— 5 —— 6 —— 7 —— 8 —— 9 —— 10

28. When you constructively and consciously direct your thoughts, you connect to the Infinite and attract that which you are focusing on into being.
1 —— 2 —— 3 —— 4 —— 5 —— 6 —— 7 —— 8 —— 9 —— 10

29. Once you secure control over you physical body, you can work towards securing control over your mind. The first step is to inhibit your thoughts. While this may last for only a couple of seconds, practicing it will increase your ability to do so.
1 —— 2 —— 3 —— 4 —— 5 —— 6 —— 7 —— 8 —— 9 —— 10

30. Continuing to practice mind control will build your mental muscle.
1 —— 2 —— 3 —— 4 —— 5 —— 6 —— 7 —— 8 —— 9 —— 10

31. Mastery takes practice and commitment.
1 —— 2 —— 3 —— 4 —— 5 —— 6 —— 7 —— 8 —— 9 —— 10

Tally your total score by adding the number you allocated for yourself in each of the 31 principles above. Your score will range from 31 to 310.

If you scored between 219 and 310, you are very adept at understanding the mechanics of the conscious and sub-conscious minds. Continue to study the teachings outlined in this book, being sure to practice the techniques shared in each segment.

If you scored between 125 and 218, you are quite familiar with the dynamics of the workings of your mind. Continue to reflect and journal about your findings, and be sure to practice the mind inhibition exercise this week.

If you scored between 31 and 124, you would be wise to integrate the teachings of this chapter into your understanding. If you need additional understanding, research the teachings on the law of attraction. Many have followed the wisdom that was imparted by Charles Haanel so long ago. Be sure to practice the mind technique outlined in this segment. Knowing is one strength, however experiencing will propel you forward on your journey of discovery.

Introspection:

1. What did you learn about yourself after completing the Comprehension Survey?
2. Was your score what you expected it to be? Why or why not?
3. What areas of the segment of the book have you mastered?
4. What are the areas in this segment of the book that you need to focus on?
5. What three "takeaways" from this segment would you share with others and why?

Exercise

Last week's exercise focused on securing control of your physical body; if you have accomplished this you are ready to advance. With this week's exercise, you will begin to control your thoughts. Always do this in the same room, the same chair, and the same position, if possible. As before, be perfectly still, but inhibit all thought; this will give you control over all thoughts of care, worry and fear, and will enable you to entertain only the kind of thoughts you desire. Continue this exercise until you gain complete mastery.

You will not be able to do this for more than a few moments at a time, but the exercise is valuable, because it will be a very practical demonstration of the great number of thoughts which are constantly trying to gain access to your mental world.

NOTES IN RESPONSE TO PERFORMING THIS EXERCISE

Be sure to journal about any findings or experiences you have as you continue to do this exercise as outlined.

Part Three

INTRODUCTION

You have found that the Individual may act on the Universal, and that the result of this action and interaction is cause and effect.

Thought, therefore, is the cause, and the experiences with which you meet in life are the effect.

Eliminate, therefore, any possible tendency to complain of conditions as they have been, or as they are, because it rests with you to change them and make them what you would like them to be.

Direct your efforts to a realization of the mental resources, always at your command, from which all real and lasting power comes.

Persist in this practice till you come to a realization of the fact that there can be no failure in the accomplishment of any proper object in life if you but understand your power and persist in your object, because the mind forces are ever ready to lend themselves to a purposeful will in the effort to crystallize thought and desire into actions, events and conditions.

Whereas in the beginning each function of life and each action is the result of conscious thought, the habitual actions become automatic and the thought that controls them passes into the realm of the subconscious; yet it is just as intelligent as before. It is necessary that it become automatic or subconscious in order that the self-conscious mind may attend to other things. The new actions will, however, in their turn, become habitual, then automatic, then subconscious in order that the mind again may he freed from this detail and advanced to still other activities.

When you realize this, you will have found a source of power which will enable you to cope with any situation in life which may develop.

---

1. The necessary interaction of the conscious and subconscious mind requires a similar interaction between the corresponding systems of nerves. Judge Troward indicates the very beautiful method in which this interaction is effected. He says: The cerebrospinal system is the organ of the conscious mind and the sympathetic is the organ of the subconscious. The cerebrospinal is the channel through which we receive conscious perception from the physical senses and exercise control over the movements of the body. This system of nerves has its center in the brain.

2. The Sympathetic System has its center in a ganglionic mass at the back of the stomach known as the Solar Plexus, and is the channel of that mental action which unconsciously supports the vital functions of the body.

3. The connection between the two systems is made by the vagus nerve which passes out of the cerebral region as a portion of the voluntary system to the thorax, sending out branches to the heart and lungs, and finally passing through the diaphragm, it loses its outer coating and be comes identified with the nerves of the Sympathetic System, forming a link between the two and making man a physical entity.

4. We have seen that every thought is received by the brain, which is the organ of the conscious; it is here subjected to our power of reasoning. When the objective mind has been satisfied that the thought is true it is sent to the Solar Plexus, or the brain of the subjective mind, to be made into our flesh, to be brought forth into the world as a reality. It is then no longer susceptible to any argument whatever. The subconscious mind cannot argue; it only acts. It accepts the conclusions of the objective mind as final.

5. The Solar Plexus has been likened to the sun of the body, because it is a central point of distribution for the energy which the body is constantly generating. This energy is very real energy, and this sun is a very real sun, and the energy is being distributed by very real nerves to all parts of the body, and is thrown off in an atmosphere which envelopes the body.

6. If this radiation is sufficiently strong the person is called magnetic; he is said to be filled with personal magnetism. Such a person may become positively radiant and wield an immense power for good. His presence alone, without a spoken word, will often bring peace and comfort to the troubled minds with which he comes in contact.

7. When the Solar Plexus is in active operation and is radiating life, and energy to every part of the body, and to every one with whom he comes in contact, the sensations are pleasant, the body is filled with health and all with whom he comes in contact experience a pleasant sensation.

8. If there is any interruption of this radiation the sensations are unpleasant, the flow of life and energy to some part of the body is stopped, and this is the cause of every ill to the human race, physical, mental or environmental.

9. Physical because the sun of the body is no longer generating sufficient energy to vitalize some part of the body; mental because the conscious mind is dependent upon the

subconscious mind for the vitality necessary to support its thought, and environmental, because the connection between the subconscious mind and the Universal mind, is being interrupted.

10. The Solar Plexus is the point at which the part meets with the whole, where the finite becomes Infinite, where the Uncreate becomes create, the Universal becomes individualized, the Invisible becomes visible. It is the point at which life appears and there is no limit to the amount of life an individual may generate from this Solar center.

11. This center of energy is Omnipotent because it is the point of contact with all life and all intelligence. It can therefore accomplish whatever it is directed to accomplish, and herein lies the power of the conscious mind; the subconscious can and will carry out such plans and ideas as may be suggested to it by the conscious mind.

12. Conscious thought, then, is master of this sun center from which the life and energy of the entire body flows and the quality of the thought which we entertain determines the quality of the thought which this sun will radiate, and the character of the thought which our conscious mind entertains will determine the character of the thought which this sun will radiate, and the nature of the thought which our conscious mind entertains will determine the nature of thought which this sun will radiate, and consequently will determine the nature of the experience which will result.

13. It is evident, therefore, that all we have to do is let our light shine; the more energy we can radiate, the more rapidly shall we be enabled to transmute undesirable conditions into sources of pleasure and profit. The important question, then, is how to let this light shine; how to generate this energy.

14. Non-resistant thought expands the Solar Plexus; resistant thought contracts it. Pleasant thought expands it; unpleas-

ant thought contracts it. Thoughts of courage, power, confidence and hope all produce a corresponding state, but the one arch enemy of the Solar Plexus which must be absolutely destroyed before there is any possibility of letting any light shine is fear. This enemy must be completely destroyed; he must be eliminated; he must be expelled forever; he is the cloud which hides the sun; which causes a perpetual gloom.

15. It is this personal devil which makes men fear the past, the present and the future; fear themselves, their friends and their enemies; fear everything and everybody. When fear is effectually and completely destroyed, your light will shine, the clouds will disperse and you will have found the source of power, energy and life.

16. When you find that you are really one with the Infinite power, and when you can consciously realize this power by a practical demonstration of your ability to overcome any adverse condition by the power of your thought, you will have nothing to fear; fear will have been destroyed and you will have come into possession of your birthright.

17. It is our attitude of mind toward life which determines the experiences with which we are to meet; if we expect nothing, we shall have nothing; if we demand much, we shall receive the greater portion. The world is harsh only as we fail to assert ourselves. The criticism of the world is bitter only to those who cannot compel room for their ideas. It is fear of this criticism that causes many ideas to fail to see the light of day.

18. But the man who knows that he has a Solar Plexus will not fear criticism or anything else; he will be too busy radiating courage, confidence, and power; he will anticipate success by his mental attitude; he will pound barriers to pieces, and leap over the chasm of doubt and hesitation which fear places in his path.

19. A knowledge of our ability to consciously radiate health, strength and harmony will bring us into a realization that there is nothing to fear because we are in touch with Infinite Strength.
20. This knowledge can be gained only by making a practical application of this information. We learn by doing; through practice the athlete becomes powerful.
21. As the following statement is of considerable importance, I will put it in several ways, so that you cannot fail to get the full significance of it. If you are religiously inclined, I would say, you can let your light shine. If your mind has a bias toward physical science, I would say you can wake the Solar Plexus; or, if you prefer the strictly scientific interpretation, I will say that you can impress your subconscious mind.
22. I have already told you what the result of this impression will be. It is the method in which you are now interested. You have already learned that the subconscious is intelligent and that it is creative, and responsive to the will of the conscious mind. What, then, is the most natural way of making the desired impression? Mentally concentrate on the object of your desire; when you are concentrating you are impressing the subconscious.
23. This is not the only way, but it is a simple and effective way, and the most direct way, and consequently the way in which the best results are secured. It is the method which is producing such extraordinary results that many think that miracles are being accomplished.
24. It is the method by which every great inventor, every great financier, every great statesman has been enabled to convert the subtle and invisible force of desire, faith and confidence into actual, tangible, concrete facts in the objective world.
25. The subconscious mind is a part of the Universal mind. The Universal is the creative principle of the Universe, a

part must be the same in kind and quality as the whole. This means that this creative power is absolutely unlimited; it is not bound by precedent of any kind, and consequently has no prior existing pattern by which to apply its constructive-principle.

26. We have found that the subconscious mind is responsive to our conscious will, which means that the unlimited creative power of the Universal Mind is within the control of the conscious mind of the individual.

27. When making a practical application of this principle, in accordance with the exercises given in subsequent lessons, it is well to remember that it is not necessary to outline the method by which the subconscious will produce the results you desire. The finite can not inform the Infinite. You are simply to say what you desire, not how you are to obtain it.

28. You are the channel by which the undifferentiated is being differentiated, and this differentiation is being accomplished by appropriation. It only requires recognition to set causes in motion which will bring about results in accordance with your desire, and this is accomplished because the Universal can act only through the individual, and the individual can act only through the Universal; they are one.

29. For your exercise this week, I will ask you to go one step further. I want you to not only be perfectly still, and inhibit all thought as far as possible, but relax, let go, let the muscles take their normal condition; this will remove all pressure from the nerves, and eliminate that tension which so frequently produces physical exhaustion.

30. Physical relaxation is a voluntary exercise of the will and the exercise will be found to be of great value, as it enables the blood to circulate freely to and from the brain and body.

31. Tension leads to mental unrest and abnormal mental activity of the mind; it produces worry, care, fear and anxiety.

Relaxation is therefore an absolute necessity in order to allow the mental faculties to exercise the greatest freedom.

32. Make this exercise as thorough and complete as possible, mentally determine that you will relax every muscle and nerve, until you feel quiet and restful and at peace with yourself and the world.

33. The Solar Plexus will then be ready to function and you will be surprised at the result.

We judge of a man's wisdom by his hope, knowing that the perception of the inexhaustibleness of Nature is an immortal youth.
—EMERSON.

STUDY GUIDE

Part Three

Summary

Tells why the necessary action and interaction of the conscious and subconscious minds requires two corresponding systems of nerves. It explains how the connection is made between these two systems of nerves. It explains and tells of a central point in the body for the distribution of energy. How this energy is distributed. How the distribution of this energy gives the individual pleasant sensations, how the interruption of this distribution brings discord, in harmony and lack and limitation of every kind. It tells of an arch enemy which must be destroyed, and tells how to destroy it. It tells what determines the experiences in life with which we are to meet, and why these experiences are under our own control. One enthusiastic reader says of this Part: "This document in my opinion is the greatest single document beneficial to mankind ever written in the history of the world; it is the first time that I have come into a true understanding of the Silent Powers that dominate and determine one's success."

1. Your thoughts are "cause" and your experiences are "effect." Provide a poignant example of how you have experienced this truth in your life.

2. You would be wise to abstain from complaining, for doing so will keep you in the state upon which you are complaining. Provide an example of how you lost yourself in a negative cycle by experiencing, then complaining about your experience.

3. When you continue to practice positive mindfulness, it eventually crystalizes in your psyche. Provide a situation or circumstance where a commitment and focus on a positive outcome came to fruition.

4. Ultimately, it is necessary for a positive mindset to become a habit that is embedded in your subconscious. Once it does, it is automatic and most powerful. Do you know of someone, either a public figure or someone in your life, who has achieved this state? Please describe them and evidence of their abilities.

Comprehension Survey

In this segment you will learn about the biology that supports your mindset. Once you have completed it, you will have a better understanding of the Solar Plexus and how energy moves within the body. For each of the principles below, choose the number that is most closely aligns to your beliefs (1 being "not at all" and 10 being "a great deal").

1. Your cerebrospinal system is the part of your neuro system that is associated with your conscious mind. Your sympathetic system is the organ of your subconscious mind.

   1 —— 2 —— 3 —— 4 —— 5 —— 6 —— 7 —— 8 —— 9 —— 10

2. Your Sympathetic System is located at your Solar Plexus/stomach and it unconscious supports the vital functions of your body.

   1 —— 2 —— 3 —— 4 —— 5 —— 6 —— 7 —— 8 —— 9 —— 10

3. The connection between the two systems is made by your vagus nerve.

   1 —— 2 —— 3 —— 4 —— 5 —— 6 —— 7 —— 8 —— 9 —— 10

4. Your objective mind receives your thoughts and once reasoned upon, sends the thoughts to the Solar Plexus and are made flesh. Once done, they cannot be argued by your subconscious mind.

   1 —— 2 —— 3 —— 4 —— 5 —— 6 —— 7 —— 8 —— 9 —— 10

5. Likened to the sun, your Solar Plexus is constantly generating energy to all parts of your body.

   1 —— 2 —— 3 —— 4 —— 5 —— 6 —— 7 —— 8 —— 9 —— 10

6. When the radiation from your Solar Plexus is sufficiently strong, you possess a magnetism and your presence alone brings peace and comfort to others.

   1 —— 2 —— 3 —— 4 —— 5 —— 6 —— 7 —— 8 —— 9 —— 10

7. When you Solar Plexus is in active operation, all in contact with its energy will experience health and wellbeing.

   1 —— 2 —— 3 —— 4 —— 5 —— 6 —— 7 —— 8 —— 9 —— 10

8. The interruption of this radiation blocks the flow of life energy and causes physical, mental and environmental illness.

   1 —— 2 —— 3 —— 4 —— 5 —— 6 —— 7 —— 8 —— 9 —— 10

9. Your physical suffers because of insufficient energy, your mental suffers because your conscious mind is dependent upon the energy fueled by your subconscious mind, and your environment suffers because the connection between minds is interrupted.

   1 —— 2 —— 3 —— 4 —— 5 —— 6 —— 7 —— 8 —— 9 —— 10

10. The Solar Plexus is the point at which the Universe becomes individualized and Infinite power is rooted and generated.
1 —— 2 —— 3 —— 4 —— 5 —— 6 —— 7 —— 8 —— 9 —— 10

11. This center is Omnipresent because it is in contact with source intelligence and all of life.
1 —— 2 —— 3 —— 4 —— 5 —— 6 —— 7 —— 8 —— 9 —— 10

12. The quality of your thoughts determines how the sun at your Solar Plexus will radiate, and will ultimately determine your life experiences.
1 —— 2 —— 3 —— 4 —— 5 —— 6 —— 7 —— 8 —— 9 —— 10

13. The more you let your light shine, the more rapidly you transmute the undesirable conditions into pleasurable and profitable ones.
1 —— 2 —— 3 —— 4 —— 5 —— 6 —— 7 —— 8 —— 9 —— 10

14. Your uplifting thoughts of courage, power, confidence and hope all produce such states. The greatest darkness that you must overcome is your fear.
1 —— 2 —— 3 —— 4 —— 5 —— 6 —— 7 —— 8 —— 9 —— 10

15. Once your fears are dispelled, you will find the source of power, energy and life
1 —— 2 —— 3 —— 4 —— 5 —— 6 —— 7 —— 8 —— 9 —— 10

16. Once you experience that you are one with Infinite power or Source, your fears will be destroyed and you will experience all that is your birthright.
1 —— 2 —— 3 —— 4 —— 5 —— 6 —— 7 —— 8 —— 9 —— 10

17. Fear is at the heart of any criticisms that get in the way of your success.
1 —— 2 —— 3 —— 4 —— 5 —— 6 —— 7 —— 8 —— 9 —— 10

18. Once you realize that you have a Solar Plexus (a connection to Source), you will overcome your doubts and fears.
1 —— 2 —— 3 —— 4 —— 5 —— 6 —— 7 —— 8 —— 9 —— 10

19. Your knowledge of your ability to radiate health, strength and harmony will override any fears that come your way.
1 —— 2 —— 3 —— 4 —— 5 —— 6 —— 7 —— 8 —— 9 —— 10

20. Like a seasoned athlete, you must practice this Truth in order to make it a reality.
    1 — 2 — 3 — 4 — 5 — 6 — 7 — 8 — 9 — 10

21. You can access Source through your beliefs in spirituality or science; either path can awakening your Solar Plexus or impact your subconscious.
    1 — 2 — 3 — 4 — 5 — 6 — 7 — 8 — 9 — 10

22. Concentrate on that which you desire, so that it can imprint upon your subconscious.
    1 — 2 — 3 — 4 — 5 — 6 — 7 — 8 — 9 — 10

23. While this is not the only way, it is the most direct way to experience miracles.
    1 — 2 — 3 — 4 — 5 — 6 — 7 — 8 — 9 — 10

24. Every great inventor, financier and statesman has used this method to achieve their success.
    1 — 2 — 3 — 4 — 5 — 6 — 7 — 8 — 9 — 10

25. Your creative power is infinite and unlimited, and unencumbered by past patterns.
    1 — 2 — 3 — 4 — 5 — 6 — 7 — 8 — 9 — 10

26. The unlimited power of the Universal Mind can be controlled by your conscious will.
    1 — 2 — 3 — 4 — 5 — 6 — 7 — 8 — 9 — 10

27. You cannot control how your desires will manifest, for your finite mind cannot inform that which is Infinite.
    1 — 2 — 3 — 4 — 5 — 6 — 7 — 8 — 9 — 10

28. You are the channel through which the Universe makes manifest your desires. All you need do is recognize this and the circle of light between you will unfold.
    1 — 2 — 3 — 4 — 5 — 6 — 7 — 8 — 9 — 10

29. In this week's exercise, illuminate the tension that creates exhaustion within your body.
    1 — 2 — 3 — 4 — 5 — 6 — 7 — 8 — 9 — 10

30. When you relax, blood flows freely throughout your brain and body.
1 — 2 — 3 — 4 — 5 — 6 — 7 — 8 — 9 — 10

31. Relaxation is absolutely necessary to quiet the active mind that produces worry, fear and anxiety.
1 — 2 — 3 — 4 — 5 — 6 — 7 — 8 — 9 — 10

32. Mentally commit to relaxing every nerve and muscle in your body until you feel at peace with yourself and the world.
1 — 2 — 3 — 4 — 5 — 6 — 7 — 8 — 9 — 10

33. Once you experience this peace, you will experience the amazing results of your Solar Plexus at work.
1 — 2 — 3 — 4 — 5 — 6 — 7 — 8 — 9 — 10

Tally your total score by adding the number you allocated for yourself in each of the 31 principles above. Your score will range from 33 to 330.

If you scored between 233 and 333, then you are already familiar with the mechanics of the Solar Plexus and how it ignites the light of creation within you. Be sure to do the prescribed exercise regularly and write about your experience in as much detail as possible.

If you scored between 133 and 232, you are quite familiar with the relationship between your nervous system, Solar Plexus and accessing the Infinite. Continue to review the 33 tenets in this segment, and do the required exercises on a daily basis. Doing so will enhance your understanding and turn knowledge into experience.

If you scored between 33 and 132, you are on your way to greater understanding. Be sure to continuously review the 33 tenets in this segment until they become fully understood. Then do the daily exercise, knowing that your commitment will drive you deeper into acquiring greater knowledge and experience of the Master Key System.

Introspection:

1. What did you learn about yourself after completing the Comprehension Survey?
2. Was your score what you expected it to be? Why or why not?
3. What areas of the segment of the book have you mastered?
4. What are the areas in this segment of the book that you need to focus on?
5. What three "takeaways" from this segment would you share with others and why?

Exercise

For your exercise this week, I will ask you to go one step further. I want you to not only be perfectly still, and inhibit all thought as far as possible, but relax, let go, let the muscles take their normal condition; this will remove all pressure from the nerves, and eliminate that tension which so frequently produces physical exhaustion. Make this exercise as thorough and complete as possible, mentally determine that you will relax every muscle and nerve, until you feel quiet and restful and at peace with yourself and the world.

NOTES IN RESPONSE TO PERFORMING THIS EXERCISE
Be sure to journal about any findings or experiences you have as you continue to do this exercise as outlined.

Part Four

INTRODUCTION

This Part will show you why what you think, or do, or feel, is an indication of what you are.

Thought is energy, and energy is power, and it is because all the religions, sciences and philosophies with which the world has heretofore been familiar have been based upon the manifestation of this energy instead of the energy itself, that the world has been limited to effects, while causes have been ignored or misunderstood.

For this reason we have God and the Devil in religion, positive and negative in science, and good and bad in philosophy.

The Master Key reverses the process; it is interested only in cause, and the letters received from readers tell a marvelous story; they indicate conclusively that adepts are finding the cause whereby they may secure for themselves health, harmony, abundance, and whatever else may be necessary for their welfare and happiness.

Life is expressive and it is our business to express ourselves harmoniously and constructively. Sorrow, misery, unhappiness, disease and poverty are not necessities and we are constantly eliminating them.

But this process of eliminating consists in rising above and beyond limitation of any kind. He who has strengthened and purified his thought need not concern himself about microbes, and he who has come into an understanding of the law of abundance will go at once to the source of supply.

It is thus that fate, fortune and destiny will be controlled as readily as a captain controls his ship, or an engineer his train.

---

1. The "I" of you is not the physical body; that is simply an instrument which the "I" uses to carry out its purposes; the "I" cannot be the Mind, for the mind is simply another instrument which the "I" uses with which to think, reason, and plan.
2. The "I" must be something which controls and directs both the body and the mind; something which determines what they shall do and how they shall act. When you come into a realization of the true nature of this "I" you will enjoy a sense of power which you have never before known.
3. Your personality is made up of countless individual characteristics, peculiarities, habits and traits of character; these are the result of your former method of thinking, but they have nothing to do with the real "I."
4. When you say "I think" the "I" tells the mind what it shall think; when you say "I go" the "I" tells the physical body where it shall go; the real nature of this "I" is spiritual, and is the source of the real power which comes to men and women when they come into a realization of their true nature.
5. The greatest and most marvelous power which this "I" has been given is the power to think, but few people know how to think constructively, or correctly, consequently they achieve only indifferent results. Most people allow their thoughts to dwell on selfish purposes, the inevitable result of an infantile mind. When a mind becomes mature, it understands that the germ of defeat is in every selfish thought.
6. The trained mind knows that every transaction must benefit every person who is in any way connected with the

transaction, and any attempt to profit by the weakness, ignorance or necessity of another will inevitably operate to his disadvantage.

7. This is because the individual is a part of the Universal. A part cannot antagonize any other part, but, on the contrary, the welfare of each part depends upon a recognition of the interest of the whole.

8. Those who recognize this principle have a great advantage in the affairs of life. They do not wear themselves out. They can eliminate vagrant thoughts with facility. They can readily concentrate to the highest possible degree on any subject. They do not waste time or money upon objects which can be of no possible benefit to them.

9. If you cannot do these things it is because you have thus far not made the necessary effort. Now is the time to make the effort. The result will be exactly in proportion to the effort expended. One of the strongest affirmations which you can use for the purpose of strengthening the will and realizing your power to accomplish, is, "I can be what I will to be."

10. Every time you repeat it realize who and what this "I" is; try to come into a thorough understanding of the true nature of the "I"; if you do, you will become invincible; that is, provided that your objects and purposes are constructive and are therefore in harmony with the creative principle of the Universe.

11. If you make use of this affirmation, use it continuously, night and morning, and as often during the day as you think of it, and continue to do so until it becomes a part of you; form the habit.

12. Unless you do this, you had better not start at all, because modern Psychology tells us that when we start something and do not complete it, or make a resolution and do not keep it, we are forming the habit of failure; absolute, ignominious failure. If you do not intend to do a thing, do not start; if you do start, see it through even if the heavens fall; if you

make up your mind to do something, do it; let nothing, no one interfere; the "I" in you has determined, the thing is settled; the die is cast, there is no longer any argument.

13. If you carry out this idea, beginning with small things which you know you can control and gradually increase the effort, but never under any circumstances allowing your "I" to be overruled, you will find that you can eventually control yourself, and many men and women have found to their sorrow that it is easier to control a kingdom than to control themselves.

14. But when you have learned to control yourself you will have found the "World Within" which controls the world without; you will have become irresistible; men and things will respond to your every wish without any apparent effort on your part.

15. This is not so strange or impossible as it may appear when you remember that the "World Within" is controlled by the "I" and that this "I" is a part or one with the Infinite "I" which is the Universal Energy or Spirit, usually called God.

16. This is not a mere statement or theory made for the purpose of confirming or establishing an idea, but it is a fact which has been accepted by the best religious thought as well as the best scientific thought.

17. Herbert Spencer says: "Amid all the mysteries by which we are surrounded, nothing is more certain than that we are ever in the presence of an Infinite and Eternal Energy from which all things proceed."

18. Lyman Abbott, in an address delivered before the Alumni of Bangor Theological Seminary, said: "We are coming to think of God as dwelling *in* man rather than as operating *on* men from without."

19. Science goes a little way in its search and stops. Science finds the everpresent Eternal Energy, but Religion finds the Power behind this energy and locates it within man.

But this is by no means a new discovery; the Bible says exactly the same thing, and the language is just as plain and convincing: "Know ye not that ye are the temple of the living God?" Here, then, is the secret of the wonderful creative power of the "World Within."

20. Here is the secret of power, of mastery. To overcome does not mean to go without things. Self-denial is not success. We cannot give unless we get; we cannot be helpful unless we are strong. The Infinite is not a bankrupt and we who are the representatives of Infinite power should not be bankrupts either, and if we wish to be of service to others we must have power and more power, but to get it we must give it; we must be of service.

21. The more we give the more we shall get; we must become a channel whereby the Universal can express activity. The Universal is constantly seeking to express itself, to be of service, and it seeks the channel whereby it can find the greatest activity, where it can do the most good, where it can be of greatest service to mankind.

22. The Universal cannot express through you as long as you are busy with your plans, your own purposes; quiet the senses, seek inspiration, focus the mental activity on the within, dwell in the consciousness of your unity with Omnipotence. "Still water runs deep;" contemplate the multitudinous opportunities to which you have spiritual access by the Omnipresence of power.

23. Visualize the events, circumstances and conditions which these spiritual connections may assist in manifesting. Realize the fact that the essence and soul of all things is spiritual and that the spiritual is the real, because it is the life of all there is; when the spirit is gone, the life is gone; it is dead; it has ceased to exist.

24. These mental activities pertain to the world within, to the world of cause; and conditions and circumstances which

result are the effect. It is thus that you become a creator. This is important work, and the higher, loftier, grander and more noble ideals which you can conceive, the more important the work will become.

25. Over-work or over-play or over bodily activity of any kind produces conditions of mental apathy and stagnation which makes it impossible to do the more important work which results in a realization of conscious power. We should, therefore, seek the Silence frequently. Power comes through repose; it is in the Silence that we can be still, and when we are still, we can think, and thought is the secret of all attainment.

26. Thought is a mode of motion and is carried by the law of vibration the same as light or electricity. It is given vitality by the emotions through the law of love; it takes form and expression by the law of growth; it is a product of the spiritual "I," hence its Divine, spiritual, and creative nature.

27. From this it is evident that in order to express power, abundance or any other constructive purpose, the emotions must be called upon to give feeling to the thought so that it will take form. How may this purpose be accomplished? This is the vital point; how may we develop the faith, the courage, the feeling, which will result in accomplishment?

28. The reply is, by exercise; mental strength is secured in exactly the same way that physical strength is secured, by exercise. We think something, perhaps with difficulty the first time; we think the same thing again, and it becomes easier this time; we think it again and again; it then becomes a mental habit. We continue to think the same thing; finally it becomes automatic; we can no longer help thinking this thing; we are now positive of what we think; there is no longer any doubt about it. We are sure; we know.

29. Last week I asked you to relax, to let go physically. This week, I am going to ask you to let go mentally. If you practiced the

exercise given you last week fifteen or twenty minutes a day in accordance with the instructions, you can no doubt relax physically; and anyone who cannot consciously do this quickly and completely is not a master of himself. He has not obtained freedom; he is still a slave to conditions. But I shall assume that you have mastered the exercise and are ready to take the next step, which is mental freedom.

30. This week, after taking your usual position, remove all tension by completely relaxing, then mentally let go of all adverse conditions, such as hatred, anger, worry, jealousy, envy, sorrow, trouble or disappointment of any kind.
31. You may say that you cannot "let go" of these things, but you can; you can do so by mentally determining to do so, by voluntary intention and persistence.
32. The reason that some cannot do this is because they allow themselves to be controlled by the emotions instead of by their intellect. But the will guided by the intellect will gain the victory. You will not succeed the first time you try, but practice makes perfect, in this as in everything else, and you must succeed in dismissing, eliminating and completely destroying these negative and destructive thoughts; because they are the seed which is constantly germinating into discordant conditions of every conceivable kind and description.

There is nothing truer than that the quality of thought which we entertain correlates certain externals in the outside world. This is the Law from which there is no escape. And it is this Law, this correlative of the thought with its object, that from time immemorial has led the people to believe in special providence.
—WILMANS.

STUDY GUIDE

Part Four

Summary

This Part tells what it is which controls that which you call yourself. "You" are not your body; the body is simply the physical instrument which the ego uses to carry out its purpose. "You" are not your mind; this is simply another instrument which the ego uses to think, reason and plan. When you say "'I' go" you tell the body where to go, when you say "'I' think" you tell the mind what to think. When you come into a realization of the true nature of the "I" you will enjoy a sense of power which nothing else can give, because you will come to know what you are, who you are, what you want, and how to get it.

1. Why do you believe that what you think, do or feel is an indication of what you are? Provide an example to illuminate your explanation.

2. The author stipulates that because we have been focused on the manifestations of the Source energy, as opposed to the Source energy itself, the world has been limited to effects and has ignored or misunderstood the causes. Where do you currently see evidence of this in the world?

3. In your own words, explain why God and Devil, positive and negative and good and bad exist in the world?

4. Why do you think shifting your focus from "effect" to "cause" will have an impact on your life? Describe what you believe the impact will be.

5. Charles Haanel asserts that "life is expressive" and that it is your business to express yourself "harmoniously and constructively." How do you currently do so? How can you further do so?

6. If you have strengthened and purified your thoughts, you need not worry about the little things. What "little things" do you currently concern yourself with?

Comprehension Survey

In this segment you will learn about the true nature of the Universal "I." Once you have completed it, you will have a greater understanding of how much you are supported by Source energy, especially when your intentions are beyond the self-serving "I." For each of the principles below, choose the number that is most closely aligns to your beliefs (1 being "not at all" and 10 being "a great deal").

1. The "I" is not your body, nor your mind. They are instruments your "I" uses to carry out its purpose and to think, reason and plan.
   1 — 2 — 3 — 4 — 5 — 6 — 7 — 8 — 9 — 10

2. Once you understand the true nature of "I," you will experience greater power.
   1 — 2 — 3 — 4 — 5 — 6 — 7 — 8 — 9 — 10

3. Your personality is a result of your former thinking and has nothing to do with the real "I."
   1 — 2 — 3 — 4 — 5 — 6 — 7 — 8 — 9 — 10

4. You will experience real power when you realize the true nature of "I" as spiritual
   1 — 2 — 3 — 4 — 5 — 6 — 7 — 8 — 9 — 10

5. When your mind matures, it will outgrow selfish thoughts.
   1 — 2 — 3 — 4 — 5 — 6 — 7 — 8 — 9 — 10

6. The trained mind knows that every transaction must be intended for the highest good of all involved.
   1 — 2 — 3 — 4 — 5 — 6 — 7 — 8 — 9 — 10

7. You, as an individual are part of the whole, thus you want not to antagonize any part of that whole.
   1 — 2 — 3 — 4 — 5 — 6 — 7 — 8 — 9 — 10

8. Once you recognize this principle, you will not burn yourself out thinking about anything less than the highest good for all.
   1 — 2 — 3 — 4 — 5 — 6 — 7 — 8 — 9 — 10

9. The greater your efforts, the greater your rewards. One of the strongest affirmations you can make is, "I can be what I will to be."
   1 — 2 — 3 — 4 — 5 — 6 — 7 — 8 — 9 — 10

10. When you repeat the affirmation and understand the true nature of the "I," you will be invincible if your thoughts are pure and harmonious.
    1 — 2 — 3 — 4 — 5 — 6 — 7 — 8 — 9 — 10

11. Repeat this affirmation until it becomes a habitual part of you.
    1 —— 2 —— 3 —— 4 —— 5 —— 6 —— 7 —— 8 —— 9 —— 10

12. Follow through on this practice, for if you do not, you will form a destructive habit of failure in your psyche.
    1 —— 2 —— 3 —— 4 —— 5 —— 6 —— 7 —— 8 —— 9 —— 10

13. While many struggle with controlling themselves, if you practice this starting with small things and see it through, you will eventually be able to control yourself.
    1 —— 2 —— 3 —— 4 —— 5 —— 6 —— 7 —— 8 —— 9 —— 10

14. When you truly find the "World Within" you, you will be magnetic and unstoppable.
    1 —— 2 —— 3 —— 4 —— 5 —— 6 —— 7 —— 8 —— 9 —— 10

15. Remember that the "World Within" is controlled by the "I" which is one with the Infinite Universal Energy.
    1 —— 2 —— 3 —— 4 —— 5 —— 6 —— 7 —— 8 —— 9 —— 10

16. This is more than a theory. It is a truth that has been accepted by both religion and science.
    1 —— 2 —— 3 —— 4 —— 5 —— 6 —— 7 —— 8 —— 9 —— 10

17. The one thing for which you can be certain is that you are always in the presence of the creative, infinite source from which all things proceed.
    1 —— 2 —— 3 —— 4 —— 5 —— 6 —— 7 —— 8 —— 9 —— 10

18. God or Source dwells within you, rather than operating outside of you.
    1 —— 2 —— 3 —— 4 —— 5 —— 6 —— 7 —— 8 —— 9 —— 10

19. When the bible states, "Know ye not that ye are the temple of the Living God?" it is referencing the creative power that lies within you.
    1 —— 2 —— 3 —— 4 —— 5 —— 6 —— 7 —— 8 —— 9 —— 10

20. You cannot give from an impoverished state. You need power to beget more power, but to get it, you must give and commit to being of service.
    1 —— 2 —— 3 —— 4 —— 5 —— 6 —— 7 —— 8 —— 9 —— 10

21. You need to be a channel through which the Universal can express itself. The more of service you can be to mankind, the more that power will make use of you.

    1 — 2 — 3 — 4 — 5 — 6 — 7 — 8 — 9 — 10

22. Still and quiet yourself. When you are busy making plans, the Universal is unable to express itself through you.

    1 — 2 — 3 — 4 — 5 — 6 — 7 — 8 — 9 — 10

23. Visualize that which you wish to manifest, knowing that spiritual connections can assist you. Realize that the spiritual is real, as life begins and ends with it.

    1 — 2 — 3 — 4 — 5 — 6 — 7 — 8 — 9 — 10

24. The more noble and grand your ambitions, the more important your work will be.

    1 — 2 — 3 — 4 — 5 — 6 — 7 — 8 — 9 — 10

25. Overdoing anything will impede upon your power. Seek silence and stillness and there you will uncover the secret of all attainment.

    1 — 2 — 3 — 4 — 5 — 6 — 7 — 8 — 9 — 10

26. As a product of the spiritual "I," your thoughts are energized by love. They are Divine spiritual and creative in nature.

    1 — 2 — 3 — 4 — 5 — 6 — 7 — 8 — 9 — 10

27. Your emotions empower your thoughts to make ideals manifest into form.

    1 — 2 — 3 — 4 — 5 — 6 — 7 — 8 — 9 — 10

28. Just as repeated exercise strengthens the body, repeated mental exercise makes what was once difficult a mental habit that is no longer questioned.

    1 — 2 — 3 — 4 — 5 — 6 — 7 — 8 — 9 — 10

29. If you have diligently done last week's exercises for 15–20 minutes each day, you are ready to do this week's exercise.

    1 — 2 — 3 — 4 — 5 — 6 — 7 — 8 — 9 — 10

30. This week, as you sit in stillness, let go of all adverse conditions such as hatred, anger, worry, jealousy, envy, sorrow, trouble or disappointment of any kind.

    1 — 2 — 3 — 4 — 5 — 6 — 7 — 8 — 9 — 10

31. Through persistence, intention and determination, you can do anything to which you set your mind.

1 —— 2 —— 3 —— 4 —— 5 —— 6 —— 7 —— 8 —— 9 —— 10

32. You must master your emotions, and allow your intellect to take over in order to overcome your negative thinking patterns.

1 —— 2 —— 3 —— 4 —— 5 —— 6 —— 7 —— 8 —— 9 —— 10

Tally your total score by adding the number you allocated for yourself in each of the 32 principles above. Your score will range from 32 to 320.

If you scored between 225 and 320, you have a strong sense of what your personal "I" self is in comparison to the more expanded "I" that is a part of the Universal Source. You see how powerful it is to see yourself as a being beyond the limitations of your personality. Continue to read through the principles outlined in this segment, and practice the exercise once each day. Be sure to write about your experience and subsequent findings.

If you scored between 129 and 224, you are quite aware of dance that you experience between the limited, small "I" self, and the more expanded and potent self that is a part of the limitless field of Universal Source Intelligence. Read through the thirty-two principles outlined in this session once again, and be sure to do the accompanying exercise several times throughout the week.

If you scored between 32 and 128, There is still a great deal more learning you can do to further integrate the wisdom of this segment of the book into your conscious and subconscious mind. Take time to read through each of the thirty-two teachings in this segment, along with the corresponding introspective questions. Be sure that you fully comprehend each by the end of the week, and continue to do the exercise on a daily basis. Write about your findings.

Introspection:

1. What did you learn about yourself after completing the Comprehension Survey?
2. Was your score what you expected it to be? Why or why not?
3. What areas of the segment of the book have you mastered?
4. What are the areas in this segment of the book that you need to focus on?
5. What three "takeaways" from this segment would you share with others and why?

Exercise

Last week you were asked you to relax, to let go physically. This week, you will focus on letting go mentally. After taking your usual position, remove all tension by completely relaxing, then mentally let go of all adverse conditions, such as hatred, anger, worry, jealousy, envy, sorrow, trouble or disappointment of any kind. You may say that you cannot "let go" of these things, but you can; you can do so by mentally determining to do so, by voluntary intention and persistence.

NOTES IN RESPONSE TO PERFORMING THIS EXERCISE

Be sure to journal about any findings or experiences you have as you continue to do this exercise as outlined.

Part Five

INTRODUCTION

After studying this Part carefully, you will see that every conceivable force or object or fact is the result of mind in action.

Mind in action is thought, and thought is creative. Men are thinking now as they never thought before. Therefore, this is a creative age, and the world is awarding its richest prizes to the thinkers.

Matter is powerless, passive, inert. Mind is force, energy power. Mind shapes and controls matter. Every form which matter takes is but the expression of some pre-existing thought.

But thought works no magic transformations; it obeys natural laws; it sets in motion natural forces; it releases natural energies; it manifests in your conduct and actions, and these in turn react upon your friends and acquaintances, and eventually upon the whole of your environment.

You can originate thought, and, since thoughts are creative, you can create for yourselves the things you desire.

1. At least ninety percent of our mental life is subconscious, so that those who fail to make use of this mental power live within very narrow limits.

2. The subconscious can and will solve any problem for us if we know how to direct it. The subconscious processes are always at work; the only question is, are we to be simply passive recipients of this activity, or are we to consciously direct the work? Shall we have a vision of the destination to be reached, the dangers to be avoided, or shall we simply drift!
3. We have found that mind pervades every part of the physical body and is always capable of being directed or impressed by authority corning from the objective or the more dominant portion of the mind.
4. The mind, which pervades the body, is largely the result of heredity, which, in turn, is simply the result of all the environments of all past generations on the responsive and ever-moving life forces. An understanding of this fact will enable us to use our authority when we find some undesirable trait of character manifesting.
5. We can consciously use all the desirable characteristics with which we have been provided and we can repress and refuse to allow the undesirable ones to manifest.
6. Again, this mind which pervades our physical body is not only the result of hereditary tendencies, but is the result of home, business and social environment, where countless thousands of impressions, ideas, prejudices and similar thoughts have been received. Much of this has been received from others, the result of opinions, suggestions or statements; much of it is the result of our own thinking, but nearly all of it has been accepted with little or no examination or consideration.
7. The idea seemed plausible, the conscious received it, passed it on to the subconscious, where it was taken up by the Sympathetic System and passed on to be built into our physical body. "The word has become flesh."
8. This, then, is the way we are constantly creating and recreating ourselves; we are today the result of our past think-

ing, and we shall be what we are thinking today, the Law of Attraction is bringing to us, not the things we should like, or the things we wish for, or the things some one else has, but it brings us "our own," the things which we have created by our thought processes, whether consciously or unconsciously. Unfortunately, many of us are creating these things unconsciously.

9. If either of us were building a home for ourselves, how careful we would be in regard to the plans; how we should study every detail; how we should watch the material and select only the best of everything; and yet how careless we are when it comes to building our Mental Home, which is infinitely more important than any physical home, as everything which can possibly enter into our lives depends upon the character of the material which enters into the construction of our Mental Home.

10. What is the character of this material? We have seen that it is the result of the impressions which we have accumulated in the past and stored away in our subconscious Mentality. If these impressions have been of fear, of worry, of care, of anxiety; if they have been despondent, negative, doubtful, then the texture of the material which we are weaving today will be of the same negative material. Instead of being of any value, it will be mildewed and rotten and will bring us only more toil and care and anxiety. We shall be forever busy trying to patch it up and make it appear at least genteel.

11. But if we have stored away nothing but courageous thought, if we have been optimistic, positive, and have immediately thrown any kind of negative thought on the scrap pile, have refused to have anything to do with it, have refused to associate with it or become identified with it in any way, what then is the result? Our mental material is now of the best kind; we can weave any kind of

material we want; we can use any color we wish; we know that the texture is firm, that the material is solid, that it will not fade, and we have no fear, no anxiety concerning the future; there is nothing to cover, there are no patches to hide.

12. These are psychological facts; there is no theory or guess work about these thinking processes; there is nothing secret about them; in fact, they are so plain that every one can understand them. The thing to do is to have a mental house-cleaning, and to have this house-cleaning every day, and keep the house clean. Mental, moral and physical cleanliness are absolutely indispensable if we are to make progress of any kind.

13. When this mental house-cleaning process has been completed, the material which is left will be suitable for the making of the kind of ideals or mental images which we desire to realize.

14. There is a fine estate awaiting a claimant. Its broad acres, with abundant crops, running water and fine timber, stretch away as far as the eye can see. There is a mansion, spacious and cheerful, with rare pictures, a well-stocked library, rich hangings, and every comfort and luxury. All the heir has to do is to assert his heirship, take possession, and use the property. He must use it; he must not let it decay; for use is the condition on which he holds it. To neglect it is to lose possession.

15. In the domain of mind and spirit, in the domain of practical power, such an estate is yours. You are the heir! You can assert your heirship, and possess, and use this rich inheritance. Power over circumstances is one of its fruits, health, harmony and prosperity are assets upon its balance sheet. It offers you poise and peace. It costs you only the labor of studying and harvesting its great resources. It demands no sacrifice, except the loss of your limitations, your ser-

vitudes, your weakness. It clothes you with self-honor, and puts a scepter in your hands.

16. To gain this estate, three processes are necessary: You must earnestly desire it. You must assert your claim. You must take possession.

17. You admit that those are not burdensome conditions.

18. You are familiar with the subject of heredity. Darwin, Huxley, Haeckel, and other physical scientists have piled evidence mountain high that heredity is a law attending progressive creation. It is progressive heredity which gives man his erect attitude, his power of motion, the organs of digestion, blood circulation, nerve force, muscular force, bone structure and a host of other faculties on the physical side. There are even more impressive facts concerning heredity of mind force. All the constitute what may be called your human heredity.

19. But there is a heredity which the physical scientists have not compassed. It lies beneath and antecedent to all their researches. At a point where they throw up their hands in despair, saying they cannot account for what they see, this divine heredity is found in full sway.

20. It is the benignant force which decrees primal creation. It thrills down from the Divine, direct into every created being. It originates life, which the physical scientist has not done, nor ever can do. It stands out among all forces supreme, unapproachable. No human heredity can approach it. No human heredity measures up to it.

21. This Infinite Life flows through you; is you. Its doorways are but the faculties which comprise your consciousness. To keep open these doors is the Secret of Power. Is it not worth while to make the effort?

22. The great fact is, that the source of all life and all power is from within. Persons, circumstances and events may suggest need and opportunities, but the insight, strength and power to answer these needs will be found within.

23. Avoid counterfeits. Build firm foundations for your consciousness upon forces which flow direct from the Infinite source, the Universal Mind of which you are the image and likeness.
24. Those who have come into possession of this inheritance are never quite the same again. They have come into possession of a sense of power hitherto undreamed of. They can never again be timid, weak, vacillating, or fearful. They are indissolubly connected with Omnipotence. Something in them has been aroused; they have suddenly discovered that they possess a tremendous latent ability of which they were heretofore entirely unconscious.
25. This power is from within, but we cannot receive it unless we give it. Use is the condition upon which we hold this inheritance. We are each of us but the channel through which the Omnipotent power is being differentiated into form; unless we give out the channel is obstructed and we can receive no more. This is true on every plane of existence and in every field of endeavor and all walks of life. The more we give, the more we get. The athlete who wishes to get strong must make use of the strength he has, and the more he gives the more he will get. The financier who wishes to make money must make use of the money he has, for only by using it can he get more.
26. The merchant who does not keep his goods going out will soon have none coming in; the corporation which fails to give efficient service will soon lack customers; the attorney who fails to get results will soon lack clients, and so it goes everywhere; power is contingent upon a proper use of the power already in our possession; what is true in every field of endeavor, every experience in life, is true of the power from which every other power known among men is begotten-spiritual power. Take away the spirit and what is left? Nothing.

27. If then the spirit is all there is, upon the recognition of this fact must depend the ability to demonstrate all power, whether physical, mental or spiritual.
28. All possession is the result of the accumulative attitude of mind, or the money consciousness; this is the magic wand which will enable you to receive the idea, and it will formulate plans for you to execute, and you will find as much pleasure in the execution as in the satisfaction of attainment and achievement.
29. Now, go to your room, take the same seat, the same position as heretofore, and mentally select a place which has pleasant associations. Make a complete mental picture of it, see the buildings, the grounds, the trees, friends, associations, everything complete. At first, you will find yourself thinking of everything under the sun, except the ideal upon which you desire to concentrate. But do not let that discourage you. Persistence will win, but persistence requires that you practice these exercises every day without fail.

Relation and connection are not somewhere and some time, but everywhere and always.
—EMERSON.

STUDY GUIDE

Part Five

Summary

This Part tells how the subconscious processes are continually at work, and it tells how we may consciously direct this work instead of being mere passive recipients of its activity. It tells how we may have a vision of the destination to be reached, the dangers and pitfalls to be avoided. It tells how "the word has become flesh," how we are constantly creating and recreating ourselves. It tells of a mental home which each of us is building for ourselves, the importance of this home, where the material is secured, the character of the furnishing, how and why many of us need a mental housecleaning in case we wish to realize our ideas. It tells of the conditions by which we may come into an inheritance of health, harmony and prosperity, and the condition is one which demands no sacrifice except the loss of our limitations, our servitudes and our weaknesses, and costs only the labor of harvesting its great resources.

1. Do you believe that every conceivable force, object or fact is a result of your mind in action? Please explain.

2. Increased thought precipitates new innovation. Where do you see evidence of this now or in history?

3. Mind is the force that shapes matter. If every form that matter takes first existed as a thought, then what are your current thoughts manifesting into future being?

4. Your thoughts obey natural laws, and react upon your entire environment. Consider something you really appreciate in your environment. What pre-existing thoughts created it? Similar, what pre-existing thoughts created something with which you are challenged in your life?

Comprehension Survey

In this segment you will learn how you can more consciously and actively participate in co-creating with the Universe. Once you have completed it, you will get a better sense of how you can inherit and plan for a better life. For each of the principles below, choose the number that is most closely aligns to your beliefs (1 being "not at all" and 10 being "a great deal").

1. At least ninety percent of your mental life is subconscious. If you don't make use of your mental power, then you live a very narrow life.
   1 — 2 — 3 — 4 — 5 — 6 — 7 — 8 — 9 — 10

2. You choose whether to navigate the vessel of your subconscious, or to allow it to simply drift.
   1 — 2 — 3 — 4 — 5 — 6 — 7 — 8 — 9 — 10

3. Your body is controlled by the most dominant part of your mind.
   1 — 2 — 3 — 4 — 5 — 6 — 7 — 8 — 9 — 10

4. If you know that the mind that pervades your body is hereditary, then you can change undesirable traits that manifest.
   1 — 2 — 3 — 4 — 5 — 6 — 7 — 8 — 9 — 10

5. You can refuse to allow undesirable characteristics to manifest in your life.
   1 — 2 — 3 — 4 — 5 — 6 — 7 — 8 — 9 — 10

6. You often receive and accept messages from your environment with little or no examination.
   1 — 2 — 3 — 4 — 5 — 6 — 7 — 8 — 9 — 10

7. The bible quote, "The word has become flesh" is literal. You receive an idea, pass it to your subconscious, which in turn takes it into your Sympathetic System and builds it into your body.
   1 — 2 — 3 — 4 — 5 — 6 — 7 — 8 — 9 — 10

8. The Law of Attraction brings us that which we created from our own conscious or subconscious thought processes—whether good or bad.
   1 — 2 — 3 — 4 — 5 — 6 — 7 — 8 — 9 — 10

9. If you took the careful planning to build your Mental Home (as you would your physical home), your life would be much improved.
   1 — 2 — 3 — 4 — 5 — 6 — 7 — 8 — 9 — 10

10. If your subconscious mind has accumulated and stored negative material of the past and you have been living that negativity, you will experience more of it.
    1 — 2 — 3 — 4 — 5 — 6 — 7 — 8 — 9 — 10

11. If you have refused negativity, then there is nothing you need repair to live your best life.
    1 —— 2 —— 3 —— 4 —— 5 —— 6 —— 7 —— 8 —— 9 —— 10

12. In order to make any kind of progress, you need to do mental, moral and physical mental house-cleaning every day.
    1 —— 2 —— 3 —— 4 —— 5 —— 6 —— 7 —— 8 —— 9 —— 10

13. When you complete your mental house-cleaning, you are left with that which you desire to realize.
    1 —— 2 —— 3 —— 4 —— 5 —— 6 —— 7 —— 8 —— 9 —— 10

14. You must make use of your positive mental mindset, for if you neglect it, you will lose it.
    1 —— 2 —— 3 —— 4 —— 5 —— 6 —— 7 —— 8 —— 9 —— 10

15. The domain of mind and spirit are your to enjoy. Its only demands are that you lose your limitations, bondage and your weaknesses.
    1 —— 2 —— 3 —— 4 —— 5 —— 6 —— 7 —— 8 —— 9 —— 10

16. There are three things you need do to make manifest your desire: You must earnestly desire it, assert your claim upon it, and take possession of it.
    1 —— 2 —— 3 —— 4 —— 5 —— 6 —— 7 —— 8 —— 9 —— 10

17. You can acknowledge that these three conditions are not difficult.
    1 —— 2 —— 3 —— 4 —— 5 —— 6 —— 7 —— 8 —— 9 —— 10

18 Evidence of heredity of your mind force are as strong as those that support your physical heredity.
    1 —— 2 —— 3 —— 4 —— 5 —— 6 —— 7 —— 8 —— 9 —— 10

19. Divine heredity exists, but is beyond the research limitations of physical science.
    1 —— 2 —— 3 —— 4 —— 5 —— 6 —— 7 —— 8 —— 9 —— 10

20. No human heredity can replicate the ability that the Divine has to create.
    1 —— 2 —— 3 —— 4 —— 5 —— 6 —— 7 —— 8 —— 9 —— 10

21. You are made of Infinite Life as it flows through you. The Secret of Power keeps the doors to that flow open and receptive.
    1 —— 2 —— 3 —— 4 —— 5 —— 6 —— 7 —— 8 —— 9 —— 10

22. Insight, strength and power are all you need, and they come from within.
    1 — 2 — 3 — 4 — 5 — 6 — 7 — 8 — 9 — 10

23. Do not sway from building your foundation from the Infinite Source.
    1 — 2 — 3 — 4 — 5 — 6 — 7 — 8 — 9 — 10

24. Once you possess this inheritance, you will possess powerful abilities in which you were previously unconscious.
    1 — 2 — 3 — 4 — 5 — 6 — 7 — 8 — 9 — 10

25. Give and you will receive. you must freely give of whatever you want to strengthen within you, in order to receive more of it.
    1 — 2 — 3 — 4 — 5 — 6 — 7 — 8 — 9 — 10

26. Your growing power is contingent upon the proper use of the power you already have.
    1 — 2 — 3 — 4 — 5 — 6 — 7 — 8 — 9 — 10

27. All of you physical, mental or spiritual power comes from God or the spiritual Source.
    1 — 2 — 3 — 4 — 5 — 6 — 7 — 8 — 9 — 10

28. You will find as much pleasure in the execution of your desires as you do in the experiencing of them coming to fruition.
    1 — 2 — 3 — 4 — 5 — 6 — 7 — 8 — 9 — 10

29. When you focus on your sanctuary in great deals, you enhance your ability to attract that which you desire.
    1 — 2 — 3 — 4 — 5 — 6 — 7 — 8 — 9 — 10

Tally your total score by adding the number you allocated for yourself in each of the 29 principles above. Your score will range from 29 to 290.

If you scored between 205 and 290, your knowledge of how the mind controls all aspects of what you experience—from body, to mind to spirit. Continue following the lessons and be sure to practice the weekly exercise, as experiencing will move beliefs into inner knowing.

If you scored between 117 and 204, you are quite knowledgeable about how the mind controls all aspects of your life. You have already learned a great deal and hopefully you have experienced the power of your mind firsthand. Continue to review the steps in this chapter, and do the daily exercise.

If you scored between 29 and 116, you have a great deal more you can learn. Take some time to review each of the 29 principles until they become familiar and understood. Be sure to do the daily exercises, as doing so will make ideology a reality.

Introspection:

1. What did you learn about yourself after completing the Comprehension Survey?
2. Was your score what you expected it to be? Why or why not?
3. What areas of the segment of the book have you mastered?
4. What are the areas in this segment of the book that you need to focus on?
5. What three "takeaways" from this segment would you share with others and why?

Exercise

Now, go to your room, take the same seat, the same position as heretofore, and mentally select a place which has pleasant associations. Make a complete mental picture of it, see the buildings, the grounds, the trees, friends, associations, everything complete. At first, you will find yourself thinking of everything under the sun, except the ideal upon which you desire to concentrate. But do not let that discourage you. Persistence will win, but persistence requires that you practice these exercises every day without fail.

NOTES IN RESPONSE TO PERFORMING THIS EXERCISE
Be sure to journal about any findings or experiences you have as you continue to do this exercise as outlined.

Part Six

INTRODUCTION

This Part will give you an excellent understanding of the most wonderful piece of mechanism which has ever been created. A mechanism whereby you may create for yourself Health, Strength, Success, Prosperity or any other condition which you desire. Necessities are demands, and demands create action, and actions bring about results. The process of evolution is constantly building our tomorrows out of our todays. Individual development, like Universal development, must be gradual with an ever-increasing capacity and volume.

The knowledge that if we infringe upon the rights of others we become moral thorns and find ourselves entangled at every turn of the road, should be an indication that success is contingent upon the highest moral ideal, which is "The greatest good to the greatest number."

Aspiration, desire and harmonious relations constantly and persistently maintained will accomplish results. The greatest hindrance is erroneous and fixed ideas.

To be in tune with eternal truth we must possess poise and harmony within. In order to receive intelligence the receiver must be in tune with the transmitter.

Thought is a product of Mind, and Mind is creative, but this does not mean that the Universal will change its modus ope-

randi to suit us or our ideas, but it does mean that we can come into harmonious relationship with the Universal, and when we have accomplished this we may ask anything to which we are entitled, and the way will be made plain.

---

1. The Universal Mind is so wonderful that it is difficult to understand its utilitarian powers and possibilities and its unlimited producing effects.
2. We have found that this Mind is not only all intelligence but all substance. How, then, is it to be differentiated in form? How are we to secure the effect which we desire?
3. Ask any electrician what the effect of electricity will be and he will reply that "Electricity is a form of motion and its effect will depend upon the mechanism to which it is attached." Upon this mechanism will depend whether we shall have heat, light, power, music or any of the other marvelous demonstrations of power to which this vital energy has been harnessed.
4. What effect can be produced by thought? The reply is that thought is mind in motion (just as wind is air in motion), and its effect will depend entirely on the "mechanism to which it is attached."
5. Here, then, is the secret of all mental power; it depends entirely on the mechanism which we attach.
6. What is this mechanism? You know something of the mechanism which has been invented by Edison, Bell, Marconi and other electrical wizards, by which place and space and time have become only figures of speech, but did you ever stop to think that the mechanism which has been given you for transforming the Universal, Omnipresent Potential Power was invented by a greater inventor than Edison?

7. We are accustomed to examining the mechanism of the implements which we use for tilling the soil, and we try to get an understanding of the mechanism of the automobile which we drive, but most of us are content to remain in absolute ignorance of the greatest piece of mechanism which has ever come into existence, the brain of man.

8. Let us examine the wonders of this mechanism; perhaps we shall thereby get a better understanding of the various effects of which it is the cause.

9. In the first place, there is the great mental world in which we live and move and have our being; this world is omnipotent, omniscient and omnipresent; it will respond to our desire in direct ratio to our purpose and faith; the purpose must be in accordance with the law of our being, that is, it must be creative or constructive; our faith must be strong enough to generate a current of sufficient strength to bring our purpose into manifestation. "As thy faith is, so be it unto thee," bears the stamp of scientific test.

10. The effects which are produced in the world without are the result of the action and reaction of the individual upon the universal; that is the process which we call thinking; the brain is the organ through which this process is accomplished; think of the wonder of it all! Do you love music, flowers, literature, art, or are you inspired by the thought of ancient or modern genius? Remember, every beauty to which you respond must have its corresponding outline in your brain before you can appreciate it.

11. There is not a single virtue or principle in the storehouse of nature which the brain cannot express. The brain is an embryonic world, ready to develop at any time as necessity may arise. If you can comprehend that this is a scientific truth and one of the wonderful laws of nature, it will be easier for you to get an understanding of the mechanism by which these extraordinary results are being accomplished.

12. The nervous system has been compared to an electric circuit with its battery of cells in which force is originated, and its white matter to insulated wires by which the current is conveyed; it is through these channels that every impulse or desire is carried through the mechanism.
13. The spinal cord is the great motor and sensory pathway by which messages are conveyed to and from the brain; then, there is the blood supply plunging through the veins and arteries, renewing our energy and strength, the perfectly arranged structure upon which the entire physical body rests, and, finally, the delicate and beautiful skin, clothing the entire mechanism in a mantle of beauty.
14. This then is the "Temple of the living God" and the individual "I" is given control and upon his understanding of the mechanism which is within his control will the result depend.
15. Every thought sets the brain cells in action; at first the substance upon which the thought is directed fails to respond, but if the thought is sufficiently refined and concentrated, the substance finally yields and expresses perfectly.
16. This influence of the mind can be exerted upon any part of the body, causing the elimination of any undesirable effect.
17. A perfect conception and understanding of the laws governing in the mental world cannot fail to be of inestimable value in the transaction of business, as it develops the power of discernment and gives a clearer understanding and appreciation of facts.
18. The man who looks within instead of without cannot fail to make use of the mighty forces which will eventually determine his course in life and so bring him into vibration with all that is best, strongest and most desirable.
19. Attention or concentration is probably the most important essential in the development of mind culture. The possibilities of attention when properly directed are so startling

that they would hardly appear credible to the uninitiated. The cultivation of attention is the distinguishing characteristic of every successful man or, woman, and is the very highest personal accomplishment which can be acquired.

20. The power of attention can be more readily understood by comparing it with a sun glass in which the rays of sunlight are focused; they possess no particular strength as long as the glass is moved about and the rays directed from one place to another; but let the glass be held perfectly still and let the rays be focused on one spot for any length of time, the effect will become immediately apparent.

21. So with the power of thought; let power be dissipated by scattering the thought from one object to another, and no result is apparent; but focus this power through attention or concentration on any single purpose for any length of time and nothing becomes impossible.

22. A very simple remedy for a very complex situation, some will say. All right, try it, you who have had no experience in concentrating the thought on a definite purpose or object. Choose any single object and concentrate your attention on it for a definite purpose for even ten minutes; you cannot do it; the mind will wander a dozen times and it will be necessary to bring it back to the original purpose, and each time the effect will have been lost and at the end of the ten minutes nothing will have been gained, because you have not been able to hold your thought steadily to the purpose.

23. It is, however, through attention that you will finally be able to overcome obstacles of any kind that appear in your path onward and upward, and the only way to acquire this wonderful power is by practice—practice makes perfect, in this as in anything else.

24. In order to cultivate the power of attention, bring a photograph with you to the same seat in the same room in the

same position as heretofore. Examine it closely at least ten minutes, note the expression of the eyes, the form of the features, the clothing, the way the hair is arranged; in fact, note every detail shown on the photograph carefully. Now cover it and close your eyes and try to see it mentally; if you can see every detail perfectly and can form a good mental image of the photograph, you are to be congratulated; if not, repeat the process until you can.

25. This step is simply for the purpose of preparing the soil; next week we shall be ready to sow the seed.
26. It is by such exercises as these that you will finally be able to control your mental moods your attitude, your consciousness.
27. Great financiers are learning to withdraw from the multitude more and more, that they may have more time for planning, thinking and generating the right mental moods.
28. Successful business men ate constantly demonstrating the fact that it pays to keep in touch with the thought of other successful business men.
29. A single idea may be worth thousands of dollars, and these ideas can only come to those who are receptive, who are prepared to receive them, who are in, a successful frame of mind.
30. Men are learning to place themselves in harmony with the Universal Mind; they are learning the unity of all things; they are learning the basic methods and principles of thinking, and this is changing conditions and multiplying results.
31. They are finding that circumstances and environment follow the trend of mental and spiritual progress; they find that growth follows knowledge; action follows inspiration; opportunity follows perception; always the spiritual first, then the transformation into the infinite and illimitable possibilities of achievement.

32. As the individual is but the channel for the differentiation of the Universal, these possibilities are necessarily inexhaustible.
33. Thought is the process by which we may absorb the Spirit of Power, and hold the result in our inner consciousness until it becomes a part of our ordinary consciousness. The method of accomplishing this result by the persistent practice of a few fundamental principles, as explained in this System, is the Master-Key which unlocks the storehouse of Universal Truth.
34. The two great forces of human suffering at present are bodily disease and mental anxiety. These may be readily traced to the infringement of some Natural Law. This is, no doubt, owing to the fact that so far knowledge has largely remained partial, but the clouds of darkness which have accumulated through long ages are beginning to roll away and with them many of the miseries that attend imperfect information.

> *That a man can change himself, improve himself,*
> *re-create himself, control his environment, and*
> *master his own destiny is the conclusion of*
> *every mind who is wide-awake to the power*
> *of right thought in constructive action.*
> —LARSEN.

STUDY GUIDE

Part Six

Summary

Tells of the unlimited possibilities of the Universal Mind, which is the life principle of every atom in existence, and explains how this mind is differentiated in form. It tells of the most marvelous piece of mechanism which has ever been constructed, and tells how the effect which will be produced depends entirely upon the "mechanism to which it is attached." It tells why we should all become familiar with the mechanism so as to secure the effects which we desire. The power to which it can be attached is unlimited, and we can accordingly secure any effect we desire when we become familiar with the mechanism, and understand how to make the proper connections. An understanding of this part will enable you to plan courageously and execute fearlessly, because you will have come into a knowledge of the source of all power and this will determine your course in life, bringing you into contact with all that is strongest and best and most desirable.

1. Your necessities are your demands. They, in turn create your actions, which bring about results. Provide an example of this process that you have experienced in your life.

2. You are building your tomorrows with your todays. Check in with your attitude and thoughts today. Are they promising and positive? If not, can you make an effort to alter them?

3. Your individual development, like Universal, must be gradual. Do you find yourself getting impatient with your progress as you focus on your desires and await their manifestation?

4. Do you live by the premise, "The greatest good to the greatest number"? Reflect and make note of the areas where you may not be living by this principle in your life.

5. Take a moment and still yourself. Go into your heart and ask yourself, "Where do I possess erroneous or fixed ideas that are impeding upon my progress?" Write about any insights you gain.

6. While the Universe does not change its modus operandi for you, you can come into harmonious relationship with it. Reflect on your life, and

write about a situation in which you felt that you responded harmoniously with the Universal flow.

Comprehension Survey

In this segment you will become more familiar with mechanism by which you create all aspects of your life—your health, strength, success, and prosperity, just to name a few. Once you have completed this Comprehension Survey, you will get a better sense of how much you actually know on this subject. For each of the principles below, choose the number that is most closely aligns to your beliefs (1 being "not at all" and 10 being "a great deal").

1. The Universal Mind is so wonderful that you have a difficult time imagining all that it can do.
   1 — 2 — 3 — 4 — 5 — 6 — 7 — 8 — 9 — 10

2. The Universal Mind is more than intelligence, it encompasses all substance.
   1 — 2 — 3 — 4 — 5 — 6 — 7 — 8 — 9 — 10

3. Just like the Universal Mind is connected to you, electricity responds to mechanism it is attached to.
   1 — 2 — 3 — 4 — 5 — 6 — 7 — 8 — 9 — 10

4. The effect that your thoughts have depends on you, the mechanism.
   1 — 2 — 3 — 4 — 5 — 6 — 7 — 8 — 9 — 10

5. Your mental power depends upon you as the mechanism that Universal Mind is attached to.
   1 — 2 — 3 — 4 — 5 — 6 — 7 — 8 — 9 — 10

6. The mechanism by which great inventors created their masterpieces was a Divine Source—a greater inventor that the individual.
   1 — 2 — 3 — 4 — 5 — 6 — 7 — 8 — 9 — 10

7. You have not fully examined your brain, the greatest mechanism in existence.
   1 — 2 — 3 — 4 — 5 — 6 — 7 — 8 — 9 — 10

8. Once you examine your brain, you will better understand the effects of which it is the cause.
   1 — 2 — 3 — 4 — 5 — 6 — 7 — 8 — 9 — 10

9. You need both purpose and faith to fully realize the constructive power of your mind.
   1 —— 2 —— 3 —— 4 —— 5 —— 6 —— 7 —— 8 —— 9 —— 10

10. Every beauty that you respond to must have its corresponding outline in your brain before you can appreciate it.
    1 —— 2 —— 3 —— 4 —— 5 —— 6 —— 7 —— 8 —— 9 —— 10

11. Your brain is capable of birthing anything within the storehouse of nature.
    1 —— 2 —— 3 —— 4 —— 5 —— 6 —— 7 —— 8 —— 9 —— 10

12. Your nervous system is like an electric circuit that carries every one of your desires through your brain (the mechanism).
    1 —— 2 —— 3 —— 4 —— 5 —— 6 —— 7 —— 8 —— 9 —— 10

13. Your entire body is creativity incarnate. Each aspect of it works in tandem to allow the mechanism to fully function.
    1 —— 2 —— 3 —— 4 —— 5 —— 6 —— 7 —— 8 —— 9 —— 10

14. Your body is the temple of the Living God and the individual "I" controls the understanding of it as the mechanism.
    1 —— 2 —— 3 —— 4 —— 5 —— 6 —— 7 —— 8 —— 9 —— 10

15. Each thought, once refined and concentrated sets your brain cells in action to perfectly express perfect outcome.
    1 —— 2 —— 3 —— 4 —— 5 —— 6 —— 7 —— 8 —— 9 —— 10

16. Your mind has power over all parts of your body, and in being so can elimination all undesirable effects.
    1 —— 2 —— 3 —— 4 —— 5 —— 6 —— 7 —— 8 —— 9 —— 10

17. Once you understand the laws of the mental world, you will thrive in business for they will cultivate discernment, appreciation and greater understanding within you.
    1 —— 2 —— 3 —— 4 —— 5 —— 6 —— 7 —— 8 —— 9 —— 10

18. When you look within for answers, you will draw the most desirable outcomes into your life.
    1 —— 2 —— 3 —— 4 —— 5 —— 6 —— 7 —— 8 —— 9 —— 10

19. Your ability to concentrate is key to your success.
    1 —— 2 —— 3 —— 4 —— 5 —— 6 —— 7 —— 8 —— 9 —— 10

20. You can liken concentration to the effect of stillness on a sun glass that sits within the rays of the sun. With the intense stillness and focus, it can create a fire.
    1 — 2 — 3 — 4 — 5 — 6 — 7 — 8 — 9 — 10

21. When you focus your thoughts, everything is possible.
    1 — 2 — 3 — 4 — 5 — 6 — 7 — 8 — 9 — 10

22. You will be unable to focus your thoughts onto one object for 10 minutes without having your thoughts wander.
    1 — 2 — 3 — 4 — 5 — 6 — 7 — 8 — 9 — 10

23. If you practice stillness and focus, you will eventually be able to acquire great power.
    1 — 2 — 3 — 4 — 5 — 6 — 7 — 8 — 9 — 10

24. For this week's exercise, sit in stillness with a photo for 10 minutes and focus on all aspects of it. Do this until you can mentally see all details of it.
    1 — 2 — 3 — 4 — 5 — 6 — 7 — 8 — 9 — 10

25. Doing this exercise is like preparing the soil to eventually sow the seed.
    1 — 2 — 3 — 4 — 5 — 6 — 7 — 8 — 9 — 10

26. Through doing these practices, you will eventually be able to control your moods, attitude and consciousness.
    1 — 2 — 3 — 4 — 5 — 6 — 7 — 8 — 9 — 10

27. By generating the right mental state, great financiers gain more and more.
    1 — 2 — 3 — 4 — 5 — 6 — 7 — 8 — 9 — 10

28. Like begets like. Successful business men and women remain connected to the thoughts of their successful peers.
    1 — 2 — 3 — 4 — 5 — 6 — 7 — 8 — 9 — 10

29. When you are in a successful frame of mind, you will receive great abundance.
    1 — 2 — 3 — 4 — 5 — 6 — 7 — 8 — 9 — 10

30. More and more, mankind is multiplying results by placing themselves in harmony with the Universal Mind.
    1 — 2 — 3 — 4 — 5 — 6 — 7 — 8 — 9 — 10

31. Once you focus first and foremost on the spiritual, everything else flows into alignment.
1 —— 2 —— 3 —— 4 —— 5 —— 6 —— 7 —— 8 —— 9 —— 10

32. Once you are focused and open, possibilities are endless.
1 —— 2 —— 3 —— 4 —— 5 —— 6 —— 7 —— 8 —— 9 —— 10

33. You will see powerful results once you know and practice the fundamental principles in the Master Key System.
1 —— 2 —— 3 —— 4 —— 5 —— 6 —— 7 —— 8 —— 9 —— 10

34. Your two greatest miseries are physical disease and mental anxiety. However, rest assured that the clouds of darkness are lifting.
1 —— 2 —— 3 —— 4 —— 5 —— 6 —— 7 —— 8 —— 9 —— 10

Tally your total score by adding the number you allocated for yourself in each of the 34 principles above. Your score will range from 34 to 340.

If you scored between 240 and 340, you are knowledgeable about how important concentration and focus are to experiencing the fruits of connection to the Universal Mind. Review the statements listed in this segment, and be sure to do the exercise repeatedly and regularly.

If you scored between 137 and 239, you are somewhat knowledgeable about the power of concentration in relation to accessing the Universal Mind. Review the contents of this segment several times, and be sure to practice the exercises often and regularly.

If you scored between 34 and 136, you need to get more familiar with the workings between concentration, focus and accessing the power of the Universal Mind. Review each of the 34 tenets of this segment, and do the exercise at least once daily.

Introspection:

1. What did you learn about yourself after completing the Comprehension Survey?

2. Was your score what you expected it to be? Why or why not?

3. What areas of the segment of the book have you mastered?

4. What are the areas in this segment of the book that you need to focus on?

5. What three "takeaways" from this segment would you share with others and why?

Exercise

In order to cultivate the power of attention, bring a photograph with you to the same seat in the same room in the same position as heretofore. Examine it closely at least ten minutes, note the expression of the eyes, the form of the features, the clothing, the way the hair is arranged; in fact, note every detail shown on the photograph carefully. Now cover it and close your eyes and try to see it mentally; if you can see every detail perfectly and can form a good mental image of the photograph, you are to be congratulated; if not, repeat the process until you can.

NOTES IN RESPONSE TO PERFORMING THIS EXERCISE
Be sure to journal about any findings or experiences you have as you continue to do this exercise as outlined.

Part Seven

INTRODUCTION

Through all the ages man has believed in an invisible power, through which and by which all things have been created and are continually being re-created.

We may personalize this power and call it God, or we may think of it as the essence or spirit, which permeates all things, but in either case the effect is the same.

So far as the individual is concerned, the objective, the physical, the visible, is the personal, that which can be recognized by the senses. It consists of body, brain and nerves. The subjective is the spiritual, the invisible, the impersonal.

The personal is conscious because it is a personal entity. The impersonal, being the same in kind and quality as all other Being, is not conscious of itself and has therefore been termed the subconscious.

The personal, or conscious, has the power of will and choice, and can therefore exercise discrimination in the selection of methods whereby to bring about the solution of difficulties.

The impersonal, or spiritual, being a part or one with the source and origin of all power, can necessarily exercise no such choice, but, on the contrary, it has Infinite resources at its command. It can and does bring about results by methods concerning which the human or individual mind can have no possible conception.

You will therefore sec that it is your privilege to depend upon the human will, with all its limitations and misconceptions, or you may utilize the potentialities of Infinity by making use of the subconscious mind. Here, then, is the scientific explanation of the wonderful power which has been put within your control, if you but understand, appreciate and recognize it.

One method of consciously utilizing this omnipotent power is outlined in Part Seven.

---

1. Visualization is the process of making mental images, and the image is the mold or model which will serve as a pattern from which your future will emerge.
2. Make the pattern clear, and make it beautiful; do not be afraid; make it grand; remember that no limitation can be placed upon you by any one but yourself; you are not limited as to cost or material; draw on the Infinite for your supply, construct it in your imagination; it will have to be there before it will ever appear anywhere else.
3. Make the image clear and clean-cut, hold it firmly in the mind and you will gradually and constantly bring the thing nearer to you. You can be what "you will to be."
4. This is another psychological fact which is well known, but unfortunately, reading about it will not bring about any result which you may have in mind; it will not even help you to form the mental image, much less bring it into manifestation. Work is necessary, labor, hard mental labor, the kind of effort which so few are willing to put forth.
5. The first step is idealization. It is likewise the most important step, because it is the plan on which you are going to

build. It must be solid; it must be permanent. The architect, when he plans a 30-story building, has every line and detail pictured in advance. The engineer, when he spans a chasm, first ascertains the strength requirements of a million separate parts.

6. They see the end before a single step is taken; so you are to picture in your mind what you want; you are sowing the seed, but before sowing any seed you want to know what the harvest is to be. This is Idealization. If you are not sure, return to the chair daily until the picture becomes plain; it will gradually unfold; first the general plan will be dim, but it will take shape, the outline will take form, then the details, and you will gradually develop the power by which you will be enabled to formulate plans which will eventually materialize in the objective world. You will come to know what the future holds for you.

7. Then comes the process of visualization. You must see the picture more and more complete, see the detail, and, as the details begin to unfold the ways and means for bringing it into manifestation will develop. One thing will lead to another. Thought will lead to action, action will develop methods, methods will develop friends, and friends will bring about circumstances, and, finally, the third step, or Materialization, will have been accomplished.

8. We all recognize that the Universe must have been thought into shape before it ever could have become a material fact. And if we are willing to follow along the lines of the Great Architect of the Universe, we shall find our thoughts taking form, just as the universe took concrete form. It is the same mind operating through the individual. There is no difference in kind or quality, the only difference is one of degree.

9. The architect visualizes his building, he sees it as he wishes it to be. His thought becomes a plastic mold from which the

building will eventually emerge, a high one or a low one, a beautiful one or plain one, his vision takes form on paper and eventually the necessary material is utilized and the building stands complete.

10. The inventor visualizes his idea in exactly the same manner, for instance, Nikola Tesla, he with the giant intellect, one of the greatest inventors of all ages, the man who has brought forth the most amazing realities, always visualizes his inventions before attempting to work them out. He does not rush to embody them in form and then spend his time in correcting defects. Having first built up the idea in his imagination, he holds it there as a mental picture, to be reconstructed and improved by his thought. "In this way," he writes in the Electrical Experimenter. "I am enabled to rapidly develop and perfect a conception without touching anything. When I have gone so far as to embody in the invention every possible improvement. I can think of, and see no fault anywhere, I put into concrete, the product of my brain. Invariably my devise works as I conceived it should; in twenty years there has not been a single exception."

11. If you can conscientiously follow these directions, you will develop Faith, the kind of Faith that is the "Substance of things hoped for, the evidence of things not seen;" you will develop confidence, the kind of confidence that leads to endurance and courage; you will develop the power of concentration which will enable you to exclude all thoughts except the ones which are associated with your purpose:

12. The law is that thought will manifest in form, and only one who knows how to be the divine thinker of his own thoughts can ever take a Master's place and speak with authority.

13. Clearness and accuracy are obtained only by repeatedly having the image in mind. Each repeated action renders the image more clear and accurate than the preceding, and in

proportion to the clearness and accuracy of the image will the outward manifestation be. You must build it firmly and securely in your mental world, the world within, before it can take form in the world without, and you can build nothing of value, even in the mental world unless you have the proper material. When you have the material you can build anything you wish, but make sure of your material. You cannot make broadcloth from shoddy.

14. This material will be brought out by millions of silent mental workers and fashioned into the form of the image which you have in mind.

15. Think of it! You have over five million of these mental workers, ready and in active use; brain cells they are called. Besides this, there is another reserve force of at least an equal number, ready to be called into action at the slightest need. Your power to think, then is almost unlimited, and this means that your power to create the kind of material which is necessary to build for yourself any kind of environment which you desire is practically unlimited.

16. In addition to these millions of mental workers, you have billions of mental workers in the body, every one of which is endowed with sufficient intelligence to understand and act upon any message or suggestion given. These cells are all busy creating and recreating the body, but, in addition to this, they are endowed with psychic activity whereby they can attract to themselves the substance necessary for perfect development.

17. They do this by the same law and in the same manner that every form of life attracts to itself the necessary material for growth. The oak, the rose, the lily, all require certain material for their most perfect expression and they secure it by silent demand, the Law of Attraction, the most certain way for you to secure what you require for your most complete development.

18. Make the Mental Image; make it clear, distinct, perfect; hold it firmly; the ways and means will develop; supply will follow the demand; you will be led to do the right thing at the right time and in the right way. Earnest Desire will bring about Confident Expectation, and this in turn must be reinforced by Firm Demand. These three cannot fail to bring about Attainment, because the Earnest Desire is the feeling, the Confident Expectation is the thought, and the Firm Demand is the will, and, as we have seen, feeling gives vitality to thought and the will holds it steadily until the law of Growth brings it into manifestation.

19. Is it not wonderful that man has such tremendous power within himself, such transcendental faculties concerning which he had no conception? Is it not strange that we have always been taught to look for strength and power "without?" We have been taught to look everywhere but "within" and whenever this power manifested in our lives we were told that it was something supernatural.

20. There are many who have come to an understanding of this wonderful power, and who make serious and conscientious efforts to realize health, power and other conditions; and seem to fail. They do not seem able to bring the Law into operation. The difficulty in nearly every case is that they are dealing with externals. They want money, power, health and abundance, but they fail to realize that these are effects and can come only when the cause is found.

21. Those who will give no attention to the world without; will seek only to ascertain the truth, will look only for wisdom, will find that this wisdom will unfold and disclose the source of all power, that it will manifest in thought and purpose which will create the external conditions desired. This truth will find expression in noble purpose and courageous action.

22. Create ideals only, give no thought to external conditions, make the world within beautiful and opulent and the world without will express and manifest the condition which you have made within. You will come into a realization of your power to create ideals and these ideals will be projected into the world of effect.
23. For instance, a man is in debt. He will be continually thinking about the debt, concentrating on it, and as thoughts are causes the result is that he not only fastens the debt closer to him, but actually creates more debt. He is putting the great law of Attraction into operation with the usual and inevitable result—Loss leads to greater "Loss."
24. What, then, is the correct principle? Concentrate on the things you want, not on the things you do not want. Think of abundance; idealize the methods and plans for putting the Law of Abundance into operation. Visualize the condition which the Law of Abundance creates; this will result in manifestation.
25. If the law operates perfectly to bring about poverty, lack and every form of limitation for those who are continually entertaining thoughts of lack and fear, it will operate with the same certainty to bring about conditions of abundance and opulence for those who entertain thoughts of courage and power.
26. This is a difficult problem for many; we are too anxious; we manifest anxiety, fear, distress; we want to do something; we want to help; we are like a child who has just planted a seed and every fifteen minutes goes out and stirs up the earth to see if it is growing. Of course, under such circumstances, the seed will never germinate, and yet this is exactly what many of us do in the mental world.
27. We must plant the seed and leave it undisturbed. This does not mean that we are to sit down and do nothing, by no means; we will do more and better work than we have ever

done before, new channels will constantly be provided, new doors will open; all that is necessary is to have an open mind, be ready to act when the time comes.

28. Thought force is the most powerful means of obtaining knowledge, and if concentrated on any subject will solve the problem. Nothing is beyond the power of human comprehension, but in order to harness thought force and make it do your bidding, work is required.

29. Remember that thought is the fire that creates the steam that turns the wheel of fortune, upon which your experiences depend

30. Ask yourself a few questions and then reverently await the response; do you not now and then feel the self within you? Do you assert this self or do you follow the majority? Remember that majorities are always led, they never lead. It was the majority that fought, tooth and nail, against the steam engine, the power loom and every other advance or improvement ever suggested.

31. For your exercise this week, visualize your friend, see him exactly as you last saw him, see the room, the furniture, recall the conversation, now see his face, see it distinctly, now talk to him about some subject of mutual interest; see his expression change, watch him smile. Can you do this? All right, you can; then arouse his interest, tell him a story of adventure, see his eyes light up with the spirit of fun or excitement. Can you do all of this? If so, your imagination is good, you are making excellent progress.

Man is mind, and evermore he takes the tool of thought, and shaping what he wills, brings forth, a thousand joys, a thousand ills. He thinks in secret and it comes to pass, Environment is but his looking glass.
—JAMES ALLEN.

STUDY GUIDE

Part Seven

Summary

Part Seven tells of a method by which you may construct the mold or model from which your future will emerge. It tells how you may make it grand and beautiful; it explains that you are not limited as to cost or material, that no one can place any limitation on it but yourself. It explains that in the construction of this model, there is much work to be done, that no one can do the work but yourself, but it tells you what to do and how to do it, it suggests methods and plans which if faithfully and persistently carried out will result in conditions exactly in accordance with the purpose and thought. It tells of millions of faithful helpers which will come to your aid if you are faithful in your work, and it tells why some who are apparently faithfully endeavoring to realize their ideal seem to fail. It is sometimes just as important to know what not to do as what to do.

1. How long do you believe man has believed in invisible power? Please explain.

2. Do you personalize the Universal Source power, or do you think of it as essence or spirit? Do you believe you would improve your perception and/or relationship with that power if you personalized your experience with it? Why or why not?

3. That which can be recognized by the senses, the physical (body, brain and nerves) is considered the "objective." The impersonal or spiritual is considered the "subjective." Are most of the thoughts you have objective or subjective?

4. The conscious or personal aspect of you has free will, and can therefore exercise discrimination. The impersonal or spiritual part of you does not have choice, but has Infinite resources at its command. Do you effectively communicate between these two aspects of yourself?

Comprehension Survey

In this segment Charles Haanel shares one method of consciously utilizing the omnipotent power within that has been referenced throughout this book. Once you have completed it, you can start to experience your life shifting in powerful and fruitful ways. For each of the principles below, choose the number that is most closely aligns to your beliefs (1 being "not at all" and 10 being "a great deal").

1. When you visualize your future, a pattern from which it will emerge will take shape.
   1 —— 2 —— 3 —— 4 —— 5 —— 6 —— 7 —— 8 —— 9 —— 10

2. When you visualize, do not limit yourself. What you desire must first be created in your imagination before it will appear anywhere else.
   1 —— 2 —— 3 —— 4 —— 5 —— 6 —— 7 —— 8 —— 9 —— 10

3. When you constantly envision what you want with clarity, you will gradually bring that nearer and nearer to you.
   1 —— 2 —— 3 —— 4 —— 5 —— 6 —— 7 —— 8 —— 9 —— 10

4. You must commit to hard mental labor to bring about change. Talking about it will not make it happen.
   1 —— 2 —— 3 —— 4 —— 5 —— 6 —— 7 —— 8 —— 9 —— 10

5. The first step in your visualization is to plan, be clear and detailed in what you imagine.
   1 —— 2 —— 3 —— 4 —— 5 —— 6 —— 7 —— 8 —— 9 —— 10

6. You must start your visualization with the end result in mind. This is Idealization. Keep returning to your still place and picture what you desire until it unfolds.
   1 —— 2 —— 3 —— 4 —— 5 —— 6 —— 7 —— 8 —— 9 —— 10

7. As you visualize, more and more details will unfold. Your thoughts lead to action, your actions will develop methods, your methods will develop friends, friends will bring about circumstances, and the circumstances will materialize.
   1 —— 2 —— 3 —— 4 —— 5 —— 6 —— 7 —— 8 —— 9 —— 10

8. The same mind that created the Universe operates through you. The only difference is one of degree.
   1 —— 2 —— 3 —— 4 —— 5 —— 6 —— 7 —— 8 —— 9 —— 10

9. Like an architect, you can visualize that which you desire with great precision and detail.
   1 —— 2 —— 3 —— 4 —— 5 —— 6 —— 7 —— 8 —— 9 —— 10

10. Tesla completely envisioned his inventions in his mind prior to manifesting them into physical form. You can do the same.
    1 —— 2 —— 3 —— 4 —— 5 —— 6 —— 7 —— 8 —— 9 —— 10

11. As you consciously follow these directions, you will develop faith, confidence, endurance, courage and power.
    1 —— 2 —— 3 —— 4 —— 5 —— 6 —— 7 —— 8 —— 9 —— 10

12. You know that you are the divine thinker of your thoughts, and they will manifest into form.
    1 —— 2 —— 3 —— 4 —— 5 —— 6 —— 7 —— 8 —— 9 —— 10

13. Repeatedly seeing your manifestation in your mind's eye will create the clarity and accuracy that it needs to take form.
    1 —— 2 —— 3 —— 4 —— 5 —— 6 —— 7 —— 8 —— 9 —— 10

14. The material from which you think, will take the shape from that which you hold in your mind.
    1 —— 2 —— 3 —— 4 —— 5 —— 6 —— 7 —— 8 —— 9 —— 10

15. You have over five million active brain cells that support your vision. Thus your power to think, then create is almost limitless.
    1 —— 2 —— 3 —— 4 —— 5 —— 6 —— 7 —— 8 —— 9 —— 10

16. Your body's cells psychically attract that which is needed to aid in developing your vision.
    1 —— 2 —— 3 —— 4 —— 5 —— 6 —— 7 —— 8 —— 9 —— 10

17. As nature models, the most certain way for the material of your desires to grow is supported by the Law of Attraction.
    1 —— 2 —— 3 —— 4 —— 5 —— 6 —— 7 —— 8 —— 9 —— 10

18. Your creation formula is as follows: Earnest Desire + Confident Expectation + Firm Demand = Attainment.
    1 —— 2 —— 3 —— 4 —— 5 —— 6 —— 7 —— 8 —— 9 —— 10

19. Despite having transcendental powers within you, you have been taught to seek outside of yourself.
    1 —— 2 —— 3 —— 4 —— 5 —— 6 —— 7 —— 8 —— 9 —— 10

20. The reason for any failure is that you have focused on money, power, health and abundance as "external goals," as opposed to internal "effects."
    1 —— 2 —— 3 —— 4 —— 5 —— 6 —— 7 —— 8 —— 9 —— 10

21. When you give no attention to the world without, the external conditions that you desire will manifest in your life.
    1 —— 2 —— 3 —— 4 —— 5 —— 6 —— 7 —— 8 —— 9 —— 10

22. When you create a beautiful world within, it is heard and the outside would will match it.
    1 —— 2 —— 3 —— 4 —— 5 —— 6 —— 7 —— 8 —— 9 —— 10

23. When your focus on "loss" you experience greater loss.
    1 —— 2 —— 3 —— 4 —— 5 —— 6 —— 7 —— 8 —— 9 —— 10

24. When you think of abundance and focus on the methods and plans for putting it into operation, the Universe will co-conspire.
    1 —— 2 —— 3 —— 4 —— 5 —— 6 —— 7 —— 8 —— 9 —— 10

25. The law will reflects abundance with as great a certainty as it does lack in your life.
    1 —— 2 —— 3 —— 4 —— 5 —— 6 —— 7 —— 8 —— 9 —— 10

26. Like an anxious child who will not let the seed she plants germinate, in your fear, you do the same.
    1 —— 2 —— 3 —— 4 —— 5 —— 6 —— 7 —— 8 —— 9 —— 10

27. Let the seed of your desires germinate, be open and ready act when appropriate.
    1 —— 2 —— 3 —— 4 —— 5 —— 6 —— 7 —— 8 —— 9 —— 10

28. Work is required from you in order to harness the power of your thoughts.
    1 —— 2 —— 3 —— 4 —— 5 —— 6 —— 7 —— 8 —— 9 —— 10

29. Your thoughts are the fire that create the steam that turns your wheel of fortune.
    1 —— 2 —— 3 —— 4 —— 5 —— 6 —— 7 —— 8 —— 9 —— 10

30. You assert yourself, unafraid to veer away from the actions of the majority.
    1 —— 2 —— 3 —— 4 —— 5 —— 6 —— 7 —— 8 —— 9 —— 10

31. If you can visualize yourself in a conversation with a good friend, then your ability to imagination is sound.
    1 —— 2 —— 3 —— 4 —— 5 —— 6 —— 7 —— 8 —— 9 —— 10

Tally your total score by adding the number you allocated for yourself in each of the 31 principles above. Your score will range from 31 to 310.

If you scored between 219 and 310, you have a solid understanding of how to cultivate your inner world so that you can harvest the fruits of your desires. Be sure to take note of the moments where you find yourself in fear or anxiety, and go within to further build your inner sanctuary on solid ground. Practice the visualization exercise, adding more and more detail as the image strengthens in your mind.

If you scored between 125 and 218, you understand the workings of your inner world, but you could further solidify your understanding as you practice the exercises provided. Within the next week, take some time to read through this chapter once again, so that the teachings can be consciously and subconsciously integrated in your mind. Be sure to do the visualization exercise provided, including as much detail as you can.

If you scored between 31 and 124, you could use some assistance in further understanding the workings of your inner world. Whenever you find yourself lost in anxiety, fear or hopelessness, practice the visualization exercise provided for you in this chapter, seeing a joyful and uplifting exchange with your friend. Be sure to practice the exercise daily, and reflects daily on the teachings in this chapter as well.

Introspection:

1. What did you learn about yourself after completing the Comprehension Survey?

2. Was your score what you expected it to be? Why or why not?

3. What areas of the segment of the book have you mastered?

4. What are the areas in this segment of the book that you need to focus on?

5. What three "takeaways" from this segment would you share with others and why?

Exercise #1 (reflect on these questions, and write out your response in your journal)

Ask yourself a few questions and then reverently await the response; do you not now and then feel the self within you? Do you assert this self or do you follow the majority? Remember that majorities are always led, they never lead. It was the majority that fought, tooth and nail, against the steam engine, the power loom and every other advance or improvement ever suggested.

Exercise #2

For your exercise this week, visualize your friend, see him exactly as you last saw him, see the room, the furniture, recall the conversation, now see his face, see it distinctly, now talk to him about some subject of mutual interest; see his expression change, watch him smile. Can you do this? All right, you can; then arouse his interest, tell him a story of adventure, see his eyes light up with the spirit of fun or excitement. Can you do all of this? If so, your imagination is good, you are making excellent progress.

NOTES IN RESPONSE TO PERFORMING THIS EXERCISE
Be sure to journal about any findings or experiences you have as you continue to do this exercise as outlined.

Part Eight

INTRODUCTION
In this Part you will find that you may freely choose what you think, but the result of your thought is governed by an immutable law! Is not this a wonderful thought? Is it not wonderful to know that our lives are not subject to caprice or variability of any kind? That they are governed by law. This stability is our opportunity, because by complying with the law we can secure the desired effect with invariable precision.

It is the Law which makes the Universe one grand pan of Harmony. If it were not for law, the Universe would be a Chaos instead of a Cosmos.

Here, then, is the secret of the origin of both good and evil: this is all the good and evil there ever was or ever will be.

Let me illustrate. Thought results in action. If your thought is constructive and harmonious, the result will be good: if your thought is destructive or inharmonious, the result will be evil.

There is therefore but one law, one principle, one cause, one Source of Power, and good and evil are simply words which have been coined to indicate the result of our action, or our compliance or non-compliance with this law.

The importance of this is well illustrated in the lives of Emerson and Carlyle. Emerson loved the good and his life was a sym-

phony of peace and harmony; Carlyle hated the bad, and his life was a record of perpetual discord and inharmony.

Here we have two grand men, each intent upon achieving the same ideal, but one makes use of constructive thought and is therefore in harmony with Natural Law, the other makes use of destructive thought and therefore brings upon himself discord of every kind and character.

It is evident therefore that we are to hate nothing, not even the "bad," because hatred is destructive, and we shall soon find that by entertaining destructive thought we are sowing the "wind" and shall reap the "whirlwind."

---

1. Thought contains a vital principle, because it is the creative principle of the Universe and by its nature will combine with other similar thoughts.
2. As the one purpose of life is growth, all principle underlying existence must contribute to give it effect. Thought, therefore, takes form and the law of growth eventually brings it into manifestation.
3. You may freely choose what you think, but the result of your thought is governed by an immutable law. Any line of thought persisted cannot fail to produce its result in the character, health and circumstances of the individual. Methods whereby we can substitute habits of constructive thinking for those which we have found produce only undesirable effects are therefore of primary importance.
4. We all know that this is by no means easy. Mental habits are difficult to control, but it can be done and the way to do it is to begin at once to substitute constructive thought for destructive thought. Form the habit of analyzing every thought. If it is necessary, if its manifestation in the objective will be a

benefit, not only to yourself, but to all whom it may affect in any way, keep it; treasure it; it is of value; it is in tune with the Infinite; it will grow and develop and produce fruit an hundred fold. On the other hand, it will be well for you to keep this quotation from George Matthews Adams, in mind, "Learn to keep the door shut, keep out of your mind, out of your office, and out of your world, every element that seeks admittance with no definite helpful end in view."

5. If your thought has been critical or destructive, and has resulted in any condition of discord or inharmony in your environment, it may be necessary for you to cultivate a mental attitude which will be conducive to constructive thought.

6. The imagination will be found to be a great assistance in this direction; the cultivation of the imagination leads to the development of the ideal out of which your future will emerge.

7. The imagination gathers up the material by which the Mind weaves the fabric in which your future is to be clothed.

8. Imagination is the light by which we can penetrate new worlds of thought and experience.

9. Imagination is the mighty instrument by which every discoverer, every inventor, opened the way from precedent to experience. Precedent said, "It cannot be done"; experience said, "It is done."

10. Imagination is a plastic power, molding the things of sense into new forms and ideals.

11. Imagination is the constructive form of thought which must precede every constructive form of action.

12. A builder cannot build a structure of any kind until he has first received the plans from the architect, and the architect must get them from his imagination.

13. The Captain of Industry cannot build a giant corporation which may coordinate hundreds of smaller corporations and thousands of employees, and utilize millions of capital until he has first created the entire work in his imagina-

tion. Objects in the material world are as clay in the potter's hand; it is in the Master Mind that the real things are created, and it is by the use of the imagination that the work is done. In order to cultivate the imagination it must be exercised. Exercise is necessary to cultivate mental muscle as well as physical muscle. It must be supplied with nourishment or it cannot grow.

14. Do not confuse Imagination with Fancy, or that form of day dreaming in which some people like to indulge. Day dreaming is a form of mental dissipation which may lead to mental disaster.

15. Constructive imagination means mental labor, by some considered to be the hardest kind of labor, but, if so, it yields the greatest returns, for all the great things in life have come to men and women who had the capacity to think, to imagine, and to make their dreams come true.

16. When you have become thoroughly conscious of the fact that Mind is the only creative principle, that it is Omnipotent, Omniscient and Omnipresent, and that you can consciously come into harmony with this Omnipotence through your power of thought, you will have taken a long step in the right direction.

17. The next step is to place yourself in position to receive this power. As it is Omnipresent, it must be within you. We know that this is so because we know that all power is from within, but it must be developed, unfolded, cultivated; in order to do this we must be receptive, and this receptivity is acquired just as physical strength is gained, by exercise.

18. The law of attraction will certainly and unerringly bring to you the conditions, environment, and experiences in life, corresponding with your habitual, characteristic, predominant mental attitude. Not what you think once in a while when you are in church, or have just read a good book, but your predominant mental attitude is what counts.

19. You can not entertain weak, harmful, negative thoughts ten hours a day and expect to bring about beautiful, strong and harmonious conditions by ten minutes of strong, positive, creative thought.
20. Real power comes from within. All power that anybody can possibly use is within man, only waiting to be brought into visibility by his first recognizing it, and then affirming it as his, working it into his consciousness until he becomes one with it.
21. People say that they desire abundant life, and so they do, but so many interpret this to mean that if they will exercise their muscles or breathe scientifically, eat certain foods in certain ways, drink so many glasses of water every day, of just a certain temperature, keep out of drafts, they will attain the abundant life they seek. The result of such methods is but indifferent. However, when man awakens to the truth, and affirms his oneness with all Life, he finds that he takes on the clear eye, the elastic stop, the vigor of youth; he finds that he has discovered the source of all power.
22. All mistakes are but the mistakes of ignorance. Knowledge gaining and consequent power is what determines growth and evolution. The recognition and demonstration of knowledge is what constitutes power, and this power is spiritual power, and this spiritual power is the power which lies at the heart of all things; it is the soul of the universe.
23. This knowledge is the result of man's ability to think; thought is therefore the germ of man's conscious evolution. When man ceases to advance in his thoughts and ideals, his forces immediately begin to disintegrate and his countenance gradually registers these changing conditions.
24. Successful men make it their business to hold ideals of the conditions which they wish to realize. They constantly hold in mind the next step necessary to the ideal for which

they are striving. Thoughts are the materials with which they build, and the imagination is their mental work-shop. Mind is the ever moving force with which they secure the persons and circumstances necessary to build their success structure, and imagination is the matrix in which all great things are fashioned.

25. If you have been faithful to your ideal, you will hear the call when circumstances are ready to materialize your plans and results will correspond in the exact ratio of your fidelity to your ideal. The ideal steadily held is what predetermines and attracts the necessary conditions for its fulfillment.

26. It is thus that you may weave a garment of spirit and power into the web of your entire existence; it is thus that you may lead a charmed life and be forever protected from all harm; it is thus that you may become a positive force whereby conditions of opulence and harmony may be attracted to you.

27. This is the leaven which is gradually permeating the general consciousness and is largely responsible for the conditions of unrest which are everywhere evident.

28. Last week you created a mental image, you brought it from the invisible into the visible; this week I want you to take an object and follow it back to its origination, see of what it really consists. If you do this you will develop imagination, insight, perception, and sagacity. These come not by the superficial observation of the multitude, but by a keen analytical observation which sees below the surface.

29. It is the few who know that the things which they see are only effects, and understand the causes by which these effects were brought into existence.

30. Take the same position as heretofore and visualize a Battleship; see the grim monster floating on the surface of the water; there appears to be no life anywhere about; all is silence; you know that by far the largest part of the vessel

is under water; out of sight; you know that the ship is as large and as heavy as a twenty story skyscraper; you know that there are hundreds of men ready to spring to their appointed task instantly; you know that every department is in charge of able, trained, killed officials who have proven themselves competent to take charge of this marvelous piece of mechanism; you know that although it lies apparently oblivious to everything else, it has eyes which see everything for miles around, and nothing is permitted to escape its watchful vision; you know that while it appears quiet, submissive and innocent, it is prepared to hurl a steel projectile weighing thousands of pounds at an enemy many miles away; this and much more you can bring to mind with comparatively no effort whatever. But how did the battleship come to be where it is; how did it come into existence in the first place? All of this you want to know if you are a careful observer.

31. Follow the great steel plates through the foundries, see the thousands of men employed in their production; go still further back, and see the ore as it comes from the mine, see it loaded on barges or cars, see it melted and properly treated; go back still further and see the architect and engineers who planned the vessel; let the thought carry you back still further in order to determine why they planned the vessel; you will see that you are now so far back that the vessel is something intangible, it no longer exists, it is now only a thought existing in the brain of the architect; but from where did the order come to plan the vessel? Probably from the Secretary of War; but probably this vessel was planned long before the war was thought of, and that Congress had to pass a bill appropriating the money; possibly there was opposition, and speeches for or against the bill. Whom do these Congressmen represent? They represent you and me, so that our line of thought begins with the Battleship and ends with ourselves, and we find in

the last analysis that our own thought is responsible for this and many other things, of which we seldom think, and a little further reflection will develop the most important fact of all and that is, if someone had not discovered the law by which this tremendous mass of steel and iron could be made to float upon the water, instead of immediately going to the bottom, the battleship could not have come into existence at all.

32. This law is that, "the specific gravity of any substance is the weight of any volume of it, compared with an equal volume of water." The discovery of this law revolutionized every kind of ocean travel, commerce and warfare, and made the existence of the battleship possible.

33. You will find exercises of this kind invaluable. When the thought has been trained to look below the surface everything takes on a different appearance, the insignificant becomes significant, the uninteresting interesting; the things which we supposed to be of no importance are seen to be the only really vital things in existence.

LOOK TO THIS DAY.
For it is Life, the very Life of Life.
In Its brief course lie all the Verities and
Realities of your existence;
The Bliss of Growth;
The Glory of Action;
The Splendor of Beauty;
For Yesterday is but a Dream,
And Tomorrow is only a Vision;
But Today well lived makes every
Yesterday a Dream of Happiness, and
Every Tomorrow a Vision of Hope.
Look well, therefore, to This Day!
—From the Sanscrit.

STUDY GUIDE

Part Eight

Summary

Part Eight tells of the creative principle of the Universe, what it is, how it takes form and how it is brought into manifestation. This principle being the underlying principle of all existence must necessarily be governed by an immutable law. It tells how the character, health and circumstances of the individual are formed, and suggests methods whereby desirable conditions and circumstances may be created. It tells how and why and when the material from which your future is to emerge is secured. It suggests methods and exercises by which you may secure complete control of the power which governs in this mighty field of action. Mighty because it is the most important work which any individual can undertake. We are making our future now, today, when it comes we shall have to accept what is given, it will be too late to change it, but we can dominate it, control it, make it what we want it to be, and this Part explains how.

1. There is stability in following the Law of Attraction. Choose a great thought, and focus on it for a week. Then make note of anything you experience in response to doing so.

2. Without the Law of Attraction, the Universe would be chaos. What evidence do you see of this in your life or in the world around you?

3. Harmonious thoughts result in good and destructive thoughts result in evil. Provide at least two examples of when you have seen each of these principles played out in history.

4. "Good and evil" are words that indicate the results of your actions. Provide examples of each in your life, and include the outcome of the choices you have made.

5. Charles Haanel references the lives of Emerson and Carlyle as examples of focusing on good and discord. Take some time to research each of these individuals, and list the ways in which their lives modeled their attitudes.

6. You are encourage to hate nothing, not even the bad. Take a moment and focus on someone with whom you struggle. Imagine seeing light emanating from your heart and traveling to theirs. See them in joy as

their hearts expand. If you cannot do this, keep trying and note any shifts you experience within yourself.

7. Like a powerful ship that is ready and waiting for battle, your mind can effortlessly launch into action, but how did your mind come into existence in the first place?

Comprehension Survey

In this segment Haanel provides methods by which you can begin to create desirable circumstances and conditions in your life. Once you have completed it, you will be one step closer to integrating the wisdom of his teachings into your psyche, so that you begin to experience more favorable outcomes in your life. For each of the principles below, choose the number that is most closely aligns to your beliefs (1 being "not at all" and 10 being "a great deal").

1. Your thoughts are vital as they are the creative principle of the Universe, thus attracting similar thoughts.
   1 — 2 — 3 — 4 — 5 — 6 — 7 — 8 — 9 — 10

2. The law of growth brings your thoughts into existence.
   1 — 2 — 3 — 4 — 5 — 6 — 7 — 8 — 9 — 10

3. Your thoughts are governed by an immutable law.
   1 — 2 — 3 — 4 — 5 — 6 — 7 — 8 — 9 — 10

4. While it's not easy, substituting destructive thoughts with constructive ones keeps the door to your mind closed on negativity.
   1 — 2 — 3 — 4 — 5 — 6 — 7 — 8 — 9 — 10

5. If you have put a destructive thought into the world, then it may be necessary for you to replace it with one that is constructive.
   1 — 2 — 3 — 4 — 5 — 6 — 7 — 8 — 9 — 10

6. Your imagination is central to developing the ideal vision from which your future can unfold.
   1 — 2 — 3 — 4 — 5 — 6 — 7 — 8 — 9 — 10

7. Your imagination gathers the material from which your Mind weaves the fabric.
   1 — 2 — 3 — 4 — 5 — 6 — 7 — 8 — 9 — 10

8. Your imagination is the light that penetrate new worlds of thoughts and experiences.
   1 — 2 — 3 — 4 — 5 — 6 — 7 — 8 — 9 — 10

9. Your imagination transforms your doubt into invention.
   1 — 2 — 3 — 4 — 5 — 6 — 7 — 8 — 9 — 10

10. Your imagination molds that which you sense into forms and ideals.
    1 — 2 — 3 — 4 — 5 — 6 — 7 — 8 — 9 — 10

11. You must imagine something before it can take form.
    1 — 2 — 3 — 4 — 5 — 6 — 7 — 8 — 9 — 10

12. Your mind's architect must imagine the plans from which it can then build the structure of any kind.
    1 — 2 — 3 — 4 — 5 — 6 — 7 — 8 — 9 — 10

13. You must exercise and nourish your Master Mind in order to make it effectively work.
    1 — 2 — 3 — 4 — 5 — 6 — 7 — 8 — 9 — 10

14. Imagination is different than day dreaming. When you daydream, you can experience disastrous results.
    1 — 2 — 3 — 4 — 5 — 6 — 7 — 8 — 9 — 10

15. It takes mental labor for you to invoke your constructive imagination.
    1 — 2 — 3 — 4 — 5 — 6 — 7 — 8 — 9 — 10

16. When you finally realize that all creation lies in the Omnipotence of the Mind, that you will be in harmony with creation.
    1 — 2 — 3 — 4 — 5 — 6 — 7 — 8 — 9 — 10

17. You need to develop receptivity, just as your physical body gains strength through exercise.
    1 — 2 — 3 — 4 — 5 — 6 — 7 — 8 — 9 — 10

18. Your life will reflect the predominant thoughts that you continuously focus upon.
    1 — 2 — 3 — 4 — 5 — 6 — 7 — 8 — 9 — 10

19. The amount of time you spend on your positive thoughts impacts the results you experience.
    1 — 2 — 3 — 4 — 5 — 6 — 7 — 8 — 9 — 10

20. Real power lies within you waiting for your recognize, affirm and become one with it.
    1 — 2 — 3 — 4 — 5 — 6 — 7 — 8 — 9 — 10

21. No regimen can create results. They come when you awaken the fact that you are part of the Oneness with all of life.
    1 — 2 — 3 — 4 — 5 — 6 — 7 — 8 — 9 — 10

22. Your mistakes are based on your ignorance. At the heart of all things is your spiritual power and connection.
    1 — 2 — 3 — 4 — 5 — 6 — 7 — 8 — 9 — 10

23. When you stop advancing in your thoughts, you experience atrophy in your life.
    1 — 2 — 3 — 4 — 5 — 6 — 7 — 8 — 9 — 10

24. Your mind is the force that secures the persons and circumstances to support your vision, and your imagination is its matrix.
    1 — 2 — 3 — 4 — 5 — 6 — 7 — 8 — 9 — 10

25. When you steadily hold faithful to your ideal, circumstances will fall into place that support it into being.
    1 — 2 — 3 — 4 — 5 — 6 — 7 — 8 — 9 — 10

26. When you weave spirit into your existence, you attract harmony and opulence into your life.
    1 — 2 — 3 — 4 — 5 — 6 — 7 — 8 — 9 — 10

27. Because much of the world does not weave spirit into their lives, they suffer from unrest.
    1 — 2 — 3 — 4 — 5 — 6 — 7 — 8 — 9 — 10

28. You make the invisible visible through keen analytical observation of what is below the surface.
    1 — 2 — 3 — 4 — 5 — 6 — 7 — 8 — 9 — 10

29. Few realize that what they see are only effects for which they do not know the cause.
    1 — 2 — 3 — 4 — 5 — 6 — 7 — 8 — 9 — 10

30. Like a powerful ship the bulk of which lies deep within the ocean, your mind is vast and ready and waiting to effortlessly launch into action.
    1 — 2 — 3 — 4 — 5 — 6 — 7 — 8 — 9 — 10

31. The creation of a battleship had to first have been a seed in the mind of someone. Then many intricate steps were taken from that starting point to bring it to existence.

1 — 2 — 3 — 4 — 5 — 6 — 7 — 8 — 9 — 10

32. The Law of gravity, volume and water revolutionized ocean travel and made the existence of the battleship possible.

1 — 2 — 3 — 4 — 5 — 6 — 7 — 8 — 9 — 10

33. Your thoughts are trained to look below the surface, everything become important and vitalized.

1 — 2 — 3 — 4 — 5 — 6 — 7 — 8 — 9 — 10

Tally your total score by adding the number you allocated for yourself in each of the 33 principles above. Your score will range from 33 to 330.

If you scored between 232 and 330, congratulations! You are very awareness of how mighty the battleship of the mind is. Continue to follow through on the exercise provided in this segment, and if you can, follow through on one different aspect of a manifestation each day. A fun exercise to practice is to express gratitude for the food you eat by following each element of your meal from its beginnings, thanking every aspect of its creation along the way. You will soon realize that a great deal more goes into your meals that you have been consciously appreciating.

If you scored between 133 and 231, you are familiar with the mightiness of your mind, however solidifying your knowledge would help you on your journey of manifesting. Practice this week's exercise daily with a subject matter. A fun exercise to practice is to express gratitude for the food you eat by following each element of your meal from its beginnings, thanking every aspect of its creation along the way. You will soon realize that a great deal more goes into your meals that you have been consciously appreciating.

If you scored between 33 and 132, you could improve upon your knowledge and experience of the mightiness that your mind possesses by practicing this week's exercise daily with a subject matter. Another fun exercise to practice is to express gratitude for the food you eat by following each element of your meal from its beginnings, thanking every aspect of its creation along the way. You will soon realize that a great deal more goes into your meals that you have been consciously appreciating.

Introspection:

1. What did you learn about yourself after completing the Comprehension Survey?

2. Was your score what you expected it to be? Why or why not?
3. What areas of the segment of the book have you mastered?
4. What are the areas in this segment of the book that you need to focus on?
5. What three "takeaways" from this segment would you share with others and why?

Exercise

Last week you created a mental image, you brought it from the invisible into the visible; this week I want you to take an object and follow it back to its origination, see of what it really consists. If you do this you will develop imagination, insight, perception, and sagacity. These come not by the superficial observation of the multitude, but by a keen analytical observation which sees below the surface.

EXAMPLE FROM THE BOOK:
THE CREATION OF A BATTLESHIP
Follow the great steel plates through the foundries, see the thousands of men employed in their production; go still further back, and see the ore as it comes from the mine, see it loaded on barges or cars, see it melted and properly treated; go back still further and see the architect and engineers who planned the vessel; let the thought carry you back still further in order to determine why they planned the vessel; you will see that you are now so far back that the vessel is something intangible, it no longer exists, it is now only a thought existing in the brain of the architect; but from where did the order come to plan the vessel? Probably from the Secretary of War; but probably this vessel was planned long before the war was thought of, and that Congress had to pass a bill appropriating the money; possibly there was opposition, and speeches for or against the bill. Whom do these Congressmen represent? They represent you and me, so that our line of thought begins with the Battleship and ends with ourselves, and we find in the last analysis that our own thought is responsible for this and many other things, of which we seldom think, and a little further reflection will develop the most important fact of all and that is, if someone had not discovered the law by which this tremendous mass of steel and iron could be made to float upon the water, instead of immediately going to the bottom, the battleship could not have come into existence at all.

NOTES IN RESPONSE TO PERFORMING THIS EXERCISE
Be sure to journal about any findings or experiences you have as you continue to do this exercise as outlined.

Part Nine

INTRODUCTION

In this Part you may learn to fashion the tools by which you may build for yourself any condition you desire.

If you wish to change conditions, you must change yourself. Your whims, your wishes, your fancies, your ambitions may be thwarted at every step, but your inmost thoughts will find expression just as certainly as the plant springs from the seed.

Suppose, then, we desire to change conditions, how are we to bring this about? The reply is simple: By the law of growth. Cause and effect are as absolute and undeviating in the hidden realm of thought as in the world of material things.

Hold in mind the condition desired; affirm it as an already existing fact. This indicates the value of a powerful affirmation. By constant repetition it becomes a part of ourselves. We are actually changing ourselves; we are making ourselves what we want to be.

Character is not a thing of chance, but it is the result of continued effort. If you are timid, vacillating, self-conscious, or if you are over-anxious or harassed by thoughts of fear or impending danger, remember that it is axiomatic that "two things cannot exist in the same place at the same time." Exactly the same thing is true in the mental and spiritual world; so that your remedy is plainly to substitute thoughts of courage, power, self-reliance and confidence, for those of fear, lack and limitation.

The easiest and most natural way to do this is to select an affirmation which seems to fit your particular case. The positive thought will destroy the negative as certainly as light destroys darkness, and the results will be just as effectual.

Act is the blossom of thought, and conditions are the result of action, so that you constantly have in your possession the tools by which you will certainly and inevitably make or unmake yourself, and joy or suffering will be the reward.

---

1. There are only three things which can possibly be desired in the "world without" and each of them can be found in the "world within." The secret of finding them is simply to apply the proper "mechanism" of attachment to the omnipotent power to which each individual has access.
2. The three things which all mankind desires and which are necessary for his highest expression and complete development are Health, Wealth and Love. All will admit that Health is absolutely essential; no one can be happy if the physical body is in pain. All will not so readily admit that Wealth is necessary, but all must admit that a sufficient supply at least is necessary, and what would be considered sufficient for one, would be considered absolute and painful lack for another; and as Nature provides not only enough but abundantly, wastefully, lavishly, we realize that any lack or limitation is only the limitation which has been made by an artificial method of distribution.
3. All will probably admit that Love is the third, or maybe some will say the first essential necessary to the happi-

ness of mankind; at any rate, those who possess all three, Health, Wealth and Love, find nothing else which can be added to their cup of happiness.

4. We have found that the Universal substance is "All Health," "All Substance," and "All Love," and that the mechanism of attachment whereby we can consciously connect with this Infinite supply is in our method of thinking. To think correctly is therefore to enter into the "Secret Place of the Most High."

5. What shall we think? If we know this we shall have found the proper mechanism of attachment which will relate us to "Whatsoever things we desire." This mechanism may seem very simple when I give it to you, but read on; you will find that it is in reality the "Master-Key," the "Aladdin's lamp," if you please; you will find that it is the foundation, the imperative condition, the absolute law of well-doing, which means, well-being.

6. To think correctly, accurately, we must know the "Truth." The truth then is the underlying principle in every business or social relation. It is a condition precedent to every right action. To know the truth, to be sure, to be confident, affords a satisfaction beside which no other is at all comparable; it is the only solid ground in a world of doubt, conflict and danger.

7. To know the Truth is to be in harmony with the Infinite and Omnipotent power. To know the truth is, therefore, to connect yourself with a power which is irresistible and which will sweep away every kind of discord, inharmony, doubt or error of any kind, because the "Truth is mighty and will prevail."

8. The humblest intellect can readily foretell the result of any action when he knows that it is based on truth, but the mightiest intellect, the most profound and penetrating mind loses its way hopelessly and can form no conception

of the results which may ensue when his hopes are based on a premise which he knows to be false.

9. Every action which is not in harmony with Truth, whether through ignorance or design, will result in discord, and eventual loss in proportion to its extent and character.

10. How then are we to know the truth in order to attach this mechanism which will relate us to the Infinite?

11. We can make no mistake about this if we realize that Truth is the vital principle of the Universal Mind and is Omnipresent. For instance, if you require health, a realization of the fact that the "I" in you is spiritual and that all spirit is one; that wherever a part is the whole must be, will bring about a condition of health, because every cell in the body must manifest the truth as you see it. If you see sickness they will manifest sickness; if you see perfection they must manifest perfection. The affirmation, "I am whole, perfect, strong, powerful, loving, harmonious and happy," will bring about harmonious conditions. The reason for this is because the affirmation is in strict accordance with the Truth, and when truth appears every form of error or discord must necessarily disappear

12. You have found that the "I" is spiritual, it must necessarily then always be no less than perfect, the affirmation. "I am whole, perfect, strong, powerful, loving, harmonious and happy" is therefore an exact scientific statement.

13. Thought is a spiritual activity and spirit is creative, therefore the result of holding this thought in mind, must necessarily bring about conditions in harmony with the thought.

14. If you require Wealth a realization of the fact that the "I" in you is one with the Universal mind which is all substance, and is Omnipotent, will assist you in bringing into operation the law of attraction which will bring you into vibration with those forces which make for success

and bring about conditions of power and affluence in direct proportion with the character and purpose of your affirmation.

15. Visualization is the mechanism of the attachment which you require. Visualization is a very different process from seeing; seeing is physical, and is therefore related to the objective world, the "world without," but Visualization is a product of the imagination, and is therefore a product of the subjective mind, the "world within." It therefore possesses vitality; it will grow. The thing visualized will manifest itself in form. The mechanism is perfect; it was created by the Master Architect who "doeth all things well," but unfortunately sometimes the operator is inexperienced or inefficient, but practice and determination will overcome this defect.

16. If you require Love try to realize that the only way to get love is by giving it, that the more you give the more you will get, and the only way in which you can give it, is to fill yourself with it, until you become a magnet. The method was explained in another lesson.

17. He who has learned to bring the greatest spiritual truths into touch with the so-called lesser things of life has discovered the secret of the solution of his problem. One is always quickened, made more thoughtful, by his nearness of approach to great ideas, great events, great natural objects, and great men. Lincoln is said to have begotten in all who came near him the feeling awakened when one approaches a mountain, and this sense asserts itself most keenly when one comes to realize that he has laid hold upon things that are eternal, the power of Truth.

18. It is sometimes an inspiration to hear from some one who has actually put these principles to the test, some one who has demonstrated them in his own life. I am today in receipt of a letter from Mr. Andrews; he says:

"Dear Friend:
You will find my experience published in Match Nautilus, and you are at liberty to make any extracts from or reference to it, that may suit your purpose.
Sincerely yours
Frederick Elias Andrews,
512 Odd Fellows Bldg.,
March 7, 1917. Indianapolis, Ind."

19. I was about thirteen years old when Dr. T. W. Marsee, since passed over, said to my mother: "There is no possible chance, Mrs. Andrews. I lost my little boy the same way, after doing everything for him that it was possible to do. I have made a special study of these cases, and I know there is no possible chance for him to get well."

20. She turned to him and said: "Doctor, what would you do if he were your boy?" and he answered, "I would fight, fight, as long as there is a breath of life to fight for."

21. That was the beginning of a long drawn-out battle, with many ups and downs, the doctors all agreeing that there was no chance for a cure, though they encouraged and cheered us the best they could.

22. But at last the victory came, and I have grown from a little, crooked, twisted, cripple, going about on my hands and knees, to a strong, straight, well formed man.

23. Now, I know you want the formula, and I will give it to you as briefly and quickly as I can.

24. I built up an affirmation for myself, taking the qualities I most needed, and affirming for myself over and over again, "I am whole, perfect, strong, powerful, loving, harmonious and happy." I kept up this affirmation, always the same, never varying, till I could wake up in the night and find myself repeating, "I am whole, perfect, strong, powerful, loving, harmonious and happy." It was the last thing on my lips at night and the first thing in the morning.

25. Not only did I affirm it for myself, but for others that I knew needed it. I want to emphasize this point. Whatever you desire for yourself, affirm it for others, and it will help you both. We reap what we sow. If we send out thoughts of love and health, they return to us like bread cast upon the waters; but if we send out thoughts of fear, worry, jealousy, anger, hate, etc., we will reap the results in our own lives.

26. It used to be said that man is completely built over every seven years, but some scientists now declare that we build ourselves over entirely every eleven months; so we are really only eleven months old. If we build the defects back into our bodies year after year, we have no one to blame but ourselves.

27. Man is the sum total of his own thoughts; so the question is, how are we going to entertain only the good thoughts and reject the evil ones? At first we can't keep the evil thoughts from coming, but we can keep from entertaining them. The only way to do this is to forget them—which means, get something for them. This is where the ready-made affirmation comes in.

28. When a thought of anger, jealousy, fear or worry creeps in, just start your affirmation going. The way to fight darkness is with light—the way to fight cold is with heat—the way to overcome evil is with good. For myself, I never could find any help in denials. Affirm the good, and the bad will vanish. Frederick Elias Andrews.

29. If there is anything you require, it will be well for you to make use of this affirmation; it cannot be improved upon. Use it just as it is; take it into the silence with you, until it sinks into your subconsciousness, so that you can use it anywhere, on the street cars, in the office, at home; this is the advantage of spiritual methods; they are always available. Spirit is omnipresent, ever ready; all that is required is a proper recognition of its omnipotence, and a willing-

ness or desire to become the recipient of its beneficent effects.

30. If our predominant mental attitude is one of power, courage, kindliness and sympathy, we shall find that our environment will reflect conditions in correspondence with these thoughts; if it is weak, critical, envious and destructive, we shall find our environment reflecting conditions corresponding to these thoughts.

31. Thoughts are causes and conditions are effects Herein is the explanation of the origin of both good and evil. Thought is creative and will automatically correlate with its object. This is a Cosmological law, the law of Attraction, the law of Cause and Effect; the recognition and application of this law will determine both beginning and end; it is the law by which in all ages and in all times the people were led to believe in the power of prayer. "As thy faith is, so be it unto thee," is simply another, a shorter and a better way of stating it.

32. This week visualize a plant; take a flower, the one you most admire, bring it from the unseen into the seen, plant the tiny seed, water it, care for it, place it where it will get the direct rays of the morning sun, see the seed burst; it is now a living thing, something which is alive and beginning to search for the means of subsistence. See the roots penetrating the earth, watch them shoot out in all directions and remember that they are living cells dividing and subdividing, and that they will soon number millions, that each cell is intelligent, that it knows what it wants and knows how to get it. See the stem shoot forward and upward, watch it burst through the surface of the earth, see it divide and form branches, see how perfect and symmetrical each branch is formed, see the leaves begin to form, and then the tiny stems, each one holding aloft a bud, and as you watch you see the bud begin to unfold and your favorite flower

comes to view; and now if you will concentrate intently you will become conscious of a fragrance; it is the fragrance of the flower as the breeze gently sways the beautiful creation which you have visualized.

33. When you are enabled to make your vision clear and complete you will be enabled to enter into the spirit of a thing; it will become very real to you; you will be learning to concentrate and the process is the same, whether you are concentrating on health, a favorite flower, an ideal, a complicated business proposition or any other problem of life.

34. Every success has been accomplished by persistent concentration upon the object in view.

In the end, thought rules the world.
There are times when impulses and passions
are more powerful, but they soon expend themselves;
while mind, acting constantly, is ever ready to drive
them back and work when their energy is exhausted.
—J. McCosh.

STUDY GUIDE

Part Nine

Summary

This Part tells of the fundamental principle, the imperative condition, the immutable law underlying every successful business relation or social condition. It tells of the law by which you may make yourself irresistible, by which you may sweep away every form of discord, inharmony and doubt. It tells the secret of the solution to every problem. It explains that there are only three things which all mankind requires for complete happiness and development. It tells what they are and how they may be had.

1. What tools do you believe you need to develop in order to build yourself the conditions which you desire?

2. If you wish to change conditions, you need to change your innermost thoughts. What thoughts are your currently thinking in your life that you believe are most destructive? How could you change them?

3. You can change your current conditions by applying the law of growth. Describe that law in your own words.

4. When you hold a desired condition in your mind, and consistently affirm it, you can change yourself. Create a short, concise affirmation that would best support you in your life.

5. State the affirmation when you arise in the morning and when. You go to sleep for at least 21 consecutive days. Write about any shifts you note in your life in response to committing to this practice.

6. Do you have any thoughts that are fearful, timid, vacillating, self-conscious or over-anxious? If so, plant thoughts of courage, power, self-reliance and confidence in their place. Practice this for at least 21 days, and note any shifts in your experiences.

7. The next time you catch yourself saying something derogatory about yourself, say "cancel, cancel" and replace that statement with a self-affirming one.

8. The actions you take are rooted in your thoughts come, and the conditions you experience are the result. Joy or suffering will be your reward. Which have you experienced more of in your life?

9. Take note of your response in question If you believe you previously experienced suffering and are still experiencing it, what do you think you will experience in the future, unless your change your mind?

Comprehension Survey

In this segment you learn of the only three desires that really exist: health, wealth and love. Once you have completed it, you will get a better sense of how much you are in alignment you're your desires, as you intensify and practice effective visualization. For each of the principles below, choose the number that is most closely aligns to your beliefs (1 being "not at all" and 10 being "a great deal").

1. The three desires you have in your outer world can be found within you. You simply need to apply the proper "mechanism" of attachment to the Universal Source of Loving Creation to access it.
   1 — 2 — 3 — 4 — 5 — 6 — 7 — 8 — 9 — 10

2. The three things that you and mankind desires are health, wealth and love. Any lack experienced does not come from Universal Source.
   1 — 2 — 3 — 4 — 5 — 6 — 7 — 8 — 9 — 10

3. Once you possess these three gifts, you need nothing more.
   1 — 2 — 3 — 4 — 5 — 6 — 7 — 8 — 9 — 10

4. When you think correctly, you gain all health, all substance and all love.
   1 — 2 — 3 — 4 — 5 — 6 — 7 — 8 — 9 — 10

5. What you think is the "Master-Key" or "Aladdin's lamp."
   1 — 2 — 3 — 4 — 5 — 6 — 7 — 8 — 9 — 10

6. In a world filled with doubt, anger and conflict the only solid ground you will find lies in knowing the "Truth."
   1 — 2 — 3 — 4 — 5 — 6 — 7 — 8 — 9 — 10

7. You experience the Truth when you are in harmony with the Infinite and Omnipotent Power.
   1 — 2 — 3 — 4 — 5 — 6 — 7 — 8 — 9 — 10

8. Your intellect plays no part in living and knowing the Truth.
   1 — 2 — 3 — 4 — 5 — 6 — 7 — 8 — 9 — 10

9. Every action you take that is not in harmony with Truth will create eventual loss in your life.
   1 — 2 — 3 — 4 — 5 — 6 — 7 — 8 — 9 — 10

10. There is a means by which you can know the Truth and attach it to the Infinite.
    1 — 2 — 3 — 4 — 5 — 6 — 7 — 8 — 9 — 10

11. The affirmation you should practice that is in accordance with the Truth is "I am whole, perfect, strong, powerful, loving, harmonious and happy."
    1 — 2 — 3 — 4 — 5 — 6 — 7 — 8 — 9 — 10

12. "I am whole, perfect, strong, powerful, loving, harmonious and happy" is an exact scientific statement.
    1 — 2 — 3 — 4 — 5 — 6 — 7 — 8 — 9 — 10

13. Because thinking is a spiritual activity, and because spirit is creative, holding the affirmations brings harmony with your thoughts.
    1 — 2 — 3 — 4 — 5 — 6 — 7 — 8 — 9 — 10

14. Realizing that you are one with the Universal Mind, it responds to your desire for wealth by vibrationally aligning you with those forces that match your affirmation.
    1 — 2 — 3 — 4 — 5 — 6 — 7 — 8 — 9 — 10

15. With practice and determination, you will master the "internal" art of visualization.
    1 — 2 — 3 — 4 — 5 — 6 — 7 — 8 — 9 — 10

16. Become a love magnet by giving it fully and you will receive it in return.
    1 — 2 — 3 — 4 — 5 — 6 — 7 — 8 — 9 — 10

17. When you bring the Eternal power of Truth to all of your life, you have discovered the solution to your problems.
    1 — 2 — 3 — 4 — 5 — 6 — 7 — 8 — 9 — 10

18. You are inspired when you hear from others who have discovered and applied the Master Key System.
    1 — 2 — 3 — 4 — 5 — 6 — 7 — 8 — 9 — 10

19. You do not stand in your power when you give in to the opinions of others.

    1 — 2 — 3 — 4 — 5 — 6 — 7 — 8 — 9 — 10

20. While you may ask the opinion of others, in the end decisions rest with you.

    1 — 2 — 3 — 4 — 5 — 6 — 7 — 8 — 9 — 10

21. While there may be ups and downs on your journey, stay true to your course.

    1 — 2 — 3 — 4 — 5 — 6 — 7 — 8 — 9 — 10

22. When you hold true to your vision and ideals, miracles can and do happen.

    1 — 2 — 3 — 4 — 5 — 6 — 7 — 8 — 9 — 10

23. There is a formula to be learned and Mr. Andrews tapped into it.

    1 — 2 — 3 — 4 — 5 — 6 — 7 — 8 — 9 — 10

24. Repeat the affirmation constantly from morning until night, and like Mr. Andrews, you will see light at the end of the tunnel.

    1 — 2 — 3 — 4 — 5 — 6 — 7 — 8 — 9 — 10

25. Affirm not only for yourself, but for others as well. Doing so will reap greater rewards for all.

    1 — 2 — 3 — 4 — 5 — 6 — 7 — 8 — 9 — 10

26. If your body rebuilds every 11 months, then if you attract disharmony to it, that is your own doing.

    1 — 2 — 3 — 4 — 5 — 6 — 7 — 8 — 9 — 10

27. While you may be unable to stop negative thoughts as they arise, you don't need to engage upon them. You would do better to replace them with a positive affirmation.

    1 — 2 — 3 — 4 — 5 — 6 — 7 — 8 — 9 — 10

28. When you note negative thoughts, stop immediately and recite your affirmation.

    1 — 2 — 3 — 4 — 5 — 6 — 7 — 8 — 9 — 10

29. You recite the affirmations anywhere and everywhere, knowing that they are having effect on your life.

    1 — 2 — 3 — 4 — 5 — 6 — 7 — 8 — 9 — 10

30. Because your predominant attitude to one of power, courage, kindness and sympathy, you attract like people and circumstances into your life.

    1 —— 2 —— 3 —— 4 —— 5 —— 6 —— 7 —— 8 —— 9 —— 10

31. The prayer, "As thy faith is, so be it unto thee" encapsulates the Law of Attraction.

    1 —— 2 —— 3 —— 4 —— 5 —— 6 —— 7 —— 8 —— 9 —— 10

32. You can visualize the growth of your favorite flower from seedling to full bloom.

    1 —— 2 —— 3 —— 4 —— 5 —— 6 —— 7 —— 8 —— 9 —— 10

33. When you can experience your vision whole and complete, you can enter into the spirit of things.

    1 —— 2 —— 3 —— 4 —— 5 —— 6 —— 7 —— 8 —— 9 —— 10

34. Your success lies in persistent concentration upon the object that you visualize.

    1 —— 2 —— 3 —— 4 —— 5 —— 6 —— 7 —— 8 —— 9 —— 10

Tally your total score by adding the number you allocated for yourself in each of the 34 principles above. Your score will range from 34 to 340.

If you scored between 240 and 340, you are very aware of how much affirmations and positive visualizations can shift you out of negative thinking. Practice the flower visualization daily, and be sure to take your time and allow all of your senses to enjoy the journey of growth.

If you scored between 137 and 239, you are well on your way to truly understanding the power of affirmation. As you practice the flower visualization exercise and replace any negative thoughts with the affirmation, you will build upon your knowledge and turn principles into practices.

If you scored between 34 and 136, you would be wise to reflect on the 34 steps in this segment several times. Applaud yourself for continuing on this journey, and allow yourself the time and space to fully experience the growing flower exercise. Doing so slowly and deliberately, while committing to enjoying the process will prove to be invaluable to you.

Introspection:

1. What did you learn about yourself after completing the Comprehension Survey?

2. Was your score what you expected it to be? Why or why not?

3. What areas of the segment of the book have you mastered?

4. What are the areas in this segment of the book that you need to focus on?

5. What three "takeaways" from this segment would you share with others and why?

Exercise

This week visualize a plant; take a flower, the one you most admire, bring it from the unseen into the seen, plant the tiny seed, water it, care for it, place it where it will get the direct rays of the morning sun, see the seed burst; it is now a living thing, something which is alive and beginning to search for the means of substitance [sustenance]. See the roots penetrating the earth, watch them shoot out in all directions and remember that they are living cells dividing and subdividing, and that they will soon number millions, that each cell is intelligent, that it knows what it wants and knows how to get it. See the stem shoot forward and upward, watch it burst through the surface of the earth, see it divide and form branches, see how perfect and symmetrical each branch is formed, see the leaves begin to form, and then the tiny stems, each one holding aloft a bud, and as you watch you see the bud begin to unfold and your favorite flower comes to view; and now if you will concentrate intently you will become conscious of a fragrance; it is the fragrance of the flower as the breeze gently sways the beautiful creation which you have visualized.

When you are enabled to make your vision clear and complete you will be enabled to enter into the spirit of a thing; it will become very real to you; you will be learning to concentrate and the process is the same, whether you are concentrating on health, a favorite flower, an ideal, a complicated business proposition or any other problem of life.

NOTES IN RESPONSE TO PERFORMING THIS EXERCISE
Be sure to journal about any findings or experiences you have as you continue to do this exercise as outlined.

Part Ten

INTRODUCTION

If you get a thorough understanding of the thought contained in Part Ten, you will have learned that nothing happens without a definite cause. You will be enabled to formulate your plans in accordance with exact knowledge. You will know how to control any situation by bringing adequate causes into play. When you win, as you will, you will know exactly why.

The ordinary man, who has no definite knowledge of cause and effect, is governed by his feelings or emotions. He thinks chiefly to justify his action. If he fails as a business man, he says that luck is against him. If he dislikes music, he says that music is an expensive luxury. If he is a poor clerk, he says that he could succeed better at some outdoor work. If he lacks friends, he says his individuality is too fine to be appreciated.

He never thinks this problem through to the end. In short, he does not know that every effect is the result of a certain definite cause, but he seeks to console himself with explanations and excuses. He thinks only in self-defense.

On the contrary, the man who understands that there is no effect without an adequate cause thinks impersonally. He gets down to absolute facts regardless of consequences. He is free to follow the path of truth wherever it may lead. He sees the issue clear to the end, and he meets the requirements fully and fairly, and the result is that the world gives him all that it has to give, in friendship, honor, love and approval.

---

1. Abundance is a natural law of the Universe. The evidence of this law is conclusive; we see it on every hand. Everywhere Nature is lavish, wasteful, extravagant. Nowhere is economy observed in any created thing. Profusion is manifested in everything. The millions and millions of trees and flowers and plants and animals and the vast scheme of reproduction where the process of creating and re-creating is forever going on, all indicates the lavishness with which Nature has made provision for man. That there is an abundance for everyone is evident, but that many fail to participate in this abundance is also evident; they have not yet come into a realization of the Universality of all substance, and that mind is the active principle whereby we are related to the things we desire.
2. All wealth is the offspring of power; possessions are of value only as they confer power. Events are significant only as they affect power; all things represent certain forms and degrees of power.
3. Knowledge of cause and effect as shown by the laws governing electricity, chemical affinity and gravitation, enables man to plan courageously and execute fearlessly. These laws are called Natural Laws, because they govern in the physical world, but all power is not physical power; there is also mental power, and there is moral and spiritual power.
4. Spiritual power is superior because it exists on a higher plane. It has enabled man to discover the law by which these wonderful forces of Nature could be harnessed and

made to do the work of hundreds and thousands of men. It has enabled man to discover laws whereby time and space have been annihilated and now apparently the law of gravitation is to be overcome.

5. In the physical world as we know it, there exists the organic and the inorganic. The inorganic or the mineral world is absolutely cut off from the plant or animal world; the passage is hermetically sealed. These barriers have never yet been crossed. No change of substance, no modification of environment, no chemistry, no electricity, no form of energy, no evolution of any kind can ever endow a single atom of the mineral world with the attribute of Life.

6. Only by the bending down into this dead world of some living form can those dead atoms be gifted with the properties of vitality; without this contact with life they remain fixed in the inorganic sphere forever. Huxley says that the doctrine of Biogenesis or life only from life, is victorious all along the line, and Tyndall is compelled to say: "I affirm that no shred of trustworthy evidence exists to prove that life in our day has ever appeared independent of antecedent life."

7. Physical laws may explain the inorganic, Biology explain and account for the development of the organic, but of the point of contact Science is silent. A similar passage exists between the Natural world and the Spiritual world; this passage is hermetically sealed on the natural side. The door is closed; no man can open it, no organic change, no mental energy, no moral effort, no progress of any kind can enable any human being to enter the spiritual world.

8. But as the plant stretches down into the mineral world beneath and touches its minerals with the mystery of Life and transforms them into a living sphere, so the Universal Mind reaches down into the human mind and endows it with its own high qualities, develops new, strange and

wonderful and even marvelous qualities. All men or women who have ever accomplished anything in the world of industry, commerce or art have accomplished because of this process.

9. Thought is the connecting link between the Infinite and the finite, between the Universal and the individual. We have seen that there is an impassible barrier between the organic and the inorganic, and that the only way that matter can unfold is to be impregnated with life; as a seed reaches down into the mineral world and begins to unfold and reach out, the dead matter begins to live, a thousand invisible fingers begin to weave a suitable environment for the new arrival, and as the low growth begins to take effect, we see the process continue until the Lily finally appears, and even "Solomon in all his glory was not arrayed like one of these."

10. Even so, a thought is dropped into the invisible substance of the Universal Mind, that substance from which all things are created, and as it takes root, the law of growth begins to take effect and we find that conditions and environment are but the objective form of our thought.

11. The law is that Thought is an active vital form of dynamic energy which has the power to correlate with its object and bring it out of the invisible substance from which all things are created into the visible or objective world. This is the law by which, and through which all things come into manifestation; it is the Master Key by which you are admitted into the Secret Place of the Most High and are "given dominion over all things." With an understanding of this law you may "decree a thing and it shall be established unto thee."

12. It could not be otherwise; if the soul of the Universe as we know it, is the Universal Spirit, then the Universe is sim-

ply the condition which the Universal Spirit has made for itself. We are simply individualized spirit and are creating the conditions for our growth in exactly the same way.

13. This creative power depends upon our recognition of the potential power of spirit or mind and must not be confused with Evolution. Creation is the calling into existence of that which does not exist in the objective world. Evolution is simply the unfolding of potentialities involved in things which already exist.

14. In taking advantage of the wonderful possibilities opened up to us through the operation of this law, we must remember that we ourselves contribute nothing to its efficacy as the Great Teacher said: "It is not I that doeth the works, but the Father that dwelleth in me, He doeth the work." We must take exactly the same position; we can do nothing to assist in the manifestation, we simply comply with the law, and the All-originating Mind will bring about the result.

15. The great error of the present day is the idea that Man has to originate the intelligence whereby the Infinite can proceed to bring about a specific purpose or result. Nothing of this kind is necessary; the Universal Mind can be depended upon to find the ways and means for bringing about any necessary manifestation. We must, however, create the ideal, and this ideal should be perfect.

16. We know that the laws governing Electricity have been formulated in such a way that this invisible power can be controlled and used for our benefit and comfort in thousands of ways. We know that messages are carried around the world, that ponderous machinery does its bidding, that it now illuminates practically the whole world, but we know too that if we consciously or ignorantly violate its law by touching a live wire, when it is not properly insulated, the

result will be unpleasant and possibly disastrous. A lack of understanding of the laws governing in the invisible world has the same result, and many are suffering the consequences all the time.

17. It has been explained that the law of causation depends upon polarity, a circuit must be formed; this circuit cannot be formed unless we operate in harmony with the law. How shall we operate in harmony with the law unless we know what the law is? How shall we know what the Law is? By study, by observation.

18. We see the law in operation everywhere; all nature testifies to the operation of the law by silently, constantly expressing itself in the law of growth. Where there is growth, there must be life; where there is life there must be harmony, so that everything that has life is constantly attracting to itself the conditions and the supply which is necessary for its most complete expression.

19. If your thought is in harmony with the creative Principle of nature, it is in tune with the Infinite Mind, and it will form the circuit, it will not return to you void; but it is possible for you to think thoughts that are not in tune with the Infinite, and there is no polarity, the circuit is not formed. What, then, is the result? What is the result when a dynamo is generating electricity, the circuit is cut off and there is no outlet? The dynamo stops.

20. It will be exactly the same with you, if you entertain thoughts which are not in accordance with the Infinite and cannot therefore be polarized; there is no circuit, you are isolated, the thoughts cling to you, harass you, worry you, and finally bring about disease and possibly death; the physician may not diagnose the case exactly in this way, he may give it some fancy name which has been manufactured for the various ills which are the result of wrong thinking, but the cause is the same nevertheless.

21. Constructive thought must necessarily be creative, but creative thought must be harmonious, and this eliminates all destructive or competitive thought.
22. Wisdom, strength, courage and all harmonious conditions are the result of power and we have seen that all power is from within; likewise, every lack, limitation or adverse circumstance is the result of weakness, and weakness is simply absence of power; it comes from nowhere, it is nothing—the remedy then is simply to develop power, and this is accomplished in exactly the same manner that all power is developed, by exercise.
23. This exercise consists in making an application of your knowledge. Knowledge will not apply itself. You must make the application. Abundance will not come to you out of the sky, neither will it drop into your lap, but a conscious realization of the law of attraction and the intention to bring it into operation for n certain, definite and specific purpose, and the will to carry out this purpose will bring about the materialization of your desire by a natural law of transference. If you are in business, it will increase and develop along regular channels, possibly new or unusual channels of distribution will be opened and when the law becomes frilly operative you will find that the things you seek are seeking you.
24. This week select a blank space on the wall, or any other convenient spot, from where you usually sit, mentally draw a black horizontal line about six inches long, try to see the line as plainly as though it were painted on the wall; now mentally draw two vertical lines connecting with this horizontal line at either end; now draw another horizontal line connecting with the two vertical lines; now you have a square. Try to see the square perfectly; when you can do so draw a circle within the square; now place a point in the center of the circle; now draw the point toward you about

10 inches; now you have a cone on a square base; you will remember that your work was all in black; change it to white, to red, to yellow.

25. If you can do this, you are making excellent progress and will soon be enabled to concentrate on any problem you may have in mind.

When any object or purpose is clearly held in thought, its precipitation, in tangible and visible form, is merely a question of time. The vision always precedes and itself determines the realization.
—LILLIAN WHITING.

STUDY GUIDE

Part Ten

Summary

This Part tells of the Law of Abundance. It shows that Nature has provided an abundance for all, and why some seem to be separated from this supply. It tells of a connecting link between the individual and the supply, explains the Law of Attraction, the law by which your "own" is brought to you. It tells why every experience in life is the result of this law. It tells why and how you attract the things to you which make up the sum total of your existence. It tells how you may place yourself in harmony with this law and thereby assist in bringing about desirable conditions in your health, environment, or finances. It shows that this Law of Attraction is fundamental and eternal and that there is no escape from the result of its operation. A knowledge of this Law is absolutely essential to those desiring to make permanent progress.

1. If you understand the principles outlined in Part Ten, you know that nothing happens without a definite cause. What caused you to purchase this book?

2. When you are unaware of cause and effect, the choices you make are based on your emotions. In what areas of your life do you still find yourself reacting emotionally to in a way that does not serve you? What might you do to shift your experience?

3. The ordinary human can find external excuses for all of their shortcomings. Reflect on your life, Are there any areas in which you find yourself making external excuses for the paradigms that you find yourself in?

4. Ordinary humans console themselves with self-defensive excuses. Write a list of the excuses you are currently making for your disappointments in life. Then after each, list the ways that you can shift your mindset to better support a positive outcome.

5. When you understand, you are able to face the facts and follow the path of truth wherever it leads you. List at least three situations where you committed to following the truth and, in turn, experienced positive results.

Comprehension Survey

In this segment you learn how and why you attract the things that you do into your experience. Once you have completed it, you will get a better sense of how you can get in greater harmony with this law and shift your life of greater results. For each of the principles below, choose the number that is most closely aligns to your beliefs (1 being "not at all" and 10 being "a great deal").

1. All substance is Universal and naturally grows. In realizing this, you see that your potential to grow in any way is unlimited and forever expanding.
   1 — 2 — 3 — 4 — 5 — 6 — 7 — 8 — 9 — 10

2. Your wealth is rooted in power. All things are.
   1 — 2 — 3 — 4 — 5 — 6 — 7 — 8 — 9 — 10

3. You possess power in four forms: physical, mental, moral and spiritual.
   1 — 2 — 3 — 4 — 5 — 6 — 7 — 8 — 9 — 10

4. Spiritual power is superior, as it exists beyond time and space.
   1 — 2 — 3 — 4 — 5 — 6 — 7 — 8 — 9 — 10

5. There are barriers between the organic (plant) and inorganic world (mineral), which have never been crossed.
   1 — 2 — 3 — 4 — 5 — 6 — 7 — 8 — 9 — 10

6. There is no proof that life ever existed independent of the Source life.
   1 — 2 — 3 — 4 — 5 — 6 — 7 — 8 — 9 — 10

7. There is no door from which you can enter into the spiritual world.
   1 — 2 — 3 — 4 — 5 — 6 — 7 — 8 — 9 — 10

8. When you accomplish something, it is because the Universal Mind has reached into yours and endowed you with the marvels that it embodies. While you cannot enter into the spiritual world, it can enter into you.
   1 — 2 — 3 — 4 — 5 — 6 — 7 — 8 — 9 — 10

9. Your thoughts are the connecting links between the Infinite and the finite worlds.
   1 — 2 — 3 — 4 — 5 — 6 — 7 — 8 — 9 — 10

10. The conditions and environments your experience are the objective forms of your thoughts.
    1 — 2 — 3 — 4 — 5 — 6 — 7 — 8 — 9 — 10

11. Your thoughts are dynamic and can turn potentiality into reality.
    1 — 2 — 3 — 4 — 5 — 6 — 7 — 8 — 9 — 10

12. You are an individualized spirit creating in the likeness of Universal spirit.
    1 — 2 — 3 — 4 — 5 — 6 — 7 — 8 — 9 — 10

13. Your understanding or Evolution is different that Creation. Creation calls into existence, whereas evolution unfolds that which already exists.
    1 — 2 — 3 — 4 — 5 — 6 — 7 — 8 — 9 — 10

14. You do nothing to make things manifest. You comply with the law and the All-originating Mind brings the results.
    1 — 2 — 3 — 4 — 5 — 6 — 7 — 8 — 9 — 10

15. You must surrender your agenda, or the means by which results will come to you. You must create the idea, and the Universal Mind will follow through with the best outcome.
    1 — 2 — 3 — 4 — 5 — 6 — 7 — 8 — 9 — 10

16. Like touching a live electrical wire, consciously violating this law can lead you to great harm.
    1 — 2 — 3 — 4 — 5 — 6 — 7 — 8 — 9 — 10

17. You operate harmoniously with this law via study and observation.
    1 — 2 — 3 — 4 — 5 — 6 — 7 — 8 — 9 — 10

18. The law is in operation all around you in the law of growth. For growth to occur, there must be life and for life to occur, there must be harmony.
    1 — 2 — 3 — 4 — 5 — 6 — 7 — 8 — 9 — 10

19. Like ineffective circuitry, your dynamics for creation will cease when you are not in tune with the Infinite Mind.
    1 — 2 — 3 — 4 — 5 — 6 — 7 — 8 — 9 — 10

20. When your thoughts are not aligned with the Infinite, illness and distress will arise in your life.
    1 — 2 — 3 — 4 — 5 — 6 — 7 — 8 — 9 — 10

21. Your creative thoughts must be harmonious, and as such eliminate destructive or competitive thoughts.
    1 — 2 — 3 — 4 — 5 — 6 — 7 — 8 — 9 — 10

22. Any weakness you possess is simply the absence of power. Develop your inner power and anything is possible.

1 —— 2 —— 3 —— 4 —— 5 —— 6 —— 7 —— 8 —— 9 —— 10

23. Your conscious realization of the Law of Attraction and your intention to bring it into operation in your life for definite purpose will bring the materialization of that which you desire.

1 —— 2 —— 3 —— 4 —— 5 —— 6 —— 7 —— 8 —— 9 —— 10

24. To further advance your ability to effectively visualize, do this basic exercise to "draw" upon the wall in front of you.

1 —— 2 —— 3 —— 4 —— 5 —— 6 —— 7 —— 8 —— 9 —— 10

25. You can effectively master this exercise, and you are well on your way to being able to concentrate on any problems you may which to transform.

1 —— 2 —— 3 —— 4 —— 5 —— 6 —— 7 —— 8 —— 9 —— 10

Tally your total score by adding the number you allocated for yourself in each of the 31 principles above. Your score will range from 25 to 250.

If you scored between 176 and 250, you are in tune with the realization that the Law of Attraction is dynamic and always evolving. You know that you are not the one that makes things happen. The Universal Mind does, and when you are in alignment with it, massive positive shifts take place in your life. Take your timing doing this week's exercise and be sure to do it more than once. Practice makes perfect!

If you scored between 100 and 175, you have a substantial understanding of how the Law of Attraction works. Be sure to continue studying the 25 principles outlined in this segment of the book. Also, practice the exercise consistently and diligently. Doing so will further strengthen your experience of that which you know intellectually.

If you scored between 25 and 99, you have a great deal more that you could learn about how the Law of Attraction functions. Take time to review and reflect on each of the 25 principles outlined in this session. Be sure to practice the visualization exercise at least daily. Doing so will turn principle into experience for you.

Introspection:

1. What did you learn about yourself after completing the Comprehension Survey?
2. Was your score what you expected it to be? Why or why not?
3. What areas of the segment of the book have you mastered?

4. What are the areas in this segment of the book that you need to focus on?

5. What three "takeaways" from this segment would you share with others and why?

Exercise

This week select a blank space on the wall, or any other convenient spot, from where you usually sit, mentally draw a black horizontal line about six inches long, try to see the line as plainly as though it were painted on the wall; now mentally draw two vertical lines connecting with this horizontal line at either end; now draw another horizontal line connecting with the two vertical lines; now you have a square. Try to see the square perfectly; when you can do so draw a circle within the square; now place a point in the center of the circle; now draw the point toward you about 10 inches; now you have a cone on a square base; you will remember that your work was all in black; change it to white, to red, to yellow.

NOTES IN RESPONSE TO PERFORMING THIS EXERCISE
Be sure to journal about any findings or experiences you have as you continue to do this exercise as outlined.

Part Eleven

INTRODUCTION

Your life is governed by law, by actual, immutable principles that never vary. Law is in operation at all times; in all places.

Fixed laws underlie all human actions. For this reason, men who control giant industries are enabled to determine with absolute precision just what percentage of every hundred thousand people will respond to any given set of conditions.

It is well, however, to remember that while every effect is the result of a cause, the effect in turn becomes a cause, which creates other effects, which in turn create still other causes; so that when you put the law of attraction into operation you must remember that you are starting a train of causation for good or otherwise which may have endless possibilities.

We frequently hear it said, "A very distressing situation came into my life, which could not have been the result of my thought, as I certainly never entertained any thought which could have such a result." We fail to remember that like attracts like in the mental world, and that the thought which we entertain brings to us certain friendships, companionships of a particular kind, and these in turn bring about conditions and environment, which in turn are responsible for the conditions of which we complain.

1. Inductive reasoning is the process of the objective mind by which we compare a number of separate instances with one another until we see the common factor that gives rise to them all.
2. Induction proceeds by comparison of facts; it is this method of studying nature which has resulted in the discovery of a reign of law which has marked an epoch in human progress.
3. It is the dividing line between superstition and intelligence; it has eliminated the elements of uncertainty and caprice from men's lives and substituted law, reason and certitude.
4. It is the "Watchman at the Gate" mentioned in a former lesson.
5. When, by virtue of this principle, the world to which the senses were accustomed, had been revolutionized; when tho sun had been arrested in his course, the apparently flat earth had been shaped into a ball and set whirling around him; when the inert matter had been resolved into active elements, and the universe presented itself wherever we directed the telescope and microscope, full of force, motion and life; we are constrained to ask by what possible means the delicate forms of organization in the midst of it are kept in order and repair.
6. Like poles and like forces repel themselves or remain impenetrable to each other, and this cause seems in general sufficient to assign a proper place and distance to stars, men and forces. As men of different virtues enter into partnership, so do opposite poles attract each other, elements that have no property in common like acids and gases cling to each other in preference and a general exchange is kept up between the surplus and the demand.
7. As the eye seeks and receives satisfaction from colors complementary to those which are given, so does need, want

and desire, in the largest sense, induce, guide and determine action.

8. It is our privilege to become conscious of the principle and act in accordance with it. Cuvier sees a tooth belonging to an extinct race of animals. This tooth wants a body for the performance of its function, and it defines the peculiar body it stands in need of with Such precision that Cuvier is able to reconstruct the frame of this animal.

9. Perturbations are observed in the motions of Uranus. Leverrier needs another star at a certain place to keep the solar system in order, and Neptune appears in the place and hour appointed.

10. The instinctive wants of the animal and the intellectual wants of Cuvier, the wants of nature and of the mind of Leverrier were alike, and thus the results; here the thoughts of an existence, there an existence. A well-defined lawful want, therefore, furnishes the reason for the more complex operations of nature.

11. Having recorded correctly the answers furnished by nature and stretched our senses with the growing science over her surface; having joined hands with the levers that move the earth; we become conscious of such a close, varied and deep contact with the world without, that our wants and purposes become no less identified with the harmonious operations of this vast organization, than the life, liberty and happiness of the citizen is identified with the existence of his government.

12. As the interests of the individual are protected by the arms of the country, added to his own; and his needs may depend upon certain supply in the degree that they are felt more universally and steadily; in the same manner does conscious citizenship in the Republic of nature secure us from the annoyances of subordinate agents by alliance with superior powers; and by appeal to the fundamental laws of

resistance or inducement offered to mechanical or chemical agents, distribute the labor to be performed between them and man to the best advantage of the inventor.

13. If Plato could have witnessed the pictures executed by the sun with the assistance of the photographer, or a hundred similar illustrations of what man does by induction, he would perhaps have been reminded of the intellectual midwifery of his master and, in his own mind might have arisen the vision of a land where all manual, mechanical labor and repetition is assigned to the power of nature, where our wants are satisfied by purely mental operations set in motion by the will, and where the supply is created by the demand.

14. However distant that land may appear, induction has taught men to make strides toward it and has surrounded him with benefits which are, at the same time, rewards for past fidelity and incentives for more assiduous devotion.

15. It is also an aid in concentrating and strengthening our faculties for the remaining part, giving unerring solution for individual as well as universal problems, by the mere operations of mind in the purest form.

16. Here we find a method, the spirit of which is, to believe that what is sought has been accomplished, in order to accomplish it: a method, bequeathed upon us by the same Plato who, outside of this sphere, could never find how the ideas became realities.

17. This conception is also elaborated by Swedenborg in his doctrine of correspondences; and a still greater teacher has said, "What things soever ye desire, when ye pray, believe that ye receive them, and ye shall have them." (Mark XI, 24 R. V.) The difference of the tenses in this passage is remarkable.

18. We are first to believe that our desire has already been fulfilled, its accomplishment will then follow. This is a concise

direction for making use of the creative power of thought by impressing on the Universal subjective mind, the particular thing which we desire as an already existing fact.

19. We are thus thinking on the plane of the absolute and eliminating all consideration of conditions or limitation and are planting a seed which, if left undisturbed, will finally germinate into external fruition.

20. To review: Inductive reasoning is the process of the objective mind, by which we compare a number of separate instances with one another until we see the common factor that gives rise to them all. We see people in every civilized country on the globe, securing results by some process which they do not seem to understand themselves, and to which they usually attach more or less mystery. Our reason is given to us for the purpose of ascertaining the law by which these results are accomplished.

21. The operation of this thought process is seen in those fortunate natures that possess everything that others must acquire by toil, who never have a struggle with conscience because they always act correctly, and can never comport themselves otherwise than with tact, learn everything easily, complete everything they begin with a happy knack, live in eternal harmony with themselves, without ever reflecting much what they do, or ever experiencing difficulty or toil.

22. The fruit of this thought is, as it were, a gift of the gods, but a gift which few as yet realize, appreciate, or understand. The recognition of the marvelous power which is possessed by the mind under proper conditions and the fact that this power can be utilized, directed, and made available for the solution of every human problem is of transcendental importance.

23. All truth is the same, whether stated in modern scientific terms or in the language of apostolic times. There are

timid souls who fail to realize that the very completeness of truth requires various statement—that no one human formula will show every side of it.

24. Changing, emphasis, new language, novel interpretations, unfamiliar perspectives, are not, as some suppose, signs of departure from truth but on the contrary, they are evidence that the truth is being apprehended in new relation to human needs, and is becoming more generally understood.

25. The truth must be told to each generation and to every people in new and different terms, so that when the Great Teacher said—"Believe that ye receive and ye shall receive" or, when Paul said—"Faith is the substance of things hoped for, the evidence of things not seen" or, when modern science says—"The law of attraction is that law by which thought correlates with its object," each statement when subjected to analysis, is found to contain exactly tho same truth. The only difference being in the form of presentation.

26. We are standing on the threshold of a new era. The time has arrived when man has learned the secrets of mastery and the way is being prepared for a new social order, more wonderful than anything ever heretofore dreamed of. The conflict of modern science with theology, the study of comparative religions, the tremendous power of new social movements, all of these are but clearing the way for the new order. They may have destroyed traditional forms which have become antiquated and impotent, but nothing of value has been lost.

27. A new faith has been born, a faith which demands a new form of expression, and this faith is taking form in a deep consciousness of power which is being manifested, in the present spiritual activity found on every hand.

28. The spirit which sleeps in the mineral, breathes in the vegetable, moves in the animal and reaches its highest devel-

opment in man is the Universal Mind, and it behooves us to span the gulf between being and doing, theory and practice by demonstrating our understanding of the dominion which we have been given.

29. By far the greatest discovery of all the centuries is the power of thought. The importance of this discovery has been a little slow in reaching the general consciousness, but it has arrived, and already in every field of research the importance of this greatest of all great discoveries is being demonstrated.

30. You ask in what does the creative power of thought consist? It consists in creating ideas, and these in turn objectify themselves by appropriating, inventing, observing, discerning, discovering, analyzing, ruling, governing, combining and applying matter and force. It can do this because it is an intelligent creative power.

31. Thought reaches its loftiest activity when plunged into its own mysterious depth; when it breaks through the narrow compass of self and passes from truth to truth to the region of eternal light, where all which is, was or ever will be, melt into one grand harmony.

32. From this process of self contemplation comes inspiration which is creative intelligence, and which is undeniably superior to every element, force or law of nature, because it can understand, modify, govern and apply them to its own ends and purposes and therefore possess them.

33. Wisdom begins with the dawn of reason, and reason is but an understanding if the knowledge and principles whereby we may know the true meaning of things. Wisdom, then, is illuminated reason, and this wisdom leads to humility, for humility is a large part of Wisdom.

34. We all know many who have achieved the seemingly impossible, who have realized life-long dreams, who have changed everything including themselves. We have some-

times marveled at the demonstration of an apparently irresistible power, which seemed to be ever available just when it was most needed, but it is all clear now. All that is required is an understanding of certain definite fundamental principles and their proper application.

35. For your exercise this week, concentrate on the quotation taken from the Bible, "Whatsoever things ye desire, when ye pray, believe that ye receive them and ye shall have them," notice that there is no limitation, "Whatsoever things" is very definite and implies that the only limitation which is placed upon us is in our ability to think, to be equal to the occasion, to rise to the emergency, to remember that Faith is not a shadow, but a substance, "the substance of things hoped for, the evidence of things not seen."

Death is but the natural process whereby all material forms are thrown into the crucible for reproduction: in fresh diversity.

STUDY GUIDE

Part Eleven

Summary

This Part tells of the means by which we have discovered that the infinitely small as well as the infinitely large is in the last analysis nothing but force, motion, life and mind. It tells of the process by which we have become familiar with the vast organization by which we are identified with the complex operations of Nature. It gives concise directions for making use of the creative power of the Universe, the power by which all things are brought into existence. It shows how this marvelous power may be utilized, directed and made available for the solution of every human problem.

1. Law is in operation at all times and in all places. Explain what this means, providing examples.

2. Provide concrete examples of how at least three industry giants have determined with absolute precision what percentage of people responded to particular conditions in a certain way.

3. Give an example of how a train of cause and effect has snowballed in your life.

4. Share an experience where you insisted you did not attract a particular person or experience into your life, only to later see how you actually did.

Comprehension Survey

In this segment, you will further your understanding that all in creation, big and small are nothing more than force, motion, life and mind. Once you have completed this Comprehension Survey, you will get a better sense of how much you are thriving from a place of positivity or struggling with negativity dominating your life. For each of the principles below, choose the number that is most closely aligns to your beliefs (1 being "not at all" and 10 being "a great deal").

1. When you use inductive reasoning, you compare separate instances with one another until you see the common factor that gives rise to them all.

    1 —— 2 —— 3 —— 4 —— 5 —— 6 —— 7 —— 8 —— 9 —— 10

2. Through inductive study of nature you discover the law that marks the rise of human progress.
   1 —— 2 —— 3 —— 4 —— 5 —— 6 —— 7 —— 8 —— 9 —— 10

3. Induction and reasoning are the dividing line between superstition and law.
   1 —— 2 —— 3 —— 4 —— 5 —— 6 —— 7 —— 8 —— 9 —— 10

4. Induction is the watchman at the gate of Universal Mind.
   1 —— 2 —— 3 —— 4 —— 5 —— 6 —— 7 —— 8 —— 9 —— 10

5. When your perceptions change, like moving from a flat earth to a round one, you note that all existence still functions in perfect order.
   1 —— 2 —— 3 —— 4 —— 5 —— 6 —— 7 —— 8 —— 9 —— 10

6. Like poles and forces naturally attract and repel, you can experience energetic exchanges with individuals who are the polar opposite of you.
   1 —— 2 —— 3 —— 4 —— 5 —— 6 —— 7 —— 8 —— 9 —— 10

7. Your needs, wants and desires naturally determines your action.
   1 —— 2 —— 3 —— 4 —— 5 —— 6 —— 7 —— 8 —— 9 —— 10

8. You are privileged to become conscious of this principle and act in alignment with it.
   1 —— 2 —— 3 —— 4 —— 5 —— 6 —— 7 —— 8 —— 9 —— 10

9. All of nature has a function to keep order in the Universe.
   1 —— 2 —— 3 —— 4 —— 5 —— 6 —— 7 —— 8 —— 9 —— 10

10. Cuvier and Leverrier's passion to explore nature drew them to the results they discovered.
    1 —— 2 —— 3 —— 4 —— 5 —— 6 —— 7 —— 8 —— 9 —— 10

11. When your consciousness is joined with the miracles of nature, then your purpose aligns with the harmonious desire for life, liberty and happiness.
    1 —— 2 —— 3 —— 4 —— 5 —— 6 —— 7 —— 8 —— 9 —— 10

12. As you are protected by the laws that govern your country and the like laws that govern the world, so too are you protected by the natural laws of the Universe.
    1 —— 2 —— 3 —— 4 —— 5 —— 6 —— 7 —— 8 —— 9 —— 10

13. If Plato had access to greater innovations, like photography, he may have been reminded of the power of nature in motion, which is effected by one's mind and will.
    1 — 2 — 3 — 4 — 5 — 6 — 7 — 8 — 9 — 10

14. While your desires may seem far away, their manifestation is being supported by your focused pursuit, commitment and passion.
    1 — 2 — 3 — 4 — 5 — 6 — 7 — 8 — 9 — 10

15. When your mind operates in the purest form, all else in your life is strengthened.
    1 — 2 — 3 — 4 — 5 — 6 — 7 — 8 — 9 — 10

16. In order to accomplish something, you need to hold the belief that you have done so.
    1 — 2 — 3 — 4 — 5 — 6 — 7 — 8 — 9 — 10

17. Mark XI, 24 R V of the bible states that whatever you desire, when you pray and believe that you have received them, you will do so.
    1 — 2 — 3 — 4 — 5 — 6 — 7 — 8 — 9 — 10

18. When you believe your desire has already been accomplished, the creative power of your thought gets impressed upon the Universal Mind.
    1 — 2 — 3 — 4 — 5 — 6 — 7 — 8 — 9 — 10

19. To manifest, eliminate any limitations when you plant a seed in your thoughts. If you can maintain this, that seed will reach full growth.
    1 — 2 — 3 — 4 — 5 — 6 — 7 — 8 — 9 — 10

20. Your reasoning assists you in understand the law that many mistakenly consider to be mystery.
    1 — 2 — 3 — 4 — 5 — 6 — 7 — 8 — 9 — 10

21. When in total integrity and alignment, you will manifest easily, effortlessly and joyfully.
    1 — 2 — 3 — 4 — 5 — 6 — 7 — 8 — 9 — 10

22. Your complete appreciation of your understanding of how to use your mind is of great spiritual importance.
    1 — 2 — 3 — 4 — 5 — 6 — 7 — 8 — 9 — 10

23. No matter what the rhetoric around it, no matter how it is stated, all truth is the same.
    1 — 2 — 3 — 4 — 5 — 6 — 7 — 8 — 9 — 10

Study Guide   205

24. As new language describes this phenomenon, it is evidence that it is understood and is evolving a new relationship to the needs of humankind.

1 —— 2 —— 3 —— 4 —— 5 —— 6 —— 7 —— 8 —— 9 —— 1 0

25. While source or form of this message may vary, the same truth exists at its core.

1 —— 2 —— 3 —— 4 —— 5 —— 6 —— 7 —— 8 —— 9 —— 1 0

26. As you stand on a new threshold of existence, as the old ways are destroy, you know that nothing of value has been lost.

1 —— 2 —— 3 —— 4 —— 5 —— 6 —— 7 —— 8 —— 9 —— 1 0

27. You are a part of a new faith that is being born into the world.

1 —— 2 —— 3 —— 4 —— 5 —— 6 —— 7 —— 8 —— 9 —— 1 0

28. As you become one with the Universal Mind, the spirit in all things is challenging you to demonstrate the power that you have been given.

1 —— 2 —— 3 —— 4 —— 5 —— 6 —— 7 —— 8 —— 9 —— 1 0

29. While slow in reaching general consciousness, the greatest discovery to mankind is the power of your thoughts.

1 —— 2 —— 3 —— 4 —— 5 —— 6 —— 7 —— 8 —— 9 —— 1 0

30. The creative power of your thoughts exist in creating ideas that represent themselves by adopting, inventing, observing, discerning, discovering, analyzing, ruling, governing, combining and applying matter and force.

1 —— 2 —— 3 —— 4 —— 5 —— 6 —— 7 —— 8 —— 9 —— 1 0

31. Your thoughts are of the highest nature when they break through your ego (or personality-self) and access the harmony of eternal light within you.

1 —— 2 —— 3 —— 4 —— 5 —— 6 —— 7 —— 8 —— 9 —— 1 0

32. The creative intelligence you can access when in self-contemplation is superior to everything, as it can affect all to meld to its commands.

1 —— 2 —— 3 —— 4 —— 5 —— 6 —— 7 —— 8 —— 9 —— 1 0

33. A large part of wisdom is humility, which comes from knowing the true meaning of all things.

1 —— 2 —— 3 —— 4 —— 5 —— 6 —— 7 —— 8 —— 9 —— 1 0

34. All you need do is understand the fundamental principles and application of this law to achieve the apparent impossible.
1 —— 2 —— 3 —— 4 —— 5 —— 6 —— 7 —— 8 —— 9 —— 10

35. Your faith exists as form and has great power to make the seemingly impossible happen.
1 —— 2 —— 3 —— 4 —— 5 —— 6 —— 7 —— 8 —— 9 —— 10

Tally your total score by adding the number you allocated for yourself in each of the 31 principles above. Your score will range from 35 to 350.

If you scored between 246 and 350, you are very aware of the potency of your thoughts, and how seeing your desires as already manifest holds great power. Continue to immerse yourself in the contents of this book, and be sure to do the exercise for this segment each day. You will heighten your awareness and experiences if you write down your findings.

If you scored between 140 and 245, you are quite familiar with the understanding that all things, large and small are governed by the same law of attraction. As you study this segment further, you will gain a greater understanding of how much power lies in seeing your desires as already manifest in the world. Review each of the 35 principles and practice the exercise daily so that you can continue on your journey from making theory into experience.

If you scored between 35 and 139, while you are well on your way to integrating these teachings into your life, you still have a ways to go. Honor yourself for having clarity on where your strengths and weaknesses lie. Take time each day to re-read through the 35 principles outlined in this segment of the book, and be sure to practice the contemplation exercise.

Introspection:

1. What did you learn about yourself after completing the Comprehension Survey?
2. Was your score what you expected it to be? Why or why not?
3. What areas of the segment of the book have you mastered?
4. What are the areas in this segment of the book that you need to focus on?
5. What three "takeaways" from this segment would you share with others and why?

Exercise

For your exercise this week, concentrate on the quotation taken from the Bible, "Whatsoever things ye desire, when ye pray, believe that ye receive them and ye shall have them," notice that there is no limitation, "Whatsoever things" is very definite and implies that the only limitation which is placed upon us is in our ability to think, to be equal to the occasion, to rise to the emergency, to remember that Faith is not a shadow, but a substance, "the substance of things hoped for, the evidence of things not seen."

NOTES IN RESPONSE TO PERFORMING THIS EXERCISE
Be sure to journal about any findings or experiences you have as you continue to do this exercise as outlined.

Part Twelve

INTRODUCTION

In the fourth paragraph you will find the following statement: "You must first have the knowledge of your power; second, the courage to dare; third, the faith to do."

If you concentrate upon the thoughts given; if you give them your entire attention, you will find a world of meaning in each sentence, and will attract to yourself other thoughts in harmony with them, and you will soon grasp the full significance of the vital knowledge upon which you are concentrating.

Knowledge does not apply itself; we as individuals must make the application, and the application consists in fertilizing the thought with a living purpose.

The time and thought which most persons waste in aimless effort would accomplish wonders if properly directed with some special object in view. In order to do this, it is necessary to center your mental force upon a specific thought and hold it there, to the exclusion of all other thoughts. If you have ever looked through the focusing screen of a camera, you found that when the object was not in focus, the impression was indistinct and possibly blurred, but when the proper focus was obtained the picture was clear and distinct. This illustrates the power of concentration. Unless you can concentrate upon the object which you have in view, you will have but a hazy, indifferent, vague, indistinct and blurred outline of your ideal and the results will be in accordance with your mental picture.

---

1. There is no purpose in life that cannot be best accomplished through a scientific understanding of the creative power of thought.
2. The power to think is common to all. Man is, because he thinks. Man's power to think is infinite, consequently his creative power is unlimited.
3. We know that thought is building for us the thing we think of and actually bringing it nearer, yet we find it difficult to banish fear, anxiety or discouragement, all of which are powerful thought forces, and which continually send the things we desire further away, so that it is often one step forward and two steps backward.
4. The only way to keep from going backward is to keep going forward. Eternal vigilance is the price of success. There are three steps, and each one is absolutely essential. You must first have the knowledge of your power; second, the courage to dare; third, the faith to do.
5. With this as a basis you can construct an ideal business, an ideal home, ideal friends, ideal environment. You are not restricted as to material or cost. Thought is omnipotent and has the power to draw on the Infinite bank of primary substance for all that it requires. Infinite resources are therefore at your command.
6. But your ideal must be sharp, clearcut, definite; to have one ideal today, another tomorrow, and a third next week, means to scatter your forces and accomplish nothing; your result will be a meaningless and chaotic combination of wasted material.

7. Unfortunately this is the result which many are securing, and the cause is self evident. If a sculptor started out with a piece of marble and a chisel and changed his ideal every fifteen minutes, what result could he expect? And why should you expect any different result in molding the greatest and most plastic of all substances, the only real substance?

8. The result of this indecision and negative thought is often found in the loss of material wealth. Supposed independence which required many years of toil and effort suddenly disappears. It is often found then that money and property are not independence at all. On the contrary, the only independence is found to be a practical working knowledge of the creative power of thought.

9. This practical working method cannot come to you, until you learn that the only real power which you can have, is the power to adjust yourself to Divine and unchangeable principles. You cannot change the Infinite, but you can come into an understanding of Natural laws. The reward of this understanding is a conscious realization of your ability to adjust your thought faculties with the Universal Thought which is Omnipresent. Your ability to co-operate with this Omnipotence will indicate the degree of success with which you meet.

10. The power of thought has many counterfeits which are more or less fascinating, but the results are harmful instead of helpful.

11. Of course, worry, fear, and all negative thoughts produce a crop after their kind; those who harbor thoughts of this kind must inevitably reap exactly what they have sown.

12. Again, there are the Phenomena seekers who gormandize on the so-called proofs and demonstrations obtained at materializing séances. They throw open their mental doors and soak themselves in the most poisonous currents which can be

found in the psychic world; They do not seem to understand that it is the ability, to become negative, receptive and passive, and thus drain themselves of all their vital force, which enables them to bring about these vibratory thought forms.

13. There are also the Hindu worshipers, who see in the materializing phenomena which are performed by the so-called adepts, a source of power, forgetting, or never seeming to realize that as soon as the will is withdrawn the forms wither, and the vibratory forces of which they are composed vanish.

14. Telepathy, or thought transference, has received considerable attention, but as it requires a negative mental state on the part of the receiver, the practice is harmful. A thought may be sent with the intention of hearing or seeing, but it will bring the penalty attached to the inversion of the principle involved.

15. Hypnotism is positively dangerous to the subject as well as the operator. No one familiar with the laws governing in the mental world would think of attempting to dominate the will of another, for by so doing he will gradually but surely divest himself of his own power.

16. All of these perversions have their temporary satisfaction and for some a keen fascination, but there is an infinitely greater fascination in a true understanding of the world of power within, a power which increases with use; is permanent instead of fleeting; which not only is potent as a remedial agency to bring about the remedy for past error or results of wrong thinking, but is a prophylactic agency protecting us from all manner and form of danger, and finally is an actual creative force with which we can build new conditions and new environment.

17. The law is, that thought will correlate with its object and bring forth in the material world the correspondence of the thing thought or produced in the mental world. We then discern the absolute necessity of seeing that every thought has the inherent germ of truth in order that the

law of growth will bring into manifestation good, for good alone can confer any permanent power.

18. The principle which gives the thought the dynamic power to correlate with its object, and therefore to master every adverse human experience, is the law of attraction, which is another name for love. This is an eternal and fundamental principle, inherent in all things, in every system of Philosophy, in every Religion and in every Science. There is no getting away from the law of love. It is feeling that imparts vitality to thought. Feeling is desire, and desire is love. Thought impregnated with love becomes invincible.

19. We find this truth emphasized wherever the power of thought is understood, The Universal Mind is not only Intelligence, but it is substance, and this substance is the attractive force which brings electrons together by the law of attraction so that they form atoms; the atoms in turn are brought together by the same law and form molecules; molecules take objective forms; and so we find that the law of love is the creative force behind every manifestation, not only of atoms, but of worlds, of the Universe, of everything of which the imagination can form any conception.

20. It is the operation of this marvelous law of attraction which has caused men in all ages and all times to believe that there must be some personal being who responded to their petitions and desires, and manipulated events in order to comply with their requirements.

21. It is the combination of Thought and Love which forms the irresistible force, called the law of attraction. All natural laws are irresistible, the law of Gravitation, or Electricity, or any other law operates with mathematical exactitude. There is no variation, it is only the channel of distribution which may be imperfect. If a bridge falls, we do not attribute the collapse to any variation of the law of gravitation. If a light fails us, we do not conclude that the laws govern-

ing electricity cannot be depended upon, and if the law of attraction seems to be imperfectly demonstrated by an inexperienced or uninformed person, we are not to conclude that the greatest and most infallible law upon which the entire system of creation depends has been suspended. We should rather conclude that a little more understanding of the law is required, for the same reason that a correct solution of a difficult problem in Mathematics is not always readily and easily obtained.

22. Things are created in the mental or spiritual world before they appear in the outward act or event. By the simple process of governing our thought forces today, we help create the events which will come into our lives in the future, perhaps even tomorrow. Educated desire is the most potent means of bringing into action the law of attraction.

23. Man is so constituted that he must first create the tools, or implements by which he gains the power to think. The mind cannot comprehend an entirely new idea until a corresponding vibratory brain cell has been prepared to receive it. This explains why it is so difficult for us to receive or appreciate an entirely new idea; we have no brain cell capable of receiving it; we are therefore incredulous; we do not believe it.

24. If, therefore, you have not been familiar with the Omnipotence of the law of attraction, and the scientific method by which it can be put into operation, or if you have not been familiar with the unlimited possibilities which it opens to those who are enabled to take advantage of the resources it offers, begin now and create the necessary brain cells which will enable you to comprehend the unlimited powers which may be yours by co-operating with Natural Law: This is done by concentration or attention.

25. The intention governs the attention. Power comes through repose. It is by concentration that deep thoughts, wise speech and all forces of high potentiality are accomplished.

26. It is in the Silence that you get into touch with the Omnipotent Power of the subconscious mind from which all power is evolved.

27. He who desires wisdom, power or permanent success of any kind will find it only within; it is an unfoldment. The unthinking may conclude that the silence is very simple and easily attained, but it should be remembered that only in absolute silence may one come into contact with Divinity itself; may learn of the unchangeable law and open for himself the channels by which persistent practice and concentration lead to perfection.

28. This week go to the same room, take the same chair, the same position as heretofore; be sure to relax, let go, both mentally and physically; always do this; never try to do any mental work under pressure; see that there are no tense muscles or nerves, that you are entirely comfortable. Now realize your unity with omnipotence; get into touch with this power, come into a deep and vital understanding, appreciation and realization of the fact that your ability to think is your ability to act upon the Universal Mind, and bring it into manifestation, realize that it will meet any and every requirement; that you have exactly the same potential ability which any individual ever did have or ever will have, because each is but an expression or manifestation of the One, all are parts of the whole, there is no difference in kind or quality, the only difference being one of degree.

Thought cannot conceive of anything that may not be brought to expression. He who first uttered it may be only the suggester, but the doer will appear.
—WILSON.

STUDY GUIDE

Part Twelve

Summary

This Part tells of numerous counterfeits and perversions by which many are led to think that something can be had for nothing. There is no royal road to success, we must give before we can get; if we cannot give money, we must give service, we must give time and thought, the Law of Compensation demands an eye for an eye. It tells how we may create the implements by which we may put into operation the laws by which we can gain access to the unlimited resources of Nature.

1. If you give your full concentration to something, you will find deeper meaning. Provide an example of where you have experienced this in your life.

2. Knowledge is not enough in and of itself. You must fertilize your knowledge of something with a living purpose in order to apply it. What is one of the most recent thoughts you have fertilized into being?

3. The ability to completely concentrate and focus upon the object of your desires is critical to manifesting them into physical form. Many people waste time wishing, but they do not take the time to singularly focus on that which they desire. For the next 24 hours, make a list of the thoughts you think that pull your focused concentration from that which you desire.

4. What mental picture are you currently focusing on in your life? Have you noted any movement since doing so? Please explain.

Comprehension Survey

In this segment, Charles Haanel emphasizes the importance and power of concentration and focus as you study and apply the principles outlined in this book. Once you have completed this survey, you will get a better sense of how much you are able to focus on that which really matters in your life. For each of the principles below, choose the number that is most closely aligns to your beliefs (1 being "not at all" and 10 being "a great deal").

1. When you understand the creative power of your thoughts, you able to be most "on purpose" in your life.
   1 — 2 — 3 — 4 — 5 — 6 — 7 — 8 — 9 — 10

2. Everyone is capable of thought, thus we are all able to tap into the power of creation.
   1 — 2 — 3 — 4 — 5 — 6 — 7 — 8 — 9 — 10

3. When your focus gets pulled in the direction of fear, anxiety and discouragement, you send that which you desire further away.
   1 — 2 — 3 — 4 — 5 — 6 — 7 — 8 — 9 — 10

4. To keep propelling you forward, you must be vigilant and have the knowledge, courage and faith.
   1 — 2 — 3 — 4 — 5 — 6 — 7 — 8 — 9 — 10

5. Because your thoughts are limitless and rooted in omnipotence, you can draw anything you desire into your life.
   1 — 2 — 3 — 4 — 5 — 6 — 7 — 8 — 9 — 10

6. If you scatter your thoughts, the results will be meaningless and chaotic.
   1 — 2 — 3 — 4 — 5 — 6 — 7 — 8 — 9 — 10

7. Like an indecisive sculpture, if you keep changing our ideal, you will not mold anything of great substance into your life.
   1 — 2 — 3 — 4 — 5 — 6 — 7 — 8 — 9 — 10

8. Material wealth is often lost when indecision and negativity set in. You will only find independence in your knowledge of the creative power of thought.
   1 — 2 — 3 — 4 — 5 — 6 — 7 — 8 — 9 — 10

9. The degree of your success is in direct relationship to your ability to adjust your thoughts to those of the omnipotent Universal Thought.
   1 — 2 — 3 — 4 — 5 — 6 — 7 — 8 — 9 — 10

10. There are many counterfeits to the power of thought whose results are harmful, as opposed to helpful.
    1 — 2 — 3 — 4 — 5 — 6 — 7 — 8 — 9 — 10

11. Worry, fear and negative thoughts produce like experiences in your life.
    1 — 2 — 3 — 4 — 5 — 6 — 7 — 8 — 9 — 10

12. Engaging on seances or opening yourself to negativity can drain your energy and manifest further negativity in your life.
    1 —— 2 —— 3 —— 4 —— 5 —— 6 —— 7 —— 8 —— 9 —— 10

13. When your will is withdrawn, then the energetic vibrations that materialize thoughts into things vanishes.
    1 —— 2 —— 3 —— 4 —— 5 —— 6 —— 7 —— 8 —— 9 —— 10

14. When you practice telepathy, as a receiver, you can be harmed by a negative mental state that can impose itself on you.
    1 —— 2 —— 3 —— 4 —— 5 —— 6 —— 7 —— 8 —— 9 —— 10

15. You are discouraged from practicing hypnotism. By dominating the will of another, you will lose your own power.
    1 —— 2 —— 3 —— 4 —— 5 —— 6 —— 7 —— 8 —— 9 —— 10

16. You will experience much greater power focusing your time and energies on the creative force within you. It is more potent, powerful and secure.
    1 —— 2 —— 3 —— 4 —— 5 —— 6 —— 7 —— 8 —— 9 —— 10

17. If the law of growth eventuates manifestation, then every thought you think has a germ of truth in it.
    1 —— 2 —— 3 —— 4 —— 5 —— 6 —— 7 —— 8 —— 9 —— 10

18. Your feelings are desire, and desire is love. When your thoughts are filled with love, you become invincible.
    1 —— 2 —— 3 —— 4 —— 5 —— 6 —— 7 —— 8 —— 9 —— 10

19. You are aware that the law of love, or attraction is inherent in everything from the tiniest atom to the entire Universe.
    1 —— 2 —— 3 —— 4 —— 5 —— 6 —— 7 —— 8 —— 9 —— 10

20. The success of law of attraction has caused mankind to believe that there is some personal being responding to their petitions.
    1 —— 2 —— 3 —— 4 —— 5 —— 6 —— 7 —— 8 —— 9 —— 10

21. If you experience failure with the law of attraction, the law is not at fault. You may need a little more understanding of the combination of thought and love—the two elements that form irresistible force.
    1 —— 2 —— 3 —— 4 —— 5 —— 6 —— 7 —— 8 —— 9 —— 10

22. By governing your thought forces today, you can experience them in physical form tomorrow.
    1 —— 2 —— 3 —— 4 —— 5 —— 6 —— 7 —— 8 —— 9 —— 10

218 Study Guide

23. You must first create the brain tool to receive a new idea. Your brain cells are not capable to receiving without being prepared.
1 —— 2 —— 3 —— 4 —— 5 —— 6 —— 7 —— 8 —— 9 —— 10

24. Start to create the necessary brain cells now that will enable you to comprehend the unlimited powers that are your when you master concentration and attention.
1 —— 2 —— 3 —— 4 —— 5 —— 6 —— 7 —— 8 —— 9 —— 10

25. Intention, repose, concentration, deep thoughts and wise speech create an environment conducive to creation.
1 —— 2 —— 3 —— 4 —— 5 —— 6 —— 7 —— 8 —— 9 —— 10

26. When you are silent, you get in touch with the Omnipotent power from which all power evolves.
1 —— 2 —— 3 —— 4 —— 5 —— 6 —— 7 —— 8 —— 9 —— 10

27. Only in absolute silence can you come in contact with Divinity and open the channels that lead to perfection.
1 —— 2 —— 3 —— 4 —— 5 —— 6 —— 7 —— 8 —— 9 —— 10

28. You have the ability to act on Universal Mind because you are an extension of the One.
1 —— 2 —— 3 —— 4 —— 5 —— 6 —— 7 —— 8 —— 9 —— 10

Tally your total score by adding the number you allocated for yourself in each of the 31 principles above. Your score will range from 28 to 280.

If you scored between 197 and 280, you have not been swayed by detrimental means by which you many engage with energy. You know how imperative it is to master the art of silence in order to reap the benefits that come with deeply connecting with the Universal Mind. Take additional time to connect with the Universal Mind in this week's silence exercise. Doing so will vastly intensify your experience.

If you scored between 113 and 196, you have quite a bit of awareness about how much your undivided focus impacts your ability to connect with Universal Mind. As you continue to study the tenets and do the exercises provided in this book, you will gain further insights and faith in your ability to connect with the benevolence of the Universal Mind.

If you scored between 28 and 112, you still have a way to go before feeling confident. As you read, re-read and allow the teachings to resonate within you, you will find that your understanding and application of these teachings will expand. Review each of the 28 principles shared in this segment, and be sure to practice the silent connection exercise that Charles Haanel suggests in this segment.

Introspection:

1. What did you learn about yourself after completing the Comprehension Survey?
2. Was your score what you expected it to be? Why or why not?
3. What areas of the segment of the book have you mastered?
4. What are the areas in this segment of the book that you need to focus on?
5. What three "takeaways" from this segment would you share with others and why?

Exercise

This week go to the same room, take the same chair, the same position as heretofore; be sure to relax, let go, both mentally and physically; always do this; never try to do any mental work under pressure; see that there are no tense muscles or nerves, that you are entirely comfortable. Now realize your unity with omnipotence; get into touch with this power, come into a deep and vital understanding, appreciation and realization of the fact that your ability to think is your ability to act upon the Universal Mind, and bring it into manifestation, realize that it will meet any and every requirement; that you have exactly the same potential ability which any individual ever did have or ever will have, because each is but an expression or manifestation of the One, all are parts of the whole, there is no difference in kind or quality, the only difference being one of degree.

NOTES IN RESPONSE TO PERFORMING THIS EXERCISE
Be sure to journal about any findings or experiences you have as you continue to do this exercise as outlined.

Part Thirteen

INTRODUCTION

Physical science is responsible for the marvelous age of invention in which we are now living, but spiritual science is now setting out on a career whose possibilities no one can foretell.

Spiritual science has heretofore been the football of the uneducated, the superstitious, the mystical; but men are now interested in definite methods and demonstrated facts only.

We have come to know that thinking is a spiritual process, that vision and imagination precede action and event, that the day of the dreamer has come. The following lines by Mr. Herbert Kaufman, relating to people who first dream and then achieve, are interesting in this connection.

"They are the architects of greatness, their vision lies within their souls, they peer beyond the veils and mists of doubt and pierce the walls of unborn Time. The belted wheel, the trail of steel, the churning screw, are shuttles in the loom on which they weave their magic tapestries. Makers of Empire, they have fought for bigger things than crowns and higher seats than thrones. Your homes are set upon a land that dreamers built to greatness. The pictures on its walls are visions from the souls of dreamers.

"They are the chosen few—the blazers of the way. Walls crumble and Empires fall, the tidal wave sweeps from the sea *and tears a fortress from its rocks. The rotting nations drop from off Time's bough, and only things the dreamers make live on."*

Part Thirteen tells why the dreams of the dreamer come true. It explains the law of causation by which dreamers, inventors, authors, organizers, bring about the realization of their desires. It explains the law by which the thing pictured upon our mind eventually becomes our own.

---

1. It has been the tendency, and, as might be proved, a necessity for science to seek the explanation of everyday facts by a generalization of those others which are less frequent and form the exception. Thus does the eruption of the volcano manifest the heat which is continually at work in the interior of the earth and to which the latter owes much of her configuration.
2. Thus does the lightning reveal a subtle power constantly busy to produce change in the inorganic world, and, as dead languages now seldom heard were once ruling among the nations, so does a giant tooth in Siberia, or a fossil in the depth of the earth, not only bear record of the evolution of past ages, but thereby explains to us the origin of the hills and valleys which we inhabit today.
3. In this way a generalization of facts which are rare, strange, or form the exception, has been the magnetic needle guiding to all the discoveries of inductive science.
4. This method is founded upon reason and experience and thereby destroyed superstition, precedent and conventionality.
5. It is more than two hundred years since Lord Bacon recommended this method of study, to which the civilized nations owe the greater part of their prosperity and the more valuable part of their knowledge; purging the mind

from narrow prejudices, denominated theories, more effectually than by the keenest irony; calling the attention of men from heaven to earth more successfully by surprising experiments than by the most forcible demonstrations of their ignorance; educating the inventive faculties more powerfully by the near prospect of useful discoveries thrown open to all, than by talk of bringing to light the innate laws of our mind.

6. The method of Bacon has seized the spirit and aim of the great philosophers of Greece and carried them into effect by the new means of observation which another age offered; thus gradually revealing a wondrous field of knowledge in the infinite space of astronomy, in the microscopic egg of embryology, and the dim age of geology; disclosing an order of the pulse which the logic of Aristotle could never have unveiled, and analyzing into formerly unknown elements the material combinations which no dialectic of the scholastics could force apart.

7. It has lengthened life it has mitigated pain; it has extinguished diseases; it has increased the fertility of the soil; it has given new securities to the mariner; it has spanned great rivers with bridges of form unknown to our fathers; it has guided the thunderbolt from heaven to earth; it has lighted up night with the splendor of day; it has extended the range of human vision; it has, multiplied the power of the human muscles; it has accelerated motion; it has annihilated distance; it has facilitated intercourse, correspondence, all friendly offices, all dispatch of business; it has enabled men to descend into the depths of the sea, to soar into the air, to penetrate securely into the noxious recesses of the earth.

8. This then is the true nature and scope of induction. But the greater the success which men have achieved in the inductive science, the more does the whole tenor of their

teachings and example impress us with the necessity of observing carefully, patiently, accurately, with all the instruments and resources at our command the individual facts before venturing upon a statement of general laws.

9. To ascertain the bearing of the spark drawn from the electric machine under every variety of circumstances, that we thus may be emboldened with Franklin to address, in the form of a kite, the question to the cloud about the nature of the lightning. To assure ourselves of the manner in which bodies fall with the exactness of a Galileo, that with Newton we may dare to ask the moon about the force that fastens it to the earth.

10. In short, by the value we set upon truth, by our hope in a steady and universal progress, not to permit a tyrannical prejudice to neglect or mutilate unwelcome facts, but to rear the superstructure of science upon the broad and unchangeable basis, of full attention paid to the most isolated as well as the most frequent phenomena.

11. An ever-increasing material may be collected by observation, but the accumulated facts are of very different value for the explanation of nature, and as we esteem most highly those useful qualities of men which are of the rarest occurrence, so does natural philosophy sift the facts and attach a pre-eminent importance to that striking class which cannot be accounted for by the usual and daily observation of life.

12. If then, we find that certain persons seem to possess unusual power, what are we to conclude? First, we may say, it is not so, which is simply an acknowledgment of our lack of information because every honest investigator admits that there are many strange and heretofore unaccountable phenomena constantly taking place. Those, however, who become acquainted with the creative power of thought, will no longer consider them unaccountable.

13. Second, we may say that they are the result of supernatural interference, but a scientific understanding of Natural Laws will convince us that there is nothing supernatural. Every phenomenon is the result of an accurate definite cause, and the cause is an immutable law or principle, which operates with invariable precision, whether the law is put into operation consciously or unconsciously.
14. Third, we may say that we are on "forbidden ground," that there are some things which we should not know. This objection was used against every advance in human knowledge. Every individual who ever advanced a new idea, whether a Columbus, a Darwin, a Galileo, a Fulton or an Emerson, was subjected to ridicule or persecution; so that this objection should receive no serious consideration; but, on the contrary, we should carefully consider every fact which is brought to our attention; by doing this we will more readily ascertain the law upon which it is based.
15. It will be found that the creative power of thought will explain every possible condition or experience, whether physical, mental or spiritual.
16. Thought will bring about conditions in correspondence with the predominant mental attitude. Therefore, if we fear disaster, as fear is a powerful form of thought, disaster will be the certain result of our thinking. It is this form of thought which frequently sweeps away the result of many years of toil and effort.
17. If we think of some form of material wealth we may secure it. By concentrated thought the required conditions will be brought about, and the proper effort put forth, which will result in bringing about the circumstances necessary to realize our desires; but we often find that when we secure the things we thought we wanted, they do not have the effect we expected. That is, the satisfaction is only temporary, or possibly is the reverse of what we expected.

18. What, then, is the proper method of procedure? What are we to think in order to secure what we really desire? What you and I desire, what we all desire, what every one is seeking, is Happiness and Harmony. If we can be truly happy we shall have everything the world can give. If we are happy ourselves we can make others happy.
19. But we cannot be happy unless we have, health, strength, congenial friends, pleasant environment, sufficient supply, not only to take care of our necessities but to provide for those comforts and luxuries to which we are entitled.
20. The old orthodox way of thinking was to be "a worm," to be satisfied with our portion whatever it is; but the modern idea is to know that we are entitled to the best of everything, that the "Father and I are one" and that the "Father" is the Universal Mind, the Creator, the Original Substance from which all things proceed.
21. Now admitting that this is all true in theory, and it has been taught for two thousand years, and is the essence of every system of Philosophy or Religion, how are we to make it practical in our lives? How are we to get the actual, tangible results here and now?
22. In the first place, we must put our knowledge into practice. Nothing can be accomplished in any other way. The athlete may read books and lessons on physical training all his life, but unless he begins to give out strength by actual work he will never receive any strength; he will eventually get exactly what he gives; but he will have to give it first. It is exactly the same with us; we will get exactly what we give, but we shall have to give it first. It will then return to us many fold, and the giving is simply a mental process, because thoughts are causes and conditions are effects; therefore in giving thoughts of courage, inspiration, health or help of any kind we are setting causes in motion which will bring about their effect.

23. Thought is a spiritual activity and is therefore creative, but make no mistake, thought will create nothing unless it is consciously, systematically and constructively directed; and herein is the difference between idle thinking, which is simply a dissipation of effort, and constructive thinking, which means practically unlimited achievement.

24. We have found that everything we get comes to us by the Law of Attraction. A happy thought cannot exist in an unhappy consciousness; therefore the consciousness must change, and, as the consciousness changes, all conditions necessary to meet the changed consciousness must gradually change, in order to meet the requirements of the new situation.

25. In creating a Mental Image or an Ideal, we are projecting a thought into the Universal Substance from which all things are created. This Universal Substance is Omnipresent, Omnipotent and Omniscient. Are we to inform the Omniscient as to the proper channel to be used to materialize our demand? Can the finite advise the Infinite? This is the cause of failure; of every failure. We recognize the Omnipresence of the Universal Substance, but we fail to appreciate the fact that this substance is not only Omnipresent, but is Omnipotent and Omniscient, and consequently will set causes in motion concerning which we may be entirely ignorant.

26. We can best conserve our interests by recognizing the Infinite Power and Infinite Wisdom of the Universal Mind, and in this way become a channel whereby the Infinite can bring about the realization of our desire. This means that recognition brings about realization, therefore for your exercise this week make use of the principle, recognize the fact that you are a part of the whole, and that a part must be the same in kind and quality as the whole; the only difference there can possibly be, is in degree.

27. When this tremendous fact begins to permeate your consciousness, when you really come into a realization of the fact that you, not your body but the Ego, the "I," the spirit which thinks is an integral part of the great whole, that it is the same in substance, in quality, in kind, that the Creator could create nothing different from Himself, you will also be able to say, "The Father and I are one" and you will come into an understanding of the beauty, the grandeur, the transcendental opportunities which have been placed at your disposal.

Increase in me that wisdom
Which discovers my truest interest,
Strengthen my resolution
To perform that which wisdom dictates.
—FRANKLIN.

STUDY GUIDE

Part Thirteen

Summary

This Part explains why certain forms of thought often result in disaster and frequently sweep away the result of a lifetime of effort. It explains the modern method of thinking and shows how actual, tangible results are thereby secured, and how conditions must change in order to meet the requirements of a changed consciousness. It explains the process by which this change is brought about and how we may hasten it.

1. Provide at least three examples of inventions that are being researched and are being launched by physical science.

2. How do you see humankind's interest have evolved from superstitions to demonstrated methods and facts? Provide at least one example.

3. Are you a dreamer? What do you dream about?

4. "Makers of the Empire, they have fought for bigger things than crowns and higher seats than thrones." Provide at least three examples of this in history or in the world today.

5. "The rotting nations drop from off Time's bought, and only things the dreamers make live on." Provide an example of a "rotting nation" in history. Why do you believe that nation fell?

6. Have you ever fallen like a "rotting nation"? If so, what was the learning you gained from the experience? Please explain.

Comprehension Survey

In this segment you will investigate why the dreams of the dreamers come true, and how you can make yours do so as well! Once you have completed this survey, you will gain further insight on how the law which the thing pictures upon in your mind can become your own. For each of the principles below, choose the number that is most closely aligns to your beliefs (1 being "not at all" and 10 being "a great deal").

1. Science seeks explanations of everyday facts by generalizations of examples that are the exception.

    1 —— 2 —— 3 —— 4 —— 5 —— 6 —— 7 —— 8 —— 9 —— 10

2. Physical manifestations from the past record the evolution of past ages, and explain the origin of what you experience today.
   1 — 2 — 3 — 4 — 5 — 6 — 7 — 8 — 9 — 10

3. Generalization of rare facts have guided the discoveries of inductive science.
   1 — 2 — 3 — 4 — 5 — 6 — 7 — 8 — 9 — 10

4. When you use this method, you destroy superstition, precedent and conventionality.
   1 — 2 — 3 — 4 — 5 — 6 — 7 — 8 — 9 — 10

5. It is because of Lord Bacon recommendation of this study method to shed light on the innate laws of your mind.
   1 — 2 — 3 — 4 — 5 — 6 — 7 — 8 — 9 — 10

6. Bacon's method set the world on a course of awakening, from Greek philosophers to present day innovators.
   1 — 2 — 3 — 4 — 5 — 6 — 7 — 8 — 9 — 10

7. This study method has made vast and extraordinary creations throughout the span of time.
   1 — 2 — 3 — 4 — 5 — 6 — 7 — 8 — 9 — 10

8. The greater the success of inductive science, the more necessary it is for you to observe carefully, patiently and accurately the facts before stating anything is a general law.
   1 — 2 — 3 — 4 — 5 — 6 — 7 — 8 — 9 — 10

9. To understand any new innovations in the world, you need to ask the individual and the natural source from which the realization was created.
   1 — 2 — 3 — 4 — 5 — 6 — 7 — 8 — 9 — 10

10. Without allowing prejudice nor neglect into the equation, with your commitment to truth, your belief in the steadiness of universal progress, and your support of the integration of Universal Mind and the natural laws of science, you can experience all phenomena.
    1 — 2 — 3 — 4 — 5 — 6 — 7 — 8 — 9 — 10

11. While you can appreciate that which you can frequently observe, that which is rare is most highly regarded.
    1 — 2 — 3 — 4 — 5 — 6 — 7 — 8 — 9 — 10

12. Once you familiarize yourself with the creative power of your thoughts, the unusual power that others possess will no longer be so extraordinary in your eyes.
1 — 2 — 3 — 4 — 5 — 6 — 7 — 8 — 9 — 10

13. Once you have a scientific understanding of the Natural Laws, that which may first appear to you as supernatural will no longer seem so.
1 — 2 — 3 — 4 — 5 — 6 — 7 — 8 — 9 — 10

14. There is no such thing as "forbidden ground" when you seek the advancement of a new idea. Leave no stone unturned in your exploration and in doing so, you will understand the law upon what the advancement is based.
1 — 2 — 3 — 4 — 5 — 6 — 7 — 8 — 9 — 10

15. All physical, mental or spiritual conditions can be explained by the creative power of thought.
1 — 2 — 3 — 4 — 5 — 6 — 7 — 8 — 9 — 10

16. As a powerful form of thought, fear can bring about disaster and sweep away many years of your efforts.
1 — 2 — 3 — 4 — 5 — 6 — 7 — 8 — 9 — 10

17. Upon receiving that which you think you desire, upon receiving it, you may find that it is not, in fact, what you expect.
1 — 2 — 3 — 4 — 5 — 6 — 7 — 8 — 9 — 10

18. What then should you pursue? If you pursue happiness and harmony, then you will be happy and you can have that effect on others as well.
1 — 2 — 3 — 4 — 5 — 6 — 7 — 8 — 9 — 10

19. You cannot be happy without health, strength, good friends, a pleasant environment, and enough sufficient supplies to support the comfortable lifestyle that is your birthright.
1 — 2 — 3 — 4 — 5 — 6 — 7 — 8 — 9 — 10

20. Tradition dictated that you should be happy with little, however the more modern belief is that, as a part of the Creative, Universal Mind, you are entitled to the best of everything.
1 — 2 — 3 — 4 — 5 — 6 — 7 — 8 — 9 — 10

21. While this is true in theory, there is a means by which you have to make it tangible in your life.

    1 —— 2 —— 3 —— 4 —— 5 —— 6 —— 7 —— 8 —— 9 —— 10

22. You must put your knowledge into practice by giving thoughts of courage, inspiration, health or help. By doing so, you are setting causes in motion that will bring about their effect.

    1 —— 2 —— 3 —— 4 —— 5 —— 6 —— 7 —— 8 —— 9 —— 10

23. While spiritual, your thoughts have to be conscious, systematic, and constructive, or they will create nothing.

    1 —— 2 —— 3 —— 4 —— 5 —— 6 —— 7 —— 8 —— 9 —— 10

24. You first must have a happy consciousness. Then all other conditions will naturally fall into place.

    1 —— 2 —— 3 —— 4 —— 5 —— 6 —— 7 —— 8 —— 9 —— 10

25. You must trust in the omnipresence of Universal substance, and in doing so, not try to manipulate the channels from which it is made manifest.

    1 —— 2 —— 3 —— 4 —— 5 —— 6 —— 7 —— 8 —— 9 —— 10

26. It is in your best interest to respectfully see yourself as a channel to the infinite power and wisdom of the Universal Mind, remembering that you are a part of that whole.

    1 —— 2 —— 3 —— 4 —— 5 —— 6 —— 7 —— 8 —— 9 —— 10

27. Once your fully embrace that you are a part of the divine Source, you will begin to fully appreciate the beauty, grandeur and transcendental opportunities that you have access to.

    1 —— 2 —— 3 —— 4 —— 5 —— 6 —— 7 —— 8 —— 9 —— 10

Tally your total score by adding the number you allocated for yourself in each of the 27 principles above. Your score will range from 31 to 270.

If you scored between 190 and 270, you have a good grasp on the principles and wisdom that is outlined in this segment. You realize that you are not the source, but the channel through which creative source can make thoughts manifest into form. Take time to allow the realization that you are a part of the divine, original, creative source. Doing so will elevate your beliefs and strengthen your inner knowing.

If you scored between 109 and 189, you have quite a good understanding of how a joyful and luxurious life is your birthright. Continue to set your intentions, knowing that you cannot dictate how things will manifest in your life. Be the channel and allow the Universal Mind to make manifest by the means through which it is governed. Then reap the benefits of your part in the creative process.

If you scored between 27 and 108, you could use further investigation and review to fully comprehend the teachings outlined in this segment. Realize that, as a part of the Universal Source, you are a channel that is deserving of all that life has to offer. Review each of the 27 tenets outlined in this session, and be sure to do the exercise on a daily basis.

Introspection:

1. What did you learn about yourself after completing the Comprehension Survey?
2. Was your score what you expected it to be? Why or why not?
3. What areas of the segment of the book have you mastered?
4. What are the areas in this segment of the book that you need to focus on?
5. What three "takeaways" from this segment would you share with others and why?

Exercise

We can best conserve our interests by recognizing the Infinite Power and Infinite Wisdom of the Universal Mind, and in this way become a channel whereby the Infinite can bring about the realization of our desire. This means that recognition brings about realization, therefore for your exercise this week make use of the principle, recognize the fact that you are a part of the whole, and that a part must be the same in kind and quality as the whole; the only difference there can possibly be, is in degree.

NOTES IN RESPONSE TO PERFORMING THIS EXERCISE
Be sure to journal about any findings or experiences you have as you continue to do this exercise as outlined.

Part Fourteen

INTRODUCTION

You have found from your study thus far that thought is a spiritual activity and is therefore endowed with creative power. This does not mean that some thought is creative. All thought is creative. And thought can be used in a negative way, through the process of denial.

The conscious and subconscious are but two phases of action in connection with one mind. The relation of the subconscious to the conscious is quite analogous to that existing between a weather-vane and the atmosphere. Just as the least pressure of the atmosphere causes an action on the part of the weather-vane, so does the least thought entertained by the conscious mind produce within your subconscious mind action in exact proportion to the depth of feeling characterizing the thought and the intensity with which the thought is indulged.

It follows that if you deny unsatisfactory conditions, you are withdrawing the creative power of your thought from these conditions. You are cutting them away at the root. You are sapping their vitality.

Remember that the law of growth necessarily governs every manifestation in the objective, so that a denial of unsatisfactory conditions will not bring about instant change. A plant will remain visible for some time after its roots have been cut, but it will gradually fade away and eventually disappear; so the withdrawal of your thought from the contemplation of unsatisfactory conditions will gradually but surely terminate these conditions.

You will see that this is an exactly opposite course from the one which we would naturally be inclined to adopt. It will therefore have an exactly opposite effect to the one usually secured. Most persons concentrate intently upon an unsatisfactory condition, thereby giving the condition that measure of energy and vitality which is necessary in order to supply a vigorous growth.

---

1. The Universal Energy in which all motion, light, heat, and color have their origin, does not partake of the limitation of the many effects of which it is the cause, but it is supreme over them all. This Universal Substance is the source of all Power, Wisdom and Intelligence.
2. To recognize this Intelligence is to acquaint yourself with the knowing quality of Mind and through it to move upon the Universal Substance, and bring it into harmonious relations in your affairs.
3. This is something that the most learned physical science teacher has not attempted—a field of discovery upon which he has not yet launched; in fact, but few of the materialistic schools have ever caught the first ray of this light. It does not seem to have dawned upon them that wisdom is just as much present everywhere as are force and substance.
4. Some will say, if these principles are true, why are we not demonstrating them? As the fundamental principle is obviously correct, why do we not get proper results? We do. We get results in exact accordance with our understanding of the law and our ability to make the proper application. We secured no results from the laws governing electricity

until some one formulated the law and showed us how to apply it.

5. This puts us in an entirely new relation to our environment, opening up possibilities hitherto undreamed of, and this by an orderly sequence of law which is naturally involved in our new mental attitude.

6. Mind is creative and the principle upon which this law is based is sound and legitimate and is inherent in the nature of things; but this creative power does not originate in the individual but in the Universal, which is the source and fountain of all energy and substance, the individual is simply the channel for the distribution of this energy. The individual is the means by which the Universal produces the various combinations which result in the formation of phenomena.

7. We know that scientists have resolved matter into an immense number of molecules; these molecules have been resolved into atoms, and the atoms into electrons. The discovery of electrons in high vacuum glass tubes containing fused terminals of hard metal, indicates conclusively that these electrons fill all space; that they exist everywhere, that they are omnipresent. They fill all material bodies and occupy the whole of what we call empty space. This, then, is the Universal Substance from which all things proceed.

8. Electrons would forever remain electrons unless directed where to go to be assembled into atoms and molecules, and this director is Mind. A number of electrons revolving around a center of force constitutes an atom; atoms unite in absolutely regular mathematical ratios and form molecules, and these unite with each other to form a multitude of compounds which unite to build the Universe.

9. The lightest known atom is hydrogen and this is 1,700 times heavier than an electron. An atom of mercury is 300,000 times heavier than an electron. Electrons are pure negative electricity, and as they have the same potential velocity as

all other cosmic energy, such as heat, light, electricity and thought, of 189,380 miles a second, neither time or space require consideration. The manner in which the velocity of light was ascertained is interesting:

10. The velocity of light was obtained by the Danish astronomer Roemer in 1676, by observing the eclipses of Jupiter's moons. When the earth was nearest to Jupiter, the eclipse appeared about eight and one-half minutes too soon for the calculations, and when the earth was most remote from Jupiter, they were about eight and one-half minutes too late. Roemer concluded the reason to be that it required 17 minutes for light from the planet to traverse the diameter of the earth's orbit, which measured the difference of the distances of the earth from Jupiter. This calculation has since been verified, and proves that light travels about 186,000 miles a second.

11. Electrons manifest in the body as cells, and possess mind and intelligence sufficient for them to perform their offices in the human physical anatomy. Every part of the body is composed of cells, some of which operate independently; others in communities. Some are busy building tissue, while others are engaged in forming the various secretions necessary for the body. Some act as carriers of material; others are the surgeons whose work it is to repair damage; others are scavengers, carrying off waste; others are constantly ready to repel invaders or other undesirable intruders of the germ family.

12. All these cells are moving for a common purpose and each one is not only a living organism, but has sufficient intelligence to enable it to perform its necessary duties. It is also endowed with sufficient intelligence to conserve the energies and perpetuate its own life. It must, therefore, secure sufficient nourishment and it has been found that it exercises choice in the selection of such nourishment.

13. Each cell is born, reproduces itself, dies and is absorbed. The maintenance of health and life itself depends upon the constant regeneration of these cells.
14. It is therefore apparent that there is mind in every atom of the body; this mind is negative mind, and the power of the individual to think makes him positive; so that he can control this negative mind. This is the scientific explanation for metaphysical healing, and will enable anyone to understand the principle upon which this remarkable phenomena rests.
15. This negative mind, which is contained in every cell of the body, has been called the subconscious mind, because it acts without our conscious knowledge. We have found that this subconscious mind is responsive to the will of the conscious mind.
16. All things have their origin in mind, and appearances are the result of thought. So that we see that Things in themselves have no origin, permanency or reality. Since they are produced by thought they can be erased by thought.
17. In mental, as in natural science, experiments are being made and each discovery lifts man one step higher toward his possible goal. We find that every man is the reflection of the thought he has entertained during his lifetime. This is stamped on his face, his form, his character, his environment.
18. Back of every effect there is a cause, and if we follow the trail to its starting point, we shall find the creative principle out of which it grew. Proofs of this are now so complete that this truth is generally accepted.
19. The objective world is controlled by an unseen and, heretofore, unexplainable power. We have, heretofore, personalized this power and called it God. We have now, however, learned to look upon it as the permeating essence or Principle of all that exists—the Infinite or Universal Mind.

20. The Universal Mind, being infinite and omnipotent, has unlimited resources at its command, and when we remember that it is also omnipresent, we cannot escape the conclusion that we must be an expression or manifestation of that Mind.
21. A recognition and understanding of the resources of the subconscious mind will indicate that the only difference between the subconscious and the Universal is one of degree. They differ only as a drop of water differs from the ocean. They are the same in kind and quality, the difference is one of degree only.
22. Do you, can you, appreciate the value of this all-important fact; do you realize that a recognition of this tremendous fact places you in touch with Omnipotence? The subconscious mind being the connecting link between the Universal Mind and the conscious mind, is it not evident that the conscious mind can consciously suggest thoughts which the subconscious mind will put into action, and as the subconscious is one with the Universal, is it not evident that no limit can be placed upon its activities.
23. A scientific understanding of this principle will explain the wonderful results which are secured through the power of prayer. The results which are secured in this way are not brought about by any special dispensations of providence, but on the contrary, they are the result of the operation of a perfectly natural law. There is, therefore, nothing either religious or mysterious about it.
24. Yet there are many who are not ready to enter into the discipline necessary to think correctly, even though it is evident that wrong thinking has brought failure.
25. Thought is the only reality; conditions are but the outward manifestations; as the thought changes, all outward or material conditions must change in order to be in harmony with their creator, which is thought.

26. But the thought must be clear cut, steady, fixed, definite, unchangeable; you cannot take one step forward and two steps backward, neither can you spend twenty or thirty years of your life building up negative conditions as the result of negative thoughts, and then expect to see them all melt away as the result of fifteen or twenty minutes of right thinking.
27. If you enter into the discipline necessary to bring about a radical change in your life, you must do so deliberately, after giving the matter careful thought and full consideration, and then you must allow nothing to interfere with your decision.
28. This discipline, this change of thought, this mental attitude will not only bring you the material things which are necessary for your highest and best welfare, but will bring health and harmonious conditions generally.
29. If you wish harmonious conditions in your life, you must develop an harmonious mental attitude.
30. Your world without will be a reflection of your world within.
31. For your exercise this week, concentrate on Harmony, and when I say concentrate, I mean all that the word implies; concentrate so deeply, so earnestly, that you will be conscious of nothing but harmony. Remember, we learn by doing. Reading these lessons will get you nowhere. It is in the practical application that the value consists.

Learn to keep the door shut, keep out of your mind and out of your world, every element that seeks admittance with no definite helpful end in view.
—George Matthew Adams.

STUDY GUIDE

Part Fourteen

Summary

This Part explains the source of all Power, Wisdom and Intelligence, and how we may bring it into harmonious relations in our affairs. It shows that those who understand the principle get results in exact accordance with their understanding and their ability to make the proper application. This opens up possibilities hitherto undreamed of and by an orderly sequence of law. It explains the source of all energy and all substance and the method by which this Universal Substance is differentiated into form. It explains the nature of electrons and of cells upon which the maintenance of health and life depend; it explains how we may bring about radical changes in our life and what the result of such changes must necessarily be.

1. All of your thoughts, negative and positive are spiritual. Take a piece of paper and create 2 columns. Title the left column "Negative" and title the right column "Positive." Then for at least the next 24 hours, list the thoughts you catch yourself thinking throughout the day in the two columns. Make a note of which thoughts you catch yourself thinking.

2. Do the same exercise, only this time, sit quietly for 10 minutes. As you think a thought, stop and write it down in either of the columns. Make a note of which column is the longest.

3. In the 24-hour exercise, you make have had selective attention, and subconsciously taken more note of positive of negative thoughts. In the 10-minute exercise, it is likely more difficult to be as selective. Do you believe the thoughts you had were accurately recorded on the list? Please explain.

4. The less you engage in conscious thoughts, the deeper your feelings, the more your mind will intensify to draw in that in which you focus. Reflect on an example in your life, where you were able to quiet your conscious mind, and uncover an innovative thought or idea in response to something that you are passionate about in your life.

5. When you cancel or disregard that which you consider unsatisfactory from your thoughts, then you are draining them of any power over you. Write about a situation where you were able to catch yourself and stop

a spiral of negative thinking, and in doing so you noted how little power they commanded over you. What was the outcome?

6. Most often it is human nature to focus your energies on unsatisfactory conditions in your life, with a hope that they will change. However doing so only energizes them and provides the fuel upon which they can grow. Write about someone in history that clearly fell into this mistaken practice. How did this ultimately affect the individual?

Comprehension Survey

In this segment you will get a much deeper understanding that the thoughts you focus on, negative or positive will take power from that of your subconscious. You are better to sit in silence than to dwell on that which is not working for you. By completing this survey, you will gain a better understand of how what you feed your subconscious has great impact on the bottom line. For each of the principles below, choose the number that is most closely aligns to your beliefs (1 being "not at all" and 10 being "a great deal").

1. All motion, light, heat and color are made of Universal Substance, which is the source of all Power, Wisdom and Intelligence.
   1 —— 2 —— 3 —— 4 —— 5 —— 6 —— 7 —— 8 —— 9 —— 10

2. To see this principle in action, focus on the "knowing" part of your mind and harmoniously connect it with the Universal Substance (the makings of all that exists).
   1 —— 2 —— 3 —— 4 —— 5 —— 6 —— 7 —— 8 —— 9 —— 10

3. Most traditional teachings have not realized that wisdom (your wise thoughts) have as much impact as force and substance
   1 —— 2 —— 3 —— 4 —— 5 —— 6 —— 7 —— 8 —— 9 —— 10

4. You may ask why you don't see examples of this if it is true. The results you get are directly related to your ability to understand and apply the law.
   1 —— 2 —— 3 —— 4 —— 5 —— 6 —— 7 —— 8 —— 9 —— 10

5. This realization puts you in a new relationship with your environment. Once you embrace it, you will evolve into a new mental attitude.
   1 —— 2 —— 3 —— 4 —— 5 —— 6 —— 7 —— 8 —— 9 —— 10

6. You are not the originator, but a channel through which Source brings phenomena into existence.
   1 —— 2 —— 3 —— 4 —— 5 —— 6 —— 7 —— 8 —— 9 —— 10

7. Electrons are the Universal Substance from which all things exist, interact and evolve.

   1 —— 2 —— 3 —— 4 —— 5 —— 6 —— 7 —— 8 —— 9 —— 10

8. Your Mind directs assembly of electrons into atoms and molecules. Thus, the Mind directs electrons to evolve around a center of force, creating atoms, which unite to form molecules, which unite to form compounds (which build the Universe).

   1 —— 2 —— 3 —— 4 —— 5 —— 6 —— 7 —— 8 —— 9 —— 10

9. Neither time nor space require consideration in the equation of how this system functions.

   1 —— 2 —— 3 —— 4 —— 5 —— 6 —— 7 —— 8 —— 9 —— 10

10. Through his studies of Jupiter, in 1676, Roemer proved that light travels at about 186,000 miles per second.

    1 —— 2 —— 3 —— 4 —— 5 —— 6 —— 7 —— 8 —— 9 —— 10

11. Electrons manifest in your body as cells. Each cell serves a specific function, some independent and others in community—all operate in tandem for your health and wellbeing.

    1 —— 2 —— 3 —— 4 —— 5 —— 6 —— 7 —— 8 —— 9 —— 10

12. You body's cells are living organisms that are intelligent enough to conserve their energies and perpetuate their own lives. You must, therefore secure nourishment from which it chooses.

    1 —— 2 —— 3 —— 4 —— 5 —— 6 —— 7 —— 8 —— 9 —— 10

13. Your health and your life depend upon the constant regeneration of your cells.

    1 —— 2 —— 3 —— 4 —— 5 —— 6 —— 7 —— 8 —— 9 —— 10

14. Within every atom of your body is a negative atom. Through metaphysical healing, your thoughts make it positive.

    1 —— 2 —— 3 —— 4 —— 5 —— 6 —— 7 —— 8 —— 9 —— 10

15. The subconscious mind is the negative mind that is contained in every cell of your body, and is responsive to your will.

    1 —— 2 —— 3 —— 4 —— 5 —— 6 —— 7 —— 8 —— 9 —— 10

16. Anything you see is created by your mind, thus can be erased by your thought.

    1 —— 2 —— 3 —— 4 —— 5 —— 6 —— 7 —— 8 —— 9 —— 10

17. Every thought you have during your lifetime is etched upon your face, for character and environment.

    1 —— 2 —— 3 —— 4 —— 5 —— 6 —— 7 —— 8 —— 9 —— 10

18. The fact that behind every effect there is a cause, is an accepted truth.

    1 —— 2 —— 3 —— 4 —— 5 —— 6 —— 7 —— 8 —— 9 —— 10

19. Humankind has personalized the unseen power (the Infinite or Universal Mind), calling it God.

    1 —— 2 —— 3 —— 4 —— 5 —— 6 —— 7 —— 8 —— 9 —— 10

20. When you realize that the Universal Mind is omnipresent, you know that you are an expression or manifestation of it.

    1 —— 2 —— 3 —— 4 —— 5 —— 6 —— 7 —— 8 —— 9 —— 10

21. Your mind and the Universal Mind are one in the same. The only difference is the degree to which are you a smaller part of the massive whole.

    1 —— 2 —— 3 —— 4 —— 5 —— 6 —— 7 —— 8 —— 9 —— 10

22. Once you realize that your subconscious mind is your connecting link with the Universal Mind, you will experience that you are a part of Omnipotent limitless potential.

    1 —— 2 —— 3 —— 4 —— 5 —— 6 —— 7 —— 8 —— 9 —— 10

23. There is nothing mysterious about the fact that prayer achieves results, once you fully embrace that it is part of the law of nature.

    1 —— 2 —— 3 —— 4 —— 5 —— 6 —— 7 —— 8 —— 9 —— 10

24. Despite the fact that people struggle with failure, many do not have the discipline to think correctly.

    1 —— 2 —— 3 —— 4 —— 5 —— 6 —— 7 —— 8 —— 9 —— 10

25. Your thoughts are the only reality. They change material conditions, that seek to be in harmony with your thoughts (their creator).

    1 —— 2 —— 3 —— 4 —— 5 —— 6 —— 7 —— 8 —— 9 —— 10

26. To be effective, your thoughts must be clear, steady, fixed, definite and unchangeable. You cannot change a lifetime of negative thoughts in 20 minutes.

    1 —— 2 —— 3 —— 4 —— 5 —— 6 —— 7 —— 8 —— 9 —— 10

27. Begin committing, you must give this new discipline careful though, and then you must allow nothing to interfere with your decision.
1 — 2 — 3 — 4 — 5 — 6 — 7 — 8 — 9 — 10

28. Disciplining yourself to change your thoughts will bring health and harmony, as well as the material things that are for your highest good.
1 — 2 — 3 — 4 — 5 — 6 — 7 — 8 — 9 — 10

29. To attraction harmonious conditions, your mental attitude must be harmonious.
1 — 2 — 3 — 4 — 5 — 6 — 7 — 8 — 9 — 10

30. The world around you is a reflect of the world inside of you.
1 — 2 — 3 — 4 — 5 — 6 — 7 — 8 — 9 — 10

31. It is imperative that you concentrate on and practice harmony. Reading and learning will have no effect unless you put these exercises into practice.
1 — 2 — 3 — 4 — 5 — 6 — 7 — 8 — 9 — 10

Tally your total score by adding the number you allocated for yourself in each of the 31 principles above. Your score will range from 31 to 310.

If you scored between 219 and 310, you are aware of the fact that your mind is a smaller part of a massive ocean of Omnipotent consciousness. You understand that your outer world is a reflection of the world that you focus on within you. Be sure to practice the harmony exercise throughout your day, and as a concentrated daily mediation. Take note of any shifts in your experiences as set your focus on harmony.

If you scored between 125 and 218, you have a pretty good understanding of the part you play in the entire natural law of attraction. You are becoming more and more aware of the power that your thoughts have. Re-read through this segment, and be sure to practice harmony—both as a daily meditation, and as an ongoing practice.

If you scored between 31 and 124, it would be wonderful for you to immerse yourself in this week's teachings. Once you fully embrace and eventually experience that creative source is not outside of you and that you are a part of it, you will vastly improve your inner and outer state. Be sure to review this week's lessons and focus are creating harmony, both as a daily exercise, but also as an ongoing daily practice.

Introspection:

1. What did you learn about yourself after completing the Comprehension Survey?

2. Was your score what you expected it to be? Why or why not?
3. What areas of the segment of the book have you mastered?
4. What are the areas in this segment of the book that you need to focus on?
5. What three "takeaways" from this segment would you share with others and why?

Exercise

For your exercise this week, concentrate on Harmony, and when I say concentrate, I mean all that the word implies; concentrate so deeply, so earnestly, that you will be conscious of nothing but harmony. Remember, we learn by doing. Reading these lessons will get you nowhere. It is in the practical application that the value consists.

NOTES IN RESPONSE TO PERFORMING THIS EXERCISE
Be sure to journal about any findings or experiences you have as you continue to do this exercise as outlined.

Part Fifteen

INTRODUCTION

Experiments with parasites found on plants indicate that even the lowest order of life is enabled to take advantage of natural law.

This experiment was made by Jaques Loeb, M.D., Ph.D., a member of the Rockefeller Institute.

"In order to obtain the material, potted rose bushes are brought into a room and placed in front of a closed window. If the plants are allowed to dry out, the aphids (parasites), previously wingless, change to winged insects. After the metamorphosis, the animals leave the plants, fly to the window and then creep upward on the glass."

It is evident that these tiny insects found that the plants on which they had been thriving were dead, and that they could therefore secure nothing more to eat and drink from this source. The only method by which they could save themselves from starvation was to grow temporary wings and fly, which they did.

Experiments such as these indicate that Omniscience as well as Omnipotence is omnipresent and that the tiniest living thing can take advantage of it in an emergency.

Part Fifteen will tell you more about the laws under which we live. It will explain that these laws operate to our advantage, that all conditions and experiences that come to us are for our ben-

efit; that we gain strength in proportion to the effort expended, and that our happiness is best attained through a conscious co-operation with natural laws.

---

1. The laws under which we live are designed solely for our advantage. These laws are immutable and we cannot escape from their operation.
2. All the great eternal forces act in solemn silence, but it is in our power to place ourselves in harmony with them and thus express a life of comparative peace and happiness.
3. Difficulties, inharmonies, and obstacles, indicate that we are either refusing to give out what we no longer need, or refusing to accept what we require.
4. Growth is attained through an exchange of the old for the new, of the good for the better; it is a conditional or reciprocal action, for each of us is a complete thought entity and this completeness makes it possible for us to receive only as we give.
5. We cannot obtain what we lack if we tenaciously cling to what we have. We are able to consciously control our conditions as we come to sense the purpose of what we attract, and are able to extract from each experience only what we require for our further growth. Our ability to do this determines the degree of harmony or happiness we attain.
6. The ability to appropriate what we require for our growth, continually increases as we reach higher planes and broader vision, and the greater our ability to know what we require, the more certain we shall be to discern its presence, to attract it and to absorb it. Nothing may reach us except what is necessary for our growth.
7. All conditions and experiences that come to us do so for our benefit. Difficulties and obstacles will continue to

come until we absorb their wisdom and gather from them the essentials of further growth.
8. That we reap what we sow is mathematically exact. We gain permanent strength exactly to the extent of the effort required to overcome difficulties.
9. The inexorable requirements of growth demand that we exert the greatest degree of attraction for what is perfectly in accord with us. Our highest happiness will be best attained through our understanding of, and conscious co-operation with natural laws.
10. Thought is creative and the principle upon which this law is based is sound and inherent in all things, but in order to possess vitality the thought must contain love.
11. It is love which imparts vitality to thought and thus enables it to germinate. The law of attraction, or the law of love, for they are one and the same, will bring to it the necessary material for its growth and maturity.
12. The first form which thought will find is language, or words; this determines the importance of words; they are the first manifestation of thought—the vessels in which thought is carried. They take hold of the ether and by setting it in motion reproduce the thought to others in the form of sound.
13. Thought may lead to action of any kind, but whatever the action, it is simply the thought attempting to express itself in visible form. It is evident, therefore, that if we wish desirable conditions, we can afford to entertain only desirable thoughts.
14. This leads to the inevitable conclusion that if we wish to express abundance in our lives, we can afford to think abundance only, and as words are only thoughts taking form, we must be especially careful to use nothing but constructive and harmonious language, which when finally crystallized into objective forms, will prove to our advantage.

15. We cannot escape from the pictures we incessantly photograph on the mind, and this photography of erroneous conceptions is exactly what is being done by the use of words, when we use any form of language which is not identified with our welfare.
16. We manifest more and more life as our thought becomes clarified and takes higher planes. This is obtained with greater facility as we use word pictures that are clearly defined, and relieved of the conceptions attached to them on lower planes of thought.
17. It is with words that we must express our thoughts, and if we are to make use of higher forms of truth, we may use only such material as has been carefully and intelligently selected with this purpose in view.
18. This wonderful power of clothing thoughts in the form of words is what differentiates man from the rest of the animal kingdom; by the use of the written word he has been enabled to look back over the centuries and see the stirring scenes by which he ha come into his present inheritance.
19. He has been enabled to come into communion with the greatest writers and thinkers of all time, and the combined record which we possess today is therefore the expression of Universal Thought as it has been seeking to take form in the mind of Man.
20. We know that the Universal Thought has for its goal the creation of form, and we know that the individual thought is likewise forever attempting to express itself in form, and we know that the word is a thought form, and a sentence is a combination of thought forms, therefore, if we wish our ideal to be beautiful or strong, we must see that the words out; of which this temple will eventually be created are exact, that they are put together carefully, because accuracy in building words and sentences is the highest form of architecture in civilization and is a passport to success.

21. Words are thoughts and are therefore an invisible and invincible power; which will finally objectify themselves in the form they are given.
22. Words may become mental palaces that will live forever, or they may become shacks which the first breeze will carry away. They may delight the eye as well as the ear; they may contain all knowledge; in them we find the history of the past as well as the hope of the future; they are living messengers from which every human and superhuman activity is born.
23. The beauty of the word consists in the beauty of the thought; the power of the word consists in the power of the thought, and the power of the thought consists in its vitality. How shall we identify a vital thought? What are its distinguishing characteristics? It must have principle. How shall we identify principle?
24. There is a principle of Mathematics, but none of error; there is a principle of health, but none of disease; there is a principle of truth, but none of dishonesty; there is a principle of light, but none of darkness, and there is a principle of abundance, but none of poverty.
25. How shall we know that this is true? Because if we apply the principle of Mathematics correctly we shall be certain of our results. Where there is health there will be no disease. If we know the Truth we cannot be deceived by error. If we let in light there can be no darkness, and where there is abundance there can be no poverty.
26. These are self-evident facts, but the all-important truth that a thought containing principle is vital and therefore contains life and consequently takes root, and eventually but surely and certainly displaces the negative thoughts, which by their very nature can contain no vitality, is one which seems to have been overlooked.
27. But this is a fact which will enable you to destroy every manner of discord, lack and limitation.

28. There can be no question but that he who "is wise enough to understand" will readily recognize that the creative power of thought places an invincible weapon in his hands and makes him a master of destiny.
29. In the physical world there is a law of compensation which is that "the appearance of a given amount of energy anywhere means the disappearance of the same amount somewhere else," and so we find that we can get only what we give; if we pledge ourselves to a certain action we must be prepared to assume the responsibility for the development of that action. The subconscious cannot reason. It takes us at our word; we have asked for something; we are now to receive it; we have made our bed, we are now to lie in it; the die has: been cast; the threads will carry out the pattern we have made.
30. For this reason Insight must be exercised so that the thought which we entertain contains no mental, moral or physical germ which we do not wish objectified in our lives.
31. Insight is a faculty of the mind whereby we are enabled to examine facts and conditions at long range, a kind of human telescope; it enables us to understand the difficulties as well as the possibilities in any undertaking.
32. Insight enables us to be prepared for the obstacles which we shall meet; we can therefore overcome them before; they' have any opportunity of causing difficulty.
33. Insight enables us to plan to advantage and turn our thought and attention in the right direction, instead of into channels which can yield no possible return.
34. Insight is therefore absolutely essential for the development of any great achievement, but with it we may enter, explore and possess any mental field.
35. Insight is a product of the world within and is developed in the Silence, by concentration.
36. For your exercise this week, concentrate on Insight; take your accustomed position and focus the thought on the

fact that to have a knowledge of the creative power of thought does not mean to possess the art of thinking. Let the thought dwell on the fact that knowledge does not apply itself. That our actions are not governed by knowledge, but by custom, precedent and habit. That the only way we can get ourselves to apply knowledge is by a determined conscious effort. Call to mind the fact that knowledge unused passes from the mind, that the value of the information is in the application of the principle; continue this line of thought until you gain sufficient insight to formulate a definite program for applying this principle to your own particular problem.

> *"Think truly, and thy thoughts*
> *Shall the world's famine feed;*
> *Speak truly, and each word of thine*
> *Shall be a fruitful seed;*
> *Live truly, and thy life shall be*
> *A great and noble creed."*
> —HORATIO BONAR.

STUDY GUIDE

Part Fifteen

Summary

This Part explains the Law of Growth, and explains why we cannot obtain if we tenaciously cling to what we have, and that difficulties, inharmonies and obstacles indicate that we are either refusing to give up what we no longer need, or refusing to accept what we require; we are holding on to worn-out and useless material, or we are allowing a deficiency to exist and are not obtaining the material necessary for our growth. It explains how the ability to appropriate what we require for our growth is secured. It explains how vitality is important to thought, and what determines the importance of words the vessels in which thought is carried. How abundance may be secured and why we must be prepared to assume the responsibility for every thought and action. It explains the necessity of Insight, its value in examining facts and conditions at long range and in turning our attention to profitable channels instead of working with problems which contain no possibility of any kind.

1. Experiments that found parasites on plants was evidence that all of life, including the lowest order can take advantage of natural law. Provide at least two other examples of how lower order takes advantage of the natural law.

2. Charles Haanel provides an example of how tiny insects actually grew wings to save themselves from starvation when they no longer had access to food and water. This is a wonderful example of manifestation. Do some research and find another element of nature that manifests as a means of survival.

3. You will learn more about conscious cooperation and how the laws operate to your advantage. Write down an account of how you and the Universal Mind co-conspired to create an experience that supported greater joy in your life.

Comprehension Survey

In this segment you will learn more about the laws under which you exist. Once you have completed this survey, you will get a better understanding of how the Universe conspires to support you. For each of the principles below, choose the number that is most closely aligns to your beliefs (1 being "not at all" and 10 being "a great deal").

1. The laws are immutable and have been designed solely to support you.
   1 —— 2 —— 3 —— 4 —— 5 —— 6 —— 7 —— 8 —— 9 —— 10

2. Place yourself in harmony with the silence eternal forces and you will find peace and happiness.
   1 —— 2 —— 3 —— 4 —— 5 —— 6 —— 7 —— 8 —— 9 —— 10

3. If you are experiencing obstacles, you are either holding onto that which no longer serves you, or you are unwilling to accept that which you are in need of.
   1 —— 2 —— 3 —— 4 —— 5 —— 6 —— 7 —— 8 —— 9 —— 10

4. Your growth reciprocal action and is an exchange of the old for the new. You receive only as you give.
   1 —— 2 —— 3 —— 4 —— 5 —— 6 —— 7 —— 8 —— 9 —— 10

5. The degree to which you will experience happiness and harmony is dependent upon how willing you are to let go of what you have and relinquish control.
   1 —— 2 —— 3 —— 4 —— 5 —— 6 —— 7 —— 8 —— 9 —— 10

6. The highest the energetic planes you reach and the broader your vision, the more you will know what you want and the more certain you are about attracting it.
   1 —— 2 —— 3 —— 4 —— 5 —— 6 —— 7 —— 8 —— 9 —— 10

7. You will continue to experience obstacles and challenges until you learn from them.
   1 —— 2 —— 3 —— 4 —— 5 —— 6 —— 7 —— 8 —— 9 —— 10

8. The fact that you will reap what you sow exemplifies that you will gain permanent strength equivalent to the effort you exerted to overcome difficulties.
   1 —— 2 —— 3 —— 4 —— 5 —— 6 —— 7 —— 8 —— 9 —— 10

9. In order to grow, while consciously co-operating with the natural law, you should exert the greatest degree of attraction towards that which is most in alignment with your needs.
   1 —— 2 —— 3 —— 4 —— 5 —— 6 —— 7 —— 8 —— 9 —— 10

10. Based on law, your thoughts are creative, but they must contain love to be energized.

    1 — 2 — 3 — 4 — 5 — 6 — 7 — 8 — 9 — 10

11. Love energizes thought to bring the necessary material for its eventual maturity.

    1 — 2 — 3 — 4 — 5 — 6 — 7 — 8 — 9 — 10

12. Your words are the vessel through which thought is carried. Through sound, they hold the spirit of thoughts and reproduce them to others.

    1 — 2 — 3 — 4 — 5 — 6 — 7 — 8 — 9 — 10

13. Action is thought expressing itself in visible form. If you want desirable outcomes, you should focus only on desirable thoughts.

    1 — 2 — 3 — 4 — 5 — 6 — 7 — 8 — 9 — 10

14. If you want abundance in your life, you must only express abundance through constructive and harmonious language.

    1 — 2 — 3 — 4 — 5 — 6 — 7 — 8 — 9 — 10

15. If you speak words that do not support your greater welfare, like pictures, they can get etched in your mind.

    1 — 2 — 3 — 4 — 5 — 6 — 7 — 8 — 9 — 10

16. When you use defined word pictures, as your thoughts become clear, you release concepts attached to lower planes of consciousness and manifest from higher planes.

    1 — 2 — 3 — 4 — 5 — 6 — 7 — 8 — 9 — 10

17. You must express your thoughts with word that are carefully and intelligently selected with higher purpose.

    1 — 2 — 3 — 4 — 5 — 6 — 7 — 8 — 9 — 10

18. The ability to wrap your thoughts into words differentiates you from the rest of the animal kingdom, and enables you to record the events that have led you to your present experiences.

    1 — 2 — 3 — 4 — 5 — 6 — 7 — 8 — 9 — 10

19. In connecting with the greatest writers and thinkers, Universal Thought has been revealed in humankind.

    1 — 2 — 3 — 4 — 5 — 6 — 7 — 8 — 9 — 10

20. You and Universal Thought have a joint goal to create. In order to create a temple of beauty and strength, you must take care and build with accuracy and highest intentions.

    1 —— 2 —— 3 —— 4 —— 5 —— 6 —— 7 —— 8 —— 9 —— 10

21. Your word are incredibly powerful, as they will eventually turn thoughts to form.

    1 —— 2 —— 3 —— 4 —— 5 —— 6 —— 7 —— 8 —— 9 —— 10

22. Your words are living energy from which every ordinary and extraordinary experience is born.

    1 —— 2 —— 3 —— 4 —— 5 —— 6 —— 7 —— 8 —— 9 —— 10

23. In order for your words, and consequent thoughts to be energized, they must be based in principle.

    1 —— 2 —— 3 —— 4 —— 5 —— 6 —— 7 —— 8 —— 9 —— 10

24. Highest principle only exists in all that seeks positive expression.

    1 —— 2 —— 3 —— 4 —— 5 —— 6 —— 7 —— 8 —— 9 —— 10

25. You know this is true because where there is high principle or truth, its opposite does not exist.

    1 —— 2 —— 3 —— 4 —— 5 —— 6 —— 7 —— 8 —— 9 —— 10

26. One of the facts that has been overlooked is that vital thoughts will eventually take over negative ones, because negativity does not possess vital energy.

    1 —— 2 —— 3 —— 4 —— 5 —— 6 —— 7 —— 8 —— 9 —— 10

27. Once you fully realize this fact, you will destroy discord, lack and limitation in your life.

    1 —— 2 —— 3 —— 4 —— 5 —— 6 —— 7 —— 8 —— 9 —— 10

28. Once you realize the power of your thoughts, you will unquestionably become a master of your destiny.

    1 —— 2 —— 3 —— 4 —— 5 —— 6 —— 7 —— 8 —— 9 —— 10

29. The law of compensation asserts that you will get what you give, thus you must take responsibility for that which you put out into the world. Your subconscious is not discerning. It takes you at your word, so be prepared to reap what you sew.

    1 —— 2 —— 3 —— 4 —— 5 —— 6 —— 7 —— 8 —— 9 —— 10

30. You must cultivate insight to ensure that your thoughts contain no mental, physical or moral germs.
1 — 2 — 3 — 4 — 5 — 6 — 7 — 8 — 9 — 10

31. Your insights allows you to look at your choices and the effects they will have from a long-range perspective.
1 — 2 — 3 — 4 — 5 — 6 — 7 — 8 — 9 — 10

32. When you have insight, you have the foresight to overcome potential obstacles before they challenge you.
1 — 2 — 3 — 4 — 5 — 6 — 7 — 8 — 9 — 10

33. Your insight enables you to turn your thoughts and attention in the right direction.
1 — 2 — 3 — 4 — 5 — 6 — 7 — 8 — 9 — 10

34. You must have insight to achieve greatness, for with it, you can enter, explore and possess any state of consciousness.
1 — 2 — 3 — 4 — 5 — 6 — 7 — 8 — 9 — 10

35. Your insights is within you, thus you develop it by concentrating in silence.
1 — 2 — 3 — 4 — 5 — 6 — 7 — 8 — 9 — 10

36. Unused knowledge will leave your mind, thus applying it once your receive it is imperative.
1 — 2 — 3 — 4 — 5 — 6 — 7 — 8 — 9 — 10

Tally your total score by adding the number you allocated for yourself in each of the 36 principles above. Your score will range from 36 to 360.

If you scored between 252 and 360, you are doing wonderfully well at understanding and integrating these teachings into your words, thoughts and actions. You have a solid understanding of how important highest truth and integrity is in your words and deeds. Practice the exercise at least once daily to experience how powerful your insights are and to affirm how important it is to take action on the insights you receive from the silence.

If you scored between 144 and 251, you are doing a fine job of learning these principles and applying them in your life. Continue to review the 36 teachings in this segment with the understanding that maintaining the highest level of purpose and integrity in your words, thoughts and deeds is of upmost importance. Be sure to do the exercise at least once each day, knowing that you ultimately need to take action on the insights you gain in the silence. If you do not, the insights will disappear.

If you scored between 36 and 143, while you are making progress, there is still a great deal more that you can learn and integrate into your life. Know that your words, thoughts and deeds carry great power, thus you must think, speak and act with the highest integrity. Be sure to do this week's exercise each day, and when possible, act upon any insights you receive while in silent contemplation. Insights without action will fade.

Introspection:

1. What did you learn about yourself after completing the Comprehension Survey?
2. Was your score what you expected it to be? Why or why not?
3. What areas of the segment of the book have you mastered?
4. What are the areas in this segment of the book that you need to focus on?
5. What three "takeaways" from this segment would you share with others and why?

Exercise

For your exercise this week, concentrate on Insight; take your accustomed position and focus the thought on the fact that to have a knowledge of the creative power of thought does not mean to possess the art of thinking. Let the thought dwell on the fact that knowledge does not apply itself. That our actions are not governed by knowledge, but by custom, precedent and habit. That the only way we can get ourselves to apply knowledge is by a determined conscious effort. Call to mind the fact that knowledge unused passes from the mind, that the value of the information is in the application of the principle; continue this line of thought until you gain sufficient insight to formulate a definite program for applying this principle to your own particular problem

NOTES IN RESPONSE TO PERFORMING THIS EXERCISE
Be sure to journal about any findings or experiences you have as you continue to do this exercise as outlined.

Part Sixteen

INTRODUCTION

The vibratory activities of the planetary Universe are governed by a law of periodicity. Everything that lives has periods of birth, growth, fruition and decline. These periods are governed by the Septimal Law.

The Law of Sevens governs the days of the week, the phases of the moon, the hay monies of sound, light, heat, electricity, magnetism, atomic structure. It governs the life of individuals and of nations, and it dominates the activities of the commercial world.

Life is growth, and growth is change. Each seven years period takes us into a new cycle. The first seven years is the period of infancy. The next seven the period of childhood, representing the beginning of individual responsibility. The next seven represents the period of adolescence. The fourth period marks the attainment of full growth. The fifth period is the constructive period, when men begin to acquire property, possessions, a home and family. The next, from thirty-five to forty-two, is a period of reactions and changes, and this in turn is followed by a period of reconstruction, adjustment and recuperation, so as to be ready for a new cycle of sevens, beginning with the fiftieth year.

There are many who think that the world is just about to pass out of the sixth period; that it will soon enter into the sev-

enth period, the period of readjustment, reconstruction and harmony; the period which is frequently referred to as the millennium.

Those familiar with these cycles will not be disturbed when things seem to go wrong, but can apply the principle outlined in The Master Key, with the full assurance that a higher law will invariably control all other laws, and that through an understanding and conscious operation of spiritual laws we can convert every seeming difficulty into a blessing.

---

1. Wealth is a product of labor. Capital is an effect, not a cause; a servant, not a master; a means, not an end.
2. The most commonly accepted definition of wealth is that it consists of all useful and agreeable things which possess exchange value. It is this exchange value which is the predominant characteristic of wealth.
3. When we consider the small addition made by wealth to the happiness of the possessor, we find that the true value consists not in its utility but in its exchange value.
4. This exchange value makes it a medium for securing the things of real value whereby our ideals may be realized.
5. Wealth should then never be desired as an end, but simply as a means of accomplishing an end. Success is contingent upon a higher ideal than the mere accumulation of riches, and he who aspires to such success must formulate an ideal for which he is willing to strive.
6. With such an ideal in mind, the ways and means can and will be provided, but the mistake must not be made of substituting the means for the end. There must be a definite fixed purpose, an ideal.
7. Prentice Mulford said: "The man of success is the man possessed of the greatest spiritual understanding and every

great fortune comes of superior and truly spiritual power." Unfortunately, there are those who fail to recognize this power; they forget that Andrew Carnegie's mother had to help support the family when they came to America, that Harriman's father was a poor clergyman with a salary of only $200 a year, that Sir Thomas Lipton started with only 25 cents. These men had no other power to depend upon, but it did not fail them.

8. The power to create depends entirely upon spiritual power; there are three steps, idealization, visualization and materialization. Every captain of industry depends upon this power exclusively. In an article in Everybody's Magazine, Henry M. Flagler, the Standard Oil multi-millionaire, admitted that the secret of his success was his power to see a thing in its completeness. The following conversation with the reporter shows his power of idealization, concentration and visualization, all spiritual powers:

9. "Did you actually vision to yourself the whole thing? I mean, did you, or could you, really close your eyes and see the tracks? And the trains running? And hear the whistles blowing? Did you go as far as that?" "Yes." "How clearly?" "Very clearly."

10. Here we have a vision of the law, we see "cause and effect," we see that thought necessarily precedes and determines action. If we are wise, we shall come into a realization of the tremendous fact that no arbitrary condition can exist for a moment, and that human experience is the result of an orderly and harmonious sequence.

11. The successful business man is more often than not an idealist and is ever striving for higher and higher standards. The subtle forces of thought as they crystallize in our daily moods is what constitutes life.

12. Thought is the plastic material with which we build images of our growing conception of life. Use determines its exis-

tence. As in all other things our ability to recognize it and use it properly is the necessary condition for attainment.

13. Premature wealth is but the forerunner of humiliation and disaster, because we cannot permanently retain anything which we do not merit or which we have not earned.
14. The conditions with which we meet in the world without, correspond to the conditions which we find in the world within. This is brought about by the law of attraction. How then shall we determine what is to enter into the world within?
15. Whatever enters the mind through the senses or the objective mind will impress the mind and result in a mental image which will become a pattern for the creative energies. These experiences are largely the result of environment, chance, past thinking and other forms of negative thought, and must be subjected to careful analysis before being entertained. On the other hand, we can form our own mental images, through our own interior processes of thought regardless of the thoughts of others, regardless of exterior conditions, regardless of environment of every kind, and it is by the exercise of this power that we can control our own destiny, body, mind and soul.
16. It is by the exercise of this power that we take our fate out of the hands of chance, and consciously make for ourselves the experiences which we desire, because when we consciously realize a condition, that condition will eventually manifest in our lives; it is therefore evident that in the last analysis thinking is the one great cause in life.
17. Therefore, to control thought is to control circumstances, conditions, environment and destiny.
18. How then are we to control thought; what is the process? To think is to create a thought, but the result of the thought will depend upon its form, its quality and its vitality.
19. The form will depend upon the mental image from which it emanates; this will depend upon the depth of the impres-

sion, the predominance of the idea, the clarity of the vision, the boldness of the image.

20. The quality depends upon its substance, and this depends upon the material of which the mind is composed; if this material has been woven from thoughts of vigor, strength, courage, determination, the thought will possess these qualities.

21. And finally, the vitality depends upon the feeling with which the thought is impregnated. If the thought is constructive, it will possess vitality; it will have life, it will grow, develop, expand; it will be creative; it will attract to itself everything necessary for its complete development.

22. If the thought is destructive, it will have within itself the germ of its own dissolution; it will die, but in the process of dying, it will bring sickness, disease, and every other form of discord.

23. This we call evil, and when we bring it upon ourselves, some of us are disposed to attribute our difficulties to a Supreme Being, but this supreme being is simply Mind in equilibrium.

24. It is neither good nor bad, it simply is.

25. Our ability to differentiate it into form is our ability to manifest good or evil.

26. Good and evil therefore are not entities, they are simply words which we use to indicate the result of our actions, and these actions are in turn predetermined by the character of our thought.

27. If our thought is constructive and harmonious we manifest good; if it is destructive and discordant we manifest evil.

28. If you desire to visualize a different environment, the process is simply to hold the ideal in mind, until your vision has been made real; give no thought to persons, places or things; these have no place in the absolute; the environ-

ment you desire will contain everything necessary; the right persons, and the right things will come at the right time and in the right place.

29. It is sometimes not plain how character, ability, attainment, achievement, environment and destiny can be controlled through the power of visualization, but this is an exact scientific fact.

30. You will readily see that what we think determines the quality of mind, and that the quality of mind in turn determines our ability and mental capacity, and you can readily understand that the improvement in our ability will naturally be followed by increase in attainment and a greater control of circumstances.

31. It will thus be seen that Natural laws work in a perfectly natural and harmonious manner; everything seems to "just happen." If you want any evidence of this fact simply compare results of your efforts in your own life, when your actions were prompted by high ideals and when you had selfish or ulterior motives in mind. You will need no further evidence.

32. If you wish to bring about the realization of any desire, form a mental picture of success in your mind, by consciously visualizing your desire; in this way you will be compelling success, you will be externalizing it in your life by scientific methods.

33. We can only see what already exists in the objective world, but what we visualize, already exists in the spiritual world, and this visualization is a substantial token of what will one day appear in the objective world, if we are faithful to our ideal. The reason for this is not difficult; visualization is a form of imagination; this process of thinking forms impressions on the mind, and these impressions in turn form concepts and ideals, and they in turn are the plans from which the Master Architect will weave the future.

34. The psychologists have come to the conclusion that there is but one sense, the sense of feeling, and that all other senses are but modifications of this one sense; this being true, we know why feeling is the very fountain head of power, why the emotions so easily overcome the intellect, and why we must put feeling into our thought, if we wish results. Thought and feeling is the irresistible combination.

35. Visualization must, of course, be directed by the will; we are to visualize exactly what we want; we must be careful not to let the imagination run riot. Imagination is a good servant but a poor master, and unless it is controlled it may easily lead us into all kinds of speculations and conclusions which have no basis or foundation of fact whatever. Every kind of plausible opinion is liable to be accepted without any analytical examination and the inevitable result is mental chaos

36. We must therefore construct only such mental images as are known to be scientifically true. Subject every idea to a searching analysis and accept nothing which: is not scientifically exact. When you do this you will attempt nothing but what you know you can carry out and success will crown your efforts; this is what business men call farsightedness; it is much the same as insight, and is one of the great secrets of success in all important undertakings.

37. For your exercise this week, try to bring yourself to a realization of the important fact that harmony and happiness are states of consciousness and do not depend upon the possession of things. That things are effects and come as a consequence of correct mental states. So that if we desire material possession of any kind our chief concern should be to acquire the mental attitude which will bring about the result desired. This mental attitude is brought about by a realization of our spiritual nature and our unity with the Universal Mind which is the substance of all things. This

realization will bring about everything which is necessary for our complete enjoyment. This is scientific or correct thinking. When we succeed in bringing about this mental attitude it is comparatively easy to realize our desire as an already accomplished fact; when we can do this we shall have found the "Truth" which makes us "free" from every lack or limitation of any kind.

A man might frame and let loose a star, to roll in its orbit; and yet not have done so memorable a thing before God as he who lets a golden-orbed thought to roll through the generations of time.
—H. W. Beecher.

STUDY GUIDE

Part Sixteen

Author's Summary

This Part explains the nature of Wealth, it shows how it is created and upon what it depends. It shows why success is contingent upon an ideal higher than the mere accumulation of riches, it shows that success depends upon creative ability and explains the necessary condition for attainment. It explains why premature wealth is but the forerunner of humiliation and disaster. It explains the methods by which we may take our fate out of the hands of chance, and consciously make for ourselves the conditions which we desire, it tells how we may compel success by the utilization of scientific and exact methods, and it explains that while we have the ability to create harmonious and constructive conditions we also have the ability to create inharmonious and destructive conditions, and unfortunately, through ignorance of the law, this is what many are doing.

1. In this session Charles Haanel introduces you to the law of periodicity. Governed by the Septimal Law, it stipulates that everything has periods of birth, growth, fruition and decline. Share examples of this law in business, human existence and in nature.

2. You can see the Law of Sevens existing in all forms of life. Select one form, and describe how the Law of Sevens is modeled within its lifespan.

3. Which of the seven-year life cycles are you currently inhabiting? Does the author's description match the stage characteristic that you are currently experiencing? Please explain.

4. Once your understand and fully embrace the life cycles, you can rest assured that a higher law controls all others. When you do this, seemingly difficult situations can be seen as blessings. List at least three circumstances where you were able to see the blessings that arose from seemingly difficult situations in your life.

Comprehension Survey

In this segment, you are introduced to the Law of Sevens. Once you complete this survey, you will a better understanding of how life cycles work, and a greater ability to embrace life's challenges as they arise. For each of the principles below, choose the number that is most closely aligns to your beliefs (1 being "not at all" and 10 being "a great deal").

1. Your wealth is a product of your labor. Any capital you gain is a means or effect of your labor, and is not an end.
   1 — 2 — 3 — 4 — 5 — 6 — 7 — 8 — 9 — 10

2. The predominant characteristic of wealth is "exchange value."
   1 — 2 — 3 — 4 — 5 — 6 — 7 — 8 — 9 — 10

3. The true value of the wealth you possess lies not in your happiness, but in its exchange value..
   1 — 2 — 3 — 4 — 5 — 6 — 7 — 8 — 9 — 10

4. Wealth is a medium for securing things of value that support the manifestation of your ideals.
   1 — 2 — 3 — 4 — 5 — 6 — 7 — 8 — 9 — 10

5. You should see your desire for wealth as a means towards your higher purpose in life, not as the accumulation of money or power.
   1 — 2 — 3 — 4 — 5 — 6 — 7 — 8 — 9 — 10

6. You must have a definite purpose or ideal in mind, or else you may mistakenly see monetary gain as your end goal.
   1 — 2 — 3 — 4 — 5 — 6 — 7 — 8 — 9 — 10

7. Any great fortune that comes your way should come from your higher purpose and your truly spiritual power.
   1 — 2 — 3 — 4 — 5 — 6 — 7 — 8 — 9 — 10

8. The secret to your success is to see that which you desire in its completeness
   1 — 2 — 3 — 4 — 5 — 6 — 7 — 8 — 9 — 10

9. When you visualize, see what you want to manifest in thorough detail, from conception to completion.
   1 — 2 — 3 — 4 — 5 — 6 — 7 — 8 — 9 — 10

10. None of your experiences are random. They are each a result of your orderly and harmonious visioning.
    1 — 2 — 3 — 4 — 5 — 6 — 7 — 8 — 9 — 10

11. Successful people are most often idealists, constantly striving for the best. The forces of their thoughts crystallize into moods that ultimately dictate their lives.
    1 — 2 — 3 — 4 — 5 — 6 — 7 — 8 — 9 — 10

12. Your ability to recognize and use your thoughts properly are the prerequisites for attaining that which you desire in your life.
    1 — 2 — 3 — 4 — 5 — 6 — 7 — 8 — 9 — 10

13. If you became wealthy before you were ready, you would not be able to maintain the wealth because you hadn't yet earned it.
    1 — 2 — 3 — 4 — 5 — 6 — 7 — 8 — 9 — 10

14. If the world around you is a reflection of your inner world, then how do you determine what enters into your inner world?
    1 — 2 — 3 — 4 — 5 — 6 — 7 — 8 — 9 — 10

15. You control your destiny, body, mind and soul by forming your own strong mental images irrespective of what your environment might be.
    1 — 2 — 3 — 4 — 5 — 6 — 7 — 8 — 9 — 10

16. By thinking your own independent inner thoughts, you exercise your greatest power, as your thinking is the one great cause in your life.
    1 — 2 — 3 — 4 — 5 — 6 — 7 — 8 — 9 — 10

17. Thus, when you control your thoughts, you control your circumstances, conditions, environment and destiny.
    1 — 2 — 3 — 4 — 5 — 6 — 7 — 8 — 9 — 10

18. The result of your thought depends upon its form, quality and vitality.
    1 — 2 — 3 — 4 — 5 — 6 — 7 — 8 — 9 — 10

19. The form of that which you create depends upon the mental image you created: the depth of its impression on your mind, the strength and focus upon the idea, the clarity of your vision, and the boldness of the image.
    1 — 2 — 3 — 4 — 5 — 6 — 7 — 8 — 9 — 10

20. The quality of that which you manifest is dependent upon whether your mind has had thoughts that are energized, strong, courageous and determined.
    1 — 2 — 3 — 4 — 5 — 6 — 7 — 8 — 9 — 10

21. The vitality of your manifestation depends upon the depth of your feeling as you thought your desire into being. If constructive, it will attract all of the necessary elements to make it manifest.
1 —— 2 —— 3 —— 4 —— 5 —— 6 —— 7 —— 8 —— 9 —— 1 0

22. If your thought is destructive, not only will it not by physicalized. It will manifest sickness, disease any every other form of disturbance.
1 —— 2 —— 3 —— 4 —— 5 —— 6 —— 7 —— 8 —— 9 —— 1 0

23. While many attribute evil to a Supreme Being (the devil), in truth it is simply mind in equilibrium. Destructive thoughts manifest physical disturbance.
1 —— 2 —— 3 —— 4 —— 5 —— 6 —— 7 —— 8 —— 9 —— 1 0

24. This equilibrium (manifestation of thought) is neither good nor bad, it just is.
1 —— 2 —— 3 —— 4 —— 5 —— 6 —— 7 —— 8 —— 9 —— 1 0

25. Your ability to differentiate this equilibrium into form is your ability to manifest good and bad.
1 —— 2 —— 3 —— 4 —— 5 —— 6 —— 7 —— 8 —— 9 —— 1 0

26. Good and evil are not entities. They are words that indicate the result of our actions that were predetermined by the nature of your thought.
1 —— 2 —— 3 —— 4 —— 5 —— 6 —— 7 —— 8 —— 9 —— 1 0

27. When your thoughts are constructive and harmonious, you manifest good. When they are destructive and inharmonious, you manifest evil.
1 —— 2 —— 3 —— 4 —— 5 —— 6 —— 7 —— 8 —— 9 —— 1 0

28. When you want to visualize a different environment, hold the ideal in mind, not giving thought to specific persons, places or things. They will come at the right time and place.
1 —— 2 —— 3 —— 4 —— 5 —— 6 —— 7 —— 8 —— 9 —— 1 0

29. It is not always clear how character, ability, attainment, achievement, environment and destiny can be controlled through visualization, but it is a scientific fact that they are.
1 —— 2 —— 3 —— 4 —— 5 —— 6 —— 7 —— 8 —— 9 —— 1 0

30. What you think affects the quality of your mind, which in turn determines your ability and mental capacity. So it is natural that your

improved ability will increase that which you can manifest and your ability to control circumstances.

1 —— 2 —— 3 —— 4 —— 5 —— 6 —— 7 —— 8 —— 9 —— 1 0

31. When you review your life, you will note that things seem to "just happen" when your intentions are harmonious and altruistic. This is evidence enough of this law.

    1 —— 2 —— 3 —— 4 —— 5 —— 6 —— 7 —— 8 —— 9 —— 1 0

32. When you form a mental picture of success in your mind by consciously visualizing your desire, you will compel success and externalize it by scientific methods,.

    1 —— 2 —— 3 —— 4 —— 5 —— 6 —— 7 —— 8 —— 9 —— 1 0

33. What you visualize already exists in the spiritual world, and will eventually appear in the objective world if you remain in integrity. Visualization is a form of imagination that forms impressions on the mind that weave your future.

    1 —— 2 —— 3 —— 4 —— 5 —— 6 —— 7 —— 8 —— 9 —— 1 0

34. If you want results, you must put feelings or passion into your thoughts. Thoughts and feelings combined are unstoppable.

    1 —— 2 —— 3 —— 4 —— 5 —— 6 —— 7 —— 8 —— 9 —— 1 0

35. Your imagination is potent, so take care not to let it run wild. Whatever it creates will be accepted, so mental chaos could result if you do not take care.

    1 —— 2 —— 3 —— 4 —— 5 —— 6 —— 7 —— 8 —— 9 —— 1 0

36. You must research around your desires and cultivate farsightedness to see the full picture. This is how the greatest businessmen and women created their successes.

    1 —— 2 —— 3 —— 4 —— 5 —— 6 —— 7 —— 8 —— 9 —— 1 0

37. Your health and happiness are not dependent upon having "things." When your mental attitude is in tune with your spiritual nature and your unity with the Universal Mind, then you will experience the "Truth" and your life will be fruitful and joyful.

    1 —— 2 —— 3 —— 4 —— 5 —— 6 —— 7 —— 8 —— 9 —— 1 0

Tally your total score by adding the number you allocated for yourself in each of the 37 principles above. Your score will range from 37 to 370.

If you scored between 259 and 370, you have a firm foundation on the principles shared in this chapter. You know that wealth is not a ends, but a means. You focus on your connection to Universal Mind, and cultivate your spiritual self, and in doing so, you experience joy and harmony in your life. Wonderful synchronicities occur in a delightful and glorious way. Be sure to contemplate the exercise for this week on a daily basis to further solidify your comprehension.

If you scored between 148 and 258, you understand a great deal about this law and are well on your way to mastering manifestation in your life. You understand that to seek wealth for its own sake will not be beneficial. Ideally, when you have a higher purpose with which you plan to use the wealth, it will naturally and easily come to you. Continue to explore the exercise for this week, contemplating the message on a daily.

If you scored between 37 and 147, honor yourself for the strides are you making as you build your knowledge and application of the lessons in this book. Take time each day to re-read each of the 37 teachings in this segment. As you do so, you will gain greater confidence in the Truth that can free you of your limited thinking.

Introspection:

1. What did you learn about yourself after completing the Comprehension Survey?
2. Was your score what you expected it to be? Why or why not?
3. What areas of the segment of the book have you mastered?
4. What are the areas in this segment of the book that you need to focus on?
5. What three "takeaways" from this segment would you share with others and why?

Exercise

For your exercise this week, try to bring yourself to a realization of the important fact that harmony and happiness are states of consciousness and do not depend upon the possession of things. That things are effects and come as a consequence of correct mental states. So that if we desire material possession of any kind our chief concern should be to acquire the mental attitude which will bring about the result desired. This mental attitude is brought about by a realization of our spiritual nature and our unity with the Universal Mind which is the substance of all things. This realization will bring about everything which is necessary for our complete enjoyment. This is scientific or correct thinking. When we succeed in bringing about this mental attitude it is comparatively easy to realize our desire as an already accomplished fact; when we can do this we shall have found the "Truth" which makes us "free" from every lack or limitation of any kind

NOTES IN RESPONSE TO PERFORMING THIS EXERCISE
Be sure to journal about any findings or experiences you have as you continue to do this exercise as outlined.

Part Seventeen

INTRODUCTION

The kind of Deity which a man, consciously or unconsciously, worships, indicates the intellectual status of the worshiper.

Ask the Indian of God, and he will describe to you a powerful chieftain of a glorious tribe. Ask the Pagan of God, and he will tell you of a God of fire, a God of water, a God of this, that and the other.

Ask the Israelite of God, and he will tell you of the God of Moses, who conceived it expedient to rule by coercive measures; hence, the Ten Commandments. Or he will tell you of Joshua, who led the Israelites into battle, confiscated property, murdered the prisoners and laid cities waste.

The so-called heathen made "graven images" of their Gods, whom they were accustomed to worship, but among the most intelligent, at least, these images were but the visible emblems which they used to facilitate mental concentration on the qualities which they desired to externalize in their lives.

We of the twentieth century worship a God of Love in theory, but in practice we make for ourselves "graven images" of "Wealth," "Power," "Fashion," "Custom" and "Conventionality." We "fall down" before them and worship them. We concentrate on them and they are thereby externalized in our lives.

The reader who masters the contents of Part Seventeen will not mistake symbols for reality; he will be interested in causes, rather than effects. He will concentrate on the realities of life, and will then not be disappointed in the results.

---

1. We are told that Man has "dominion over all things"; this dominion is established through Mind. Thought is the activity which controls every principle beneath it. The highest principle by reason of its superior essence and qualities necessarily determines the circumstances, aspects and relation of everything with which it comes in contact.
2. The vibrations of Mental forces are the finest and consequently the most powerful in existence. To those who perceive the nature and transcendency of mental force, all physical power sinks into insignificance.
3. We are accustomed to look upon the Universe with a lens of five senses, and from these experiences our anthropomorphic conceptions originate, but true conceptions are only secured by spiritual insight. This insight requires a quickening of the vibrations of the Mind, and is only secured when the mind is continuously concentrated in a given direction.
4. Continuous concentration means an even, unbroken flow of thought and is the result of patient, persistent, persevering and well-regulated system.
5. Great discoveries are the result of long-continued investigation. The science of mathematics requires years of concentrated effort to master it, and the greatest science—that of the Mind—is revealed only through concentrated effort.
6. Concentration is much misunderstood; there seems to be an idea of effort or activity associated with it, when just

the contrary is necessary. The greatness of an actor lies in the fact that he forgets himself in the portrayal of his character, becoming so identified with it, that the audience is swayed by the realism of the performance. This will give you a good idea of true concentration; you should be so interested in your thought, so engrossed in your subject, as to be conscious of nothing else. Such concentration leads to intuitive perception and immediate insight into the nature of the object concentrated upon.

7. All knowledge is the result of concentration of this kind; it is thus that the secrets of Heaven and Earth have been wrested; it is thus that the mind becomes a magnet and the desire to know draws the knowledge, irresistibly attracts it, makes it your own.

8. Desire is largely subconscious; conscious desire rarely realizes its object when the latter is out of immediate reach. Subconscious desire arouses the latent faculties of the mind, and difficult problems seem to solve themselves.

9. The subconscious mind may be aroused and brought into action in any direction and made to serve us for any purpose, by concentration. The practice of concentration requires the control of the physical, mental and psychical being; all modes of consciousness whether physical, mental or psychical, must be under control.

10. Spiritual Truth is therefore the controlling factor; it is this which will enable you to grow out of limited attainment and reach a point where you will be able to translate modes of thought into character and consciousness.

11. Concentration does not mean mere thinking of thoughts, but the transmutation of these thoughts into practical values; the average person has no conception of the meaning of concentration. There is always the cry "to have" but never the cry "to be"; they fail to understand that they cannot have one without the other, that they must first find the "king-

dom" before they can have the "things added." Momentary enthusiasm is of no value; it is only by unbounded self-confidence that the goal is reached.

12. The mind may place the ideal a little too high and fall short of the mark; it may attempt to soar on untrained wings and instead of flying, fall to earth; but that is no reason for not making another attempt.

13. Weakness is the only barrier to mental attainment; attribute your weakness to physical limitations or mental uncertainties and try again; ease and perfection are gained by repetition.

14. The astronomer centers his mind on the stars and they give forth their secrets; the geologist centers his mind on the construction of the earth and we have geology; so with all things. Men center their minds on the problems of life, and the result is apparent in the vast and complex social order of the day.

15. All mental discovery and attainment are the result of desire plus concentration; desire is the strongest mode of action; the more persistent the desire, the more authoritative the revelation. Desire added to concentration will wrench any secret from nature.

16. In realizing great thoughts, in experiencing great emotions that correspond with great thoughts, the mind is in a state where it appreciates the value of higher things.

17. The intensity of one moment's earnest concentration and the intense longing to become and to attain may take you further than years of slow normal and forced effort; it will unfasten the prison bars of unbelief, weakness, impotence and self-belittlement, and you will come into a realization of the joy of overcoming.

18. The spirit of initiative and originality is developed through persistence and continuity of mental effort. Business teaches the value of concentration and encourages decision

of character; it develops practical insight and quickness of conclusion. The mental element in every commercial pursuit is dominant as the controlling factor, and desire is the predominating force; all commercial relations are the externalization of desire.
19. Many of the sturdy and substantial virtues are developed in commercial employment; the mind is steadied and directed; it becomes efficient. The principal necessity is the strengthening of the mind so that it rises superior to the distractions and wayward impulses of instinctive life and thus successfully overcomes in the conflict between the higher and lower self.
20. All of us are dynamos, but the dynamo of itself is nothing; the mind must work the dynamo; then it is useful and its energy can be definitely concentrated. The mind is an engine whose power is undreamed; thought is an omni-working power. It is the ruler and creator of all form and all events occurring in form. Physical energy is nothing in comparison with the omnipotence of thought, because thought enables man to harness all other natural power.
21. Vibration is the action of thought; it is vibration which reaches out and attracts the material necessary to construct and build. There is nothing mysterious concerning the power of thought; concentration simply implies that consciousness can be focalized to the point where it becomes identified with the object of its attention. As food absorbed is the essence of the body, so the mind absorbs the object of its attention, gives it life and being.
22. If you concentrate on some matter of importance, the intuitive power will be set in operation, and help will come in the nature of information which will lead to success.
23. Intuition arrives at conclusions without the aid of experience or memory. Intuition often solves problems that are beyond the grasp of the reasoning power. Intuition often

comes with a suddenness that is startling; it reveals the truth for which we are searching, so directly that it seems to come from a higher power. Intuition can be cultivated and developed; in order to do this it must be recognized and appreciated; if the intuitive visitor is given a royal welcome when he comes, he will come again; the more cordial the welcome the more frequent his visits will become, but if he is ignored or neglected he will make his visits few and far apart.

24. Intuition usually comes in the Silence; great minds seek solitude frequently; it is here that all the larger problems of life are worked out. For this reason every business man who can afford it has a private office, where he will not be disturbed; if you cannot afford a private office you can at least find somewhere, where you can be alone a few minutes each day, to train the thought along lines which will enable you to develop that invincible power which is necessary to achieve.

25. Remember that fundamentally the subconscious is omnipotent; there is no limit to the things that can be done when it is given the power to act. Your degree of success is determined by the nature of your desire. If the nature of your desire is in harmony with Natural Law or the Universal Mind, it will gradually emancipate the mind and give you invincible courage.

26. Every obstacle conquered, every victory gained, will give you more faith in your power, and you will have greater ability to win. Your strength is determined by your mental attitude; if this attitude is one of success, and is permanently held with an unswerving purpose, you will attract to you from the invisible domain the things you silently demand.

27. By keeping the thought in mind, it will gradually take tangible form. A definite purpose sets causes in motion which

go out in the invisible world and find the material necessary to serve your purpose.

28. You may be pursuing the symbols of power, instead of power itself. You may be pursuing fame instead of honor, riches instead of wealth, position instead of service; in either event you will find that they turn to ashes just as you overtake them.

29. Premature wealth or position cannot be retained because it has not been earned; we get only what we give, and those who try to get without giving always find that the law of compensation is relentlessly bringing about an exact equilibrium.

30. The race has hitherto been for money and other mere symbols of power, but with an understanding of the true source of power, we can afford to ignore the symbols. The man with a large bank account finds it unnecessary to load his pockets down with gold; so with the man who has found the true source of power; he is no longer interested in its shams or pretentions.

31. Thought ordinarily leads outwardly in evolutionary directions, but it can be turned within where it will take hold of the basic principles of things, the heart of things, the spirit of things. When you get to the heart of things it is comparatively easy to understand and command them.

32. This is because the Spirit of a thing is the thing itself, the vital part of it, the real substance. The form is simply the outward manifestation of the spiritual activity within.

33. For your exercise this week concentrate as nearly as possible in accordance with the method outlined in this lesson; let there be no conscious effort or activity associated with your purpose. Relax completely, avoid any thought of anxiety as to results. Remember that power comes through repose. Let the thought dwell upon your object, until it is

completely identified with it, until you are conscious of nothing else.
34. If you wish to eliminate fear concentrate on courage.
35. If you wish to eliminate lack concentrate on abundance.
36. If you wish to eliminate disease concentrate on health.
37. Always concentrate on the ideal as an already existing fact; this is the Elohim, the germ cell, the life principle which goes forth, and enters in, and becomes, sets in motion those causes which guide, direct and bring about the necessary relation which eventually manifest in form.

Thought is the property of those only who can entertain it.
—EMERSON.

STUDY GUIDE

Part Seventeen

Summary

This Part tells of the Law of Vibration and why the highest principle necessarily determines the circumstances, aspects and relations of everything with which it comes in contact. It tells why and how a knowledge of these higher forces makes all physical force sink into insignificance. It explains the nature of concentration; it tells something of the practice of concentration, tells something of the results of concentration. It tells how the mind may become a magnet, how it may irresistibly attract the conditions which it desires; it tells why it is necessary "to be" in order "to have." It tells how to unfasten the prison bars of weakness, impotence and self-belittlement and realize the joy of overcoming obstacles. It tells how the intuitive power is set in operation and how this inevitably leads to success. It tells of the difference between real power and the symbols of power, and why the symbols turn to ashes just as we overtake them.

1. According to the author, what you worship is an indication of your intellect. Describe in detail what you believe yourself to worship.

2. Various cultures believed in various Gods. They were visible emblems that possessed qualities these cultures wanted to externalize in their lives. What were your religious beliefs in your youth?

3. What qualities did the "God(s)" you followed possess? Did these qualities reflect those that you aspire to? Please explain.

4. Do you still hold true to these beliefs? If not, what beliefs do you now follow and why?

5. Charles Haanel suggests that in the twentieth century people started worshipping "wealth, power, fashion, custom and conventionality" as concentration shifted from Gods to things. Do you believe your concentration has shifted from divine connection to acquiring "stuff" in your life? Please explain.

Comprehension Survey

In this segment you will learn how to avoid mistaking symbols for reality. Once you have completed it, you may have a greater awareness of the false Gods that you have been pursuing.. For each of the principles below, choose the number that is most closely aligns to your beliefs (1 being "not at all" and 10 being "a great deal").

1. Your thoughts are controlled by your principles. By reason of its heightened state, your highest principles determine the quality of your experiences.

   1 — 2 — 3 — 4 — 5 — 6 — 7 — 8 — 9 — 10

2. All physical power is nothing in comparison to the vibrations of your mental forces.

   1 — 2 — 3 — 4 — 5 — 6 — 7 — 8 — 9 — 10

3. True manifestations only come from spiritual insight. To have this, you need to continuously concentrate in a given direction. Doing so quickens the vibration of your mind.

   1 — 2 — 3 — 4 — 5 — 6 — 7 — 8 — 9 — 10

4. In order to continuously concentrate, you need an unbroken flow to thought that comes from patience, persistence, perseverance and a structured and organized system.

   1 — 2 — 3 — 4 — 5 — 6 — 7 — 8 — 9 — 10

5. Like any sound science, you can only master the Mind through long term, ongoing investigation.

   1 — 2 — 3 — 4 — 5 — 6 — 7 — 8 — 9 — 10

6. The belief that concentration takes effort is incorrect. When concentrating, you should be highly engrossed in your subject. This then leads to intuitive perceptions and immediate insights on that which you are focusing.

   1 — 2 — 3 — 4 — 5 — 6 — 7 — 8 — 9 — 10

7. Your mind is a magnet and your desire to know that irresistibly attracts that which you concentrate upon, so that it becomes your own.

   1 — 2 — 3 — 4 — 5 — 6 — 7 — 8 — 9 — 10

8. Your desires are largely subconscious. They awaken hidden capabilities of your mind, and challenges seem to solve themselves.

   1 — 2 — 3 — 4 — 5 — 6 — 7 — 8 — 9 — 10

9. Through concentration and control of your physical, mental and psychic self, you can awaken your subconscious mind.

   1 — 2 — 3 — 4 — 5 — 6 — 7 — 8 — 9 — 10

10. Spiritual Truth is at the heart of your ability to translate your thoughts into material manifestations.

    1 —— 2 —— 3 —— 4 —— 5 —— 6 —— 7 —— 8 —— 9 —— 10

11. You reach your goals through absolute self-confidence. You need to focus your energies on "being" as opposed to "having."

    1 —— 2 —— 3 —— 4 —— 5 —— 6 —— 7 —— 8 —— 9 —— 10

12. You may set your sights too high, but if you do not succeed, you can try again.

    1 —— 2 —— 3 —— 4 —— 5 —— 6 —— 7 —— 8 —— 9 —— 10

13. Repetition is key. Realize that your weakness is in the physical limitations or mental reservations that you face. Just try again.

    1 —— 2 —— 3 —— 4 —— 5 —— 6 —— 7 —— 8 —— 9 —— 10

14. If you focus your energy on the problems in your life, like so many others, you will experience even more problems.

    1 —— 2 —— 3 —— 4 —— 5 —— 6 —— 7 —— 8 —— 9 —— 10

15. Your passionate desire in conjunction with your deep concentration will evoke any of nature's secrets into existence.

    1 —— 2 —— 3 —— 4 —— 5 —— 6 —— 7 —— 8 —— 9 —— 10

16. When you have heightened thoughts and deep emotions, your mind appreciates the value of greater things.

    1 —— 2 —— 3 —— 4 —— 5 —— 6 —— 7 —— 8 —— 9 —— 10

17. One moment of deep, passionate, heartfelt concentration can break you free from years of slow, forced effort.

    1 —— 2 —— 3 —— 4 —— 5 —— 6 —— 7 —— 8 —— 9 —— 10

18. Whether your pursuits be personal or business, originality comes from the same core features of persistence, strong desire and deep concentration.

    1 —— 2 —— 3 —— 4 —— 5 —— 6 —— 7 —— 8 —— 9 —— 10

19. In business, you are wise to strengthen your mind so that you are not swayed by impulses that lack integrity and higher purpose.

    1 —— 2 —— 3 —— 4 —— 5 —— 6 —— 7 —— 8 —— 9 —— 10

20. Your thoughts rule over everything, because they are all-powerful.

    1 —— 2 —— 3 —— 4 —— 5 —— 6 —— 7 —— 8 —— 9 —— 10

21. There is no mystery in the power of your thoughts. Like your body absorbs food, your mind absorbs the objects of your attention and intention.

    1 — 2 — 3 — 4 — 5 — 6 — 7 — 8 — 9 — 10

22. When you focus on something of importance, your intuition will draw you to the right information.

    1 — 2 — 3 — 4 — 5 — 6 — 7 — 8 — 9 — 10

23. Intuition requires your upmost respect and can be developed. It can come suddenly from higher power, and must be recognized, appreciated, and acted upon. The more you follow and respect it, the more it will make itself known.

    1 — 2 — 3 — 4 — 5 — 6 — 7 — 8 — 9 — 10

24. Intuition comes in silence, so it is important for you to find a time and place to be silent and connect with it each day. When you do, you will develop extraordinary power. Successful business people practice this.

    1 — 2 — 3 — 4 — 5 — 6 — 7 — 8 — 9 — 10

25. If the nature of your desires aligns with Universal Mind, your mind will eventually be freed of the imprisonment of lower states of thinking and being. You will have unstoppable courage.

    1 — 2 — 3 — 4 — 5 — 6 — 7 — 8 — 9 — 10

26. Each time you succeed, you build more stability and unwavering purpose. You will attract all that you silently demand from the invisible realm.

    1 — 2 — 3 — 4 — 5 — 6 — 7 — 8 — 9 — 10

27. When you keep a thought in your mind, your commitment makes tangible the form that is made from material found in the invisible world.

    1 — 2 — 3 — 4 — 5 — 6 — 7 — 8 — 9 — 10

28. You may be pursuing from a place of ego gratification, where you want fame instead of honor, riches instead of True wealth, or position instead of purpose. If this is the case, they will quickly disappear just as you manifest them.

    1 — 2 — 3 — 4 — 5 — 6 — 7 — 8 — 9 — 10

29. If you gain wealth or position before you have earned it, the situation will not work out because the law of compensation is about exact equilibrium.
1 — 2 — 3 — 4 — 5 — 6 — 7 — 8 — 9 — 10

30. Once you experience the richness that comes from deep connection with Universal Source, you will no longer need the symbols of pseudo-power and material prosperity.
1 — 2 — 3 — 4 — 5 — 6 — 7 — 8 — 9 — 10

31. Turning your thoughts inward takes you to the heart of things where it is easy to understand and take charge of them.
1 — 2 — 3 — 4 — 5 — 6 — 7 — 8 — 9 — 10

32. This is because the outward form of anything is a manifestation of the spiritual activity within it.
1 — 2 — 3 — 4 — 5 — 6 — 7 — 8 — 9 — 10

33. You are most effectively when you are relaxed and exerting no effort as you visualize what you desire.
1 — 2 — 3 — 4 — 5 — 6 — 7 — 8 — 9 — 10

34. When you focus on courage, you eliminate fearfulness.
1 — 2 — 3 — 4 — 5 — 6 — 7 — 8 — 9 — 10

35. When you focus on abundance, you eliminate any sense of lack.
1 — 2 — 3 — 4 — 5 — 6 — 7 — 8 — 9 — 10

36. When you focus on health, you eliminate disease.
1 — 2 — 3 — 4 — 5 — 6 — 7 — 8 — 9 — 10

37. You are most powerful when you focus on your desires as if they already exist in the present.
1 — 2 — 3 — 4 — 5 — 6 — 7 — 8 — 9 — 10

Tally your total score by adding the number you allocated for yourself in each of the 37 principles above. Your score will range from 37 to 370.

If you scored between 259 and 370, you are aware of the importance of concentration and relaxation. You understand how important it is for you to focus not on the problem, but on the solution as if it is already in existence. Be sure to practice the exercise on a daily basis, and take note of how your experience shifts in response to doing so.

If you scored between 148 and 258, you are growing more aware of how much your commitment to concentration, relaxation and focused attention on your intention is key. You are aware of how important it is to take the moral high ground when you are planning on manifesting something in your life. Review each of the 37 lessons outlined in this step, and be sure to do the contemplation relaxation exercise daily.

If you scored between 37 and 147, you struggle with some of the teachings outlined in this segment of the book. Be sure to re-read each of the 37 lessons within this step, along with the corresponding study guide number above. Doing this, along with doing to prescribed exercise daily will assist you in gaining additional knowledge and practical experience with the teachings.

Introspection:

1. What did you learn about yourself after completing the Comprehension Survey?
2. Was your score what you expected it to be? Why or why not?
3. What areas of the segment of the book have you mastered?
4. What are the areas in this segment of the book that you need to focus on?
5. What three "takeaways" from this segment would you share with others and why?

Exercise

For your exercise this week concentrate as nearly as possible in accordance with the method outlined in this lesson; let there be no conscious effort or activity associated with your purpose. Relax completely, avoid any thought of anxiety as to results. Remember that power comes through repose. Let the thought dwell upon your object, until it is completely identified with it, until you are conscious of nothing else.

NOTES IN RESPONSE TO PERFORMING THIS EXERCISE
Be sure to journal about any findings or experiences you have as you continue to do this exercise as outlined.

Part Eighteen

INTRODUCTION

In order to grow we must obtain what is necessary for our growth. This is brought about through the law of attraction. This principle is the sole means by which the individual is differentiated from the Universal.

Think for a moment, what would a man be if he were not a husband, father or brother, if he were not interested in the social, economical, political or religious world? He would be nothing but an abstract theoretical ego. He exists, therefore, only in his relation to the whole, in his relation to other men, in his relation to society. This relation constitutes his environment; he exists, therefore, in his relation to his environment and in no other way.

Hence it is evident that the individual is simply the differentiation of the one Universal Mind "which lighteth every man that cometh into the world," and his so-called individuality or personality consists of nothing but the manner in which he relates with the whole.

This we call his environment and it is brought about by the law of attraction. Part Eighteen has something more to say concerning this important law.

1. There is change in the thought of the world. This change is silently transpiring in our midst, and is more important than any which the world has undergone since the downfall of Paganism.
2. The present revolution in the opinions of all classes of men, the highest and most cultured of men as well as those of the laboring class, stands unparalleled in the history of the world.
3. Science has of late made such vast discoveries, has revealed such an infinity of resources, has unveiled such enormous possibilities and such unsuspected forces, that scientific men more and more hesitate to affirm certain theories as established and indubitable or to deny other theories as absurd or impossible.
4. A new civilization is being born; customs, creeds, and precedent are passing; vision, faith and service are taking their place. The fetters of tradition are being melted off from humanity, and as the dross of materialism is being consumed, thought is being liberated and truth is rising full orbed before an astonished multitude.
5. The whole world is on the eve of a new consciousness, a new power, and a new realization within the self.
6. Physical Science has resolved matter into molecules, molecules into atoms, atoms into energy, and it has remained for Mr. J. A. Fleming, in an address before the Royal Institution, to resolve this energy into mind. He says: "In its ultimate essence, energy may be incomprehensible by us except as an exhibition of the direct operation of that which we call Mind or Will."
7. And this mind is the indwelling and ultimate. It is imminent in matter as in spirit. It is the sustaining, energizing, allpervading Spirit of the universe.
8. Every living thing must be sustained by this omnipotent Intelligence, and we find the difference in individual

lives to be largely measured by the degree of this intelligence, which they manifest. It is greater intelligence that places the animal in a higher scale of being than the plant, the man higher than the animal, and we find that this increased intelligence is again indicated by the power of the individual to control modes of action and thus to consciously adjust himself to his environment."

9. It is this adjustment that occupies the attention of th greatest minds, and this adjustment consists in nothing else than the recognition of an existing order in the universal mind, for it is well known that this mind will obey us precisely in proportion as we first obey it.

10. It is the recognition of Natural Laws that has enabled us to annihilate time and space, to soar in the air and to make iron float, and the greater the degree of intelligence the greater will be our recognition of these Natural Laws and the greater will be the power we can possess.

11. It is the recognition of the self as an individualization of this Universal Intelligence that enables the individual to control those forms of intelligence which have not yet reached this level of self-recognition; they do not know that this Universal Intelligence permeates all things ready to be called into action; they do not know that it is responsive to every demand, and they are therefore in bondage to the law of their own being.

12. Thought is creative and the principle on which the law is based is sound and legitimate and is inherent in the nature of things; but this creative power does not originate in the individual, but in the universal, which is the source and fountain of all energy and substance; the individual is simply the channel for the distribution of this energy.

13. The individual is simply the means by which the universal produces the various combinations which result in the

formation of phenomena, which depends upon the law of vibration, whereby various rates of rapidity of motion in the primary substance form new substances only in certain exact numerical ratios.

14. Thought is the invisible link by which the individual comes into communication with the Universal, the finite with the Infinite, the seen with the Unseen. Thought is the magic by which the human is transformed into a being who thinks and knows and feels and acts.

15. As the proper apparatus has enabled the eye to discover worlds without number millions of miles away, so, with the proper understanding, man has been enabled to communicate with the Universal Mind, the source of all power.

16. The Understanding which is usually developed is about as valuable as telephone box without wires or a central station; in fact, it is usually nothing more than a "belief" which means nothing at all. The Indians believe something and so do the savages of the Cannibal Islands; but that proves nothing.

17. The only belief which is of any value to any one is a belief that has been put to a test and demonstrated to be a fact; it is then no longer a belief, but has become a living Faith or the Truth.

18. And this Truth has been put to the test by hundreds of thousands of people and has been found to be the Truth exactly in proportion to the usefulness of the apparatus which they used.

19. A man would not expect to locate stars hundreds of millions of miles away without a sufficiently strong telescope, and for this reason Science is continually engaged in building larger and more powerful telescopes and is continually rewarded by additional knowledge of the heavenly bodies.

20. So with understanding; men are continually making progress in the methods which they use to come into communication with the Universal Mind and its infinite possibilities.
21. The Universal Mind manifests itself in the objective, through the principle of attraction that each atom has for every other atom, in infinite degrees of intensity.
22. It is by this principle of combining and attracting that things are brought together. This principle is of universal application and is the sole means whereby the purpose of existence is carried into effect.
23. The expression of growth is met in a most beautiful manner through the instrumentality of this Universal Principle.
24. In order to grow we must obtain what is essential for our growth, but as we are at all times a complete thought entity, this completeness makes it possible for us to receive only as we give; growth is therefore conditioned on reciprocal action, and we find that on the mental plane like attracts like, that mental vibrations respond only to the extent of their vibratory harmony.
25. It is clear, therefore, that thoughts of abundance will respond only to similar thoughts; the wealth of the individual is seen to be what he inherently is. Affluence within is found to be the secret of attraction for affluence without. The ability to produce is found to be the real source of wealth of the individual. It is for this reason that he who has his heart in his work is certain to meet with unbounded success. He will give and continually give, and the more he gives the more he will receive.
26. What do the great financiers of Wall Street, the captains of industry, the statesmen, the great corporation attorneys, the inventors, the physicians, tho authors—what do each of these contribute to the sum of human happiness but the power of their thought?

27. Thought is the energy by which the law of attraction is brought into operation, which eventually manifests in abundance.
28. The Universal Mind is static Mind, or Substance in equilibrium. It is differentiated into form by our power to think. Thought is the dynamic phase of mind.
29. Power depends upon consciousness of power; unless we use it, we shall lose it, and unless we are conscious of it we cannot use it.
30. The use of this power depends upon attention; the degree of attention determines our capacity for the acquirement of knowledge which is another name for power.
31. Attention has been held to be the distinguishing mark of genius. The cultivation of attention depends upon practice.
32. The incentive of attention is interest; the greater the interest, the greater the attention; the greater the attention, the greater the interest, action and reaction; begin by paying attention; before long you will have aroused interest; this interest will attract more attention, and this attention will produce more interest, and so on. This practice will enable you to cultivate the power of attention.
33. This week concentrate upon your power to create; seek insight, perception; try to find a logical basis for the faith which is in you. Let the thought dwell on the fact that the physical man lives and moves and has his being in the sustainer of all organic life air, that he must breathe to live. Then let the thought rest on the fact that the spiritual man also lives and moves and has his being in a similar but subtler energy upon which he must depend for life, and that as in the physical world no life assumes form until after a seed is sown, and no higher fruit than that of the parent stock can be produced; so in the spiritual world no

effect can be produced until the seed is sown and the fruit will depend upon the nature of the seed, so that the results which you secure depend upon your perception of law in the mighty domain of causation, the highest evolution of human consciousness.

There is no thought in my mind but it
quickly tends to convert itself into a power and
organizes a huge instrumentality of means.
—EMERSON.

STUDY GUIDE

Part Eighteen

Summary

This Part tells of a change in the thought of men, a change which is silently transpiring in our midst and which is unparalleled in the history of the world. The fetters of tradition are being melted off from humanity and truth is rising full orbed before an astonished multitude. It tells how the individual is enabled to control every form of intelligence which has not yet reached this level of self-recognition. It tells when and how the creative power originates, it tells how the Universal produces the various combinations which result in the formation of phenomena, it explains the principle of attraction by which things are brought together, which is the sole means by which existence is carried into effect. It explains the real source of wealth of the individual. It explains the method by which attention and concentration may be developed and shows why the power of attention is the distinguishing characteristic of every man of ability.

1. What differentiates yourself from the Universal?
2. Man's existence is defined by his relationships. Explain what this means, providing specific examples.
3. Your personality is defined by the manner in which you relate to the whole. What does this mean?
4. How do you anticipate environment is related to the law of attraction?

Comprehension Survey

In this segment you will learn more about how much your identity and all you do is relationship-based. Once you have completed this survey and this segment of the book, you will have a better understanding of the part that environment plays in The Master Key System. For each of the principles below, choose the number that is most closely aligns to your beliefs (1 being "not at all" and 10 being "a great deal").

1. You are a part of change in the thought of the world that is the most important since the fall of Paganism.

    1 —— 2 —— 3 —— 4 —— 5 —— 6 —— 7 —— 8 —— 9 —— 10

2. Based on the opinions of all, from the richest to the most impoverished of men, this revolution stands unmatched in the history of the world.

   1 — 2 — 3 — 4 — 5 — 6 — 7 — 8 — 9 — 10

3. This revolution has brought about question throughout the scientific world.

   1 — 2 — 3 — 4 — 5 — 6 — 7 — 8 — 9 — 10

4. There is an extraordinary new civilization being born, stripping away the old and liberating the masses.

   1 — 2 — 3 — 4 — 5 — 6 — 7 — 8 — 9 — 10

5. The whole world is experiencing a new consciousness and a power that rests within you.

   1 — 2 — 3 — 4 — 5 — 6 — 7 — 8 — 9 — 10

6. Energy is a direct operation in response to the Mind or Will.

   1 — 2 — 3 — 4 — 5 — 6 — 7 — 8 — 9 — 10

7. In your mind dwells the ultimate Spirit that sustains and energizes all.

   1 — 2 — 3 — 4 — 5 — 6 — 7 — 8 — 9 — 10

8. The more intelligent you are, the better you manifest and the more you are able to consciously adjust yourself to your environment by controlling your actions.

   1 — 2 — 3 — 4 — 5 — 6 — 7 — 8 — 9 — 10

9. The Universal Mind will obey you, as you first obey it.

   1 — 2 — 3 — 4 — 5 — 6 — 7 — 8 — 9 — 10

10. The greater your knowledge and recognition of the Natural Laws, the greater the power that you possess.

    1 — 2 — 3 — 4 — 5 — 6 — 7 — 8 — 9 — 10

11. Through your recognition of yourself as a part of the Universal Intelligence you can control that which has not yet fully realized itself as a part of the Source.

    1 — 2 — 3 — 4 — 5 — 6 — 7 — 8 — 9 — 10

12. Creative power originates in the Source, not in you. You are a channel for its distribution.

    1 — 2 — 3 — 4 — 5 — 6 — 7 — 8 — 9 — 10

13. You are the means by which the Universe produces various combinations to create phenomenon, each of which depends upon various rates of vibration in specific numerical ratios to form new substances.
    1 — 2 — 3 — 4 — 5 — 6 — 7 — 8 — 9 — 10

14. Thought is the invisible link by which the unseen is manifest, and the human is transformed to a being who knows, feels and acts.
    1 — 2 — 3 — 4 — 5 — 6 — 7 — 8 — 9 — 10

15. Just as telescopes help humankind to see galaxies millions of miles away, so too, with the proper understanding are you able to communicate with the source of all power, Universal Mind.
    1 — 2 — 3 — 4 — 5 — 6 — 7 — 8 — 9 — 10

16. A shallow understanding of this law is merely a belief and is useless without application.
    1 — 2 — 3 — 4 — 5 — 6 — 7 — 8 — 9 — 10

17. Your understanding becomes a living Faith or the Truth when you put it to the test and demonstrate it.
    1 — 2 — 3 — 4 — 5 — 6 — 7 — 8 — 9 — 10

18. This Truth has been put to the test by thousands, and has been found to be true in proportion to its usefulness.
    1 — 2 — 3 — 4 — 5 — 6 — 7 — 8 — 9 — 10

19. Science continually builds stronger telescopes and in doing so is rewarded additional knowledge.
    1 — 2 — 3 — 4 — 5 — 6 — 7 — 8 — 9 — 10

20. So too is the case with the law of attraction. As we make more progress, we are able to experience more.
    1 — 2 — 3 — 4 — 5 — 6 — 7 — 8 — 9 — 10

21. Thus the Universal Mind manifests through atoms, which are attracted to one another in infinite degrees of intensity.
    1 — 2 — 3 — 4 — 5 — 6 — 7 — 8 — 9 — 10

22. The principle of universal application involves the act of combining and attracting, which is the means by which existence is brought into being.
    1 — 2 — 3 — 4 — 5 — 6 — 7 — 8 — 9 — 10

23. This Universal Principle is the instrument though which growth is beautifully experienced.
    1 — 2 — 3 — 4 — 5 — 6 — 7 — 8 — 9 — 10

24. Mental vibrations only respond to the extent that you are in vibrational harmony with them.
    1 — 2 — 3 — 4 — 5 — 6 — 7 — 8 — 9 — 10

25. Your ability to produce is the real source of wealth. If your heart is fully engaged in your work, you will want to give and will be highly successful.
    1 — 2 — 3 — 4 — 5 — 6 — 7 — 8 — 9 — 10

26. Every genius in all areas of expertise contribute the power of their thoughts towards human happiness.
    1 — 2 — 3 — 4 — 5 — 6 — 7 — 8 — 9 — 10

27. Your thoughts are the energy through which the law of attraction operates and manifests.
    1 — 2 — 3 — 4 — 5 — 6 — 7 — 8 — 9 — 10

28. Your thoughts power the Universal Mind which is static, until they make it dynamic.
    1 — 2 — 3 — 4 — 5 — 6 — 7 — 8 — 9 — 10

29. Your power depends upon your consciousness of it. If you unaware that you have it, you will lose it.
    1 — 2 — 3 — 4 — 5 — 6 — 7 — 8 — 9 — 10

30. The use of your power is dependent upon the attention that you give it.
    1 — 2 — 3 — 4 — 5 — 6 — 7 — 8 — 9 — 10

31. To give your power the necessary attention, you need to practice cultivating it.
    1 — 2 — 3 — 4 — 5 — 6 — 7 — 8 — 9 — 10

32. Interest is the key. Show more interest, and you will cultivate the power of attention.
    1 — 2 — 3 — 4 — 5 — 6 — 7 — 8 — 9 — 10

33. The results your experience depend upon the nature of the seed (the power of your intentions, how high they are, and how much attention you give to them).

1 —— 2 —— 3 —— 4 —— 5 —— 6 —— 7 —— 8 —— 9 —— 10

Tally your total score by adding the number you allocated for yourself in each of the 31 principles above. Your score will range from 33 to 330.

If you scored between 231 and 330, you understand that your thoughts ae energy and are your link to the invisible world. You make the invisible visible by giving attention to your intentions. Continue with your studies, and read the exercise each day, contemplating it's mean and integrating it into your subconscious mind. Doing so will support you further on this journey.

If you scored between 132 and 230, you have a pretty good understanding of the contents of this segment of the book. Re-read each of the 33 lessons, along with the corresponding statements above. Also, be sure to contemplate the exercises at least daily. Doing so will give rise to greater understanding and application. For, as you just learned, attention brings intention into being.

If you scored between 33 and 131, you are on your path towards greater understanding. Re-read each of the 33 lessons, along with the survey questions above and contemplate on each, giving them attention, time and energy to sink into your psyche. Doing so will open the door of your subconscious and allow them the permeate your thoughts.

Introspection:

1. What did you learn about yourself after completing the Comprehension Survey?
2. Was your score what you expected it to be? Why or why not?
3. What areas of the segment of the book have you mastered?
4. What are the areas in this segment of the book that you need to focus on?
5. What three "takeaways" from this segment would you share with others and why?

Exercise

This week concentrate upon your power to create; seek insight, perception; try to find a logical basis for the faith which is in you. Let the thought dwell on the fact that the physical man lives and moves and has his being in the sustainer of all organic life air, that he must breathe to live. Then let the thought rest on the fact that the spiritual man also lives and moves and has his being in a similar but subtler energy upon which he must depend for life, and that as in the physical world no life assumes form until after a seed is sown, and no higher fruit than that of the parent stock can be produced; so in the spiritual world no effect can be produced until the seed is sown and the fruit will depend upon the nature of the seed, so that the results which you secure depend upon your perception of law in the mighty domain of causation, the highest evolution of human consciousness.

NOTES IN RESPONSE TO PERFORMING THIS EXERCISE
Be sure to journal about any findings or experiences you have as you continue to do this exercise as outlined.

Part Nineteen

INTRODUCTION

Fear is a powerful form of thought. It paralyzes the nerve centers, thus affecting the circulation of the blood. This, in turn, paralyzes the muscular system, so that fear affects the entire being, body, brain and nerve, physical, mental and muscular.

Of course the way to overcome fear is to become conscious of power. What is this mysterious vital force which we call power? We do not know; neither do we know what electricity is. But we do know that by conforming to the requirements of the law by which electricity is governed, it will be our obedient servant; that it will light our homes, our cities, run our machinery and serve us in many useful capacities.

And so it is with vital force. Although we do not know what it is, and possibly may never know, we do know that it is a primary force which manifests through living bodies, and that by complying with the laws and principles by which it is governed, we can open ourselves to a more abundant inflow of this vital energy, and thus express the highest possible degree of mental, moral and spiritual efficiency.

Part Nineteen, which follows, tells of a very simple way of developing this vital force. If you put into practice the information outlined in this Part you will soon develop the sense of power which has ever been the distinguishing mark of genius.

1. The search for truth is no longer a haphazard adventure, but it is a systematic process, and is logical in its operation. Every kind of experience is given a voice in shaping its decision.
2. In seeking the truth we are seeking ultimate cause; we know that every human experience is an effect; then if we may ascertain the cause, and if we shall find that this cause is one which we can consciously control, the effect or the experience will be within our control also.
3. Human experience will then no longer be the football of fate; a man will not be the child of fortune, but destiny, fate and fortune will be controlled as readily as a captain controls his vessel, or an engineer his train.
4. All things are finally resolvable into the same element and as they are thus translatable, one into the other, they must ever be in relation and may never be in opposition to one another.
5. In the physical world there are innumerable contrasts, and these may for convenience sake, be designated by distinctive names. There are sides, colors, shades or ends to all things. There is a North Pole, and a South Pole, an inside and an outside, a seen and an unseen, but these expressions merely serve to place extremes in contrast.
6. They are names given to two different parts of one quantity. The two extremes are relative; they are not separate entities, but are two parts or aspects of the whole.
7. In the mental world we find the same law; we speak of knowledge and ignorance, but ignorance is but a lack of knowledge and is therefore found to be simply a word to express the absence of knowledge; it has no principle in itself.
8. In the Moral World we again find the same law; we speak of good and evil, but Good is a reality, something tangible, while Evil is found to be simply a negative condition, the

absence of Good. Evil is sometimes thought to be a very real condition, but it has no principle, no vitality, no life; we know this because it can always be destroyed by Good; just as Truth destroys Error and light destroys darkness, so Evil vanishes when Good appears; there is therefore but one principle in the Moral World.

9. We find exactly the same law obtaining in the Spiritual world; we speak of Mind and Matter as two separate entities, but clearer insight makes it evident that there is but one operative principle and that is Mind.

10. Mind is the real and the eternal. Matter is forever changing; we know that in the eons of time a hundred years is but as a day. If we stand in any large city and let the eye rest on the innumerable large and magnificent buildings, the railroads, the electric cars, the telephones, the electric lights and all the other conveniences of modern civilization, we may remember that not one of them was there 100 years ago, and if we could stand on the same spot in a hundred years from now, in all probability we should find that but few of them remained.

11. In the animal kingdom we find the same law of change. The millions and millions of animals come and go, a few years constituting their span of life. In the plant world the change is still more rapid. Many plants and nearly all grasses come and go in a single year. When we pass to the inorganic, we expect to find something more substantial, but as we gaze on the apparently solid continent, we are told that it arose from the ocean; we see the giant mountain and are told that the place where it now stands was once a lake; and as we stand in awe before the great cliffs in the Yosemite Valley we can easily trace the path of the glaciers which carried all before them.

12. We are in the presence of continual change, and we know that this change is but the evolution of the Universal Mind,

the grand process whereby all things are continually being created anew, and we come to know that matter is but a form which Mind takes and is therefore simply a condition. Matter has no principle; Mind is the only principle.

13. We have then come to know that Mind is the only principle which is operative in the physical, mental, moral and spiritual world.
14. We also know that this mind is static, mind at rest, we also know that the ability of the individual to think is his ability to act upon the Universal Mind and convert it into dynamic mind, or mind in motion.
15. In order to do this fuel must be applied in the form of food, for man cannot think without eating, and so we find that even a spiritual activity such as thinking cannot be converted into sources of pleasure and profit except by making use of material means.
16. It requires energy of some kind to collect electricity and convert it into a dynamic power, it requires the rays of the sun to give the necessary energy to sustain plant life, so it also requires energy in the form of food to enable the individual to think and thereby act upon the Universal Mind.
17. You may know that thought constantly, eternally is taking form, is forever seeking expression, or you may not, but the fact remains that if your thought is powerful, constructive, and positive, this will be plainly evident in the state of your health, your business and your environment; if your thought is weak, critical, destructive and negative generally, it will manifest in your body as fear, worry and nervousness, in your finance as lack and limitation; and in discordant conditions in your environment.
18. All wealth is the offspring of power; possessions are of value only as they confer power. Events are significant only

as they affect power; all things represent certain forms and degrees of power.
19. A knowledge of cause and effect as shown by the laws governing steam, electricity, chemical affinity and gravitation enables men to plan courageously and to execute fearlessly. These laws are called Natural Laws, because they govern the physical world, but all power is not physical power; there is also mental power, and there is moral and spiritual power.
20. What are our schools, our universities, but mental power-houses, places where mental power is being developed?
21. As there are many mighty powerhouses for the application of power to ponderous machinery, whereby raw material is collected and converted into the necessities and comforts of life, so the mental power-houses collect the raw material and cultivate and develop it into a power which is infinitely superior to all the forces of Nature, marvelous though they be.
22. What is this raw material which is being collected in these thousands of mental power-houses all over the world and developed into a power which is evidently controlling every other power? In its static form it is Mind, in its dynamic form it is Thought.
23. This power is superior because it exists on a higher plane, because it has enabled man to discover the law by which these wonderful forces of Nature could be harnessed and made to do the work of hundreds and thousands of men. It has enabled man to discover laws whereby time and space have been annihilated, and now apparently the law of gravitation is to be overcome.
24. Thought is the vital force or energy which is being developed and which has produced such startling results in the last half century as to bring about a world which would

be absolutely inconceivable to a man existing only fifty or even twenty-five years ago. If such results have been secured by organizing these mental power-houses in fifty years, what may not be expected in another fifty years?

25. The substance from which all things are created is infinite in quantity; we know that light travels at the rate of 186,000 miles per second, and we know that there are stars so remote that it takes light 2,000 years to reach us, and we know that such stars exist in all parts of the heaven; we know, too, that this light comes in waves, so that if the ether on which these waves travel was not continuous the light would fail to reach us; we can then only come to the conclusion that this substance, or ether, or raw material, is universally present.

26. How, then, does it manifest in form? In electrical science a battery is formed by connecting the opposite poles of zinc and copper, which causes a current to flow from one to the other and so provides energy. This same process is repeated in respect to every polarity, and as all form simply depends upon the rate of vibration and consequent relations of atoms to each other, if we wish to change the form of manifestation we must change the polarity. This is the principle of causation.

27. For your exercise this week, concentrate, and when I use the word concentrate, I mean all that the word implies; become so absorbed in the object of your thought that you are conscious of nothing else, and do this a few minutes every day. You take the necessary time to eat in order that the body may be nourished, why not take the time to assimilate your mental food?

28. Let the thought rest on the fact that appearances are deceptive. The earth is not flat, neither is it stationary; the sky is not a dome, the sun does not move, the stars are not small specks of light, and matter which was once sup-

posed to be fixed has been found to be in a state of perpetual flux.

29. Try to realize that the day is fast approaching—its dawn is now at hand—when modes of thought and action must be adjusted to rapidly increasing knowledge of the operation of eternal principles.

*Silent thought, is, after all, the
mightiest agent in human affairs.*
—CHANNING.

STUDY GUIDE

Part Nineteen

Summary

This Part tells of the search for truth, which is another name for ultimate cause. If we can find the truth we shall have found the cause for every effect, and having found the cause we shall be in a position to control the effect. It explains that all things are finally resolvable into one thing, and that as they are thus translatable they must ever be in relation and can never be in opposition to one another. It explains that a knowledge of this primary substance is power; it explains that a knowledge of cause and effect is power, that wealth is the offspring of power, that events and conditions are significant only as they effect power, and finally that all things represent certain forms and decrees of power. It tells of a certain form of power which can control every other power, why it is superior and how we may make use of this superior power.

1. Fear starts a chain reaction in your body that ultimately affects all of your systems. Contemplate on what your fears are, and list them. Take some time to do this. We are often not fully aware of just how fearful we are.

2. While you don't know what electricity is, by using you empower it. Likewise, when you become conscious of your power, even if you can't fully see it, you will empower it. Write a list of the powerful traits that you have, remembering that you are a part of creative source.

3. Reflect on all that vital or primary force has created in this world. Then invite that force into your heart and mind, appreciating it for the abundance that it brings to you and to the world. Note any shifts in your attitude as you do this. Write about your experience.

4. How are you currently building vital force within you?

Comprehension Survey

In this segment you will get a deeper and more profound understanding of vital source and how it works through you. Once you have completed it, you will get a greater understanding of the part you play in turning vital force into material manifestation. For each of the principles below, choose the number that is most closely aligns to your beliefs (1 being "not at all" and 10 being "a great deal").

1. There is a system by which you should search for truth. It is a specific path that is not accidental or to be lightly tread upon.
   1 —— 2 —— 3 —— 4 —— 5 —— 6 —— 7 —— 8 —— 9 —— 10

2. When you seek the truth you know that your experiences are the effects, so you are looking for the cause. You can consciously control the cause as well as the experience.
   1 —— 2 —— 3 —— 4 —— 5 —— 6 —— 7 —— 8 —— 9 —— 10

3. As a captain controls his ship, so too can you control your destiny, fate and fortune.
   1 —— 2 —— 3 —— 4 —— 5 —— 6 —— 7 —— 8 —— 9 —— 10

4. Anything can ultimately be resolved, as long they are in harmonious relationship, and not in opposition.
   1 —— 2 —— 3 —— 4 —— 5 —— 6 —— 7 —— 8 —— 9 —— 10

5. In the physical world there are expressions that serve to place extremes in contrast.
   1 —— 2 —— 3 —— 4 —— 5 —— 6 —— 7 —— 8 —— 9 —— 10

6. The two extremes are separate. They are two parts of the same whole.
   1 —— 2 —— 3 —— 4 —— 5 —— 6 —— 7 —— 8 —— 9 —— 10

7. The same law applies to the mental world. Ignorance is lack of knowledge, thus has not principle in and of itself.
   1 —— 2 —— 3 —— 4 —— 5 —— 6 —— 7 —— 8 —— 9 —— 10

8. Similarly, evil is the absence of good, and thus will vanish when good appears.
   1 —— 2 —— 3 —— 4 —— 5 —— 6 —— 7 —— 8 —— 9 —— 10

9. Thus mind and matter are not separate. There is one operative principle and that is mind.
   1 —— 2 —— 3 —— 4 —— 5 —— 6 —— 7 —— 8 —— 9 —— 10

10. Your mind is real and eternal, while matter is constantly changing.
    1 —— 2 —— 3 —— 4 —— 5 —— 6 —— 7 —— 8 —— 9 —— 10

11. You see the laws of change at work in the smallest to the largest elements of nature.
    1 —— 2 —— 3 —— 4 —— 5 —— 6 —— 7 —— 8 —— 9 —— 10

12. Mind is the only principle from which all is created anew. Matter is a form, a condition which Mind takes.

    1 —— 2 —— 3 —— 4 —— 5 —— 6 —— 7 —— 8 —— 9 —— 10

13. You know that Mind is the principle in the physical, mental, moral and spiritual world.

    1 —— 2 —— 3 —— 4 —— 5 —— 6 —— 7 —— 8 —— 9 —— 10

14. Your ability to think is your ability to act upon the Universal Mind and convert it to mind in motion.

    1 —— 2 —— 3 —— 4 —— 5 —— 6 —— 7 —— 8 —— 9 —— 10

15. You must fuel in the form of food. This is evidence that spiritual activity needs to use material means to function.

    1 —— 2 —— 3 —— 4 —— 5 —— 6 —— 7 —— 8 —— 9 —— 10

16. Like all of nature requires fuel, you require fuel in the form of food to think and subsequently act upon the Universal Mind.

    1 —— 2 —— 3 —— 4 —— 5 —— 6 —— 7 —— 8 —— 9 —— 10

17. Your thought is constantly seeking expression and taking form. Whether positive or negative, it will be reflected in your life experiences.

    1 —— 2 —— 3 —— 4 —— 5 —— 6 —— 7 —— 8 —— 9 —— 10

18. All things—your wealth, possessions and events each represent certain forms and degrees of power.

    1 —— 2 —— 3 —— 4 —— 5 —— 6 —— 7 —— 8 —— 9 —— 10

19. There is more than physical power. There is also mental, moral and spiritual power.

    1 —— 2 —— 3 —— 4 —— 5 —— 6 —— 7 —— 8 —— 9 —— 10

20. Our learning institutions are mental powerhouses where mental power is being developed.

    1 —— 2 —— 3 —— 4 —— 5 —— 6 —— 7 —— 8 —— 9 —— 10

21. The mental power-house collects raw material and is infinitely superior to all of the forces of nature.

    1 —— 2 —— 3 —— 4 —— 5 —— 6 —— 7 —— 8 —— 9 —— 10

22. Mind is the raw material and thought is its dynamic form.

    1 —— 2 —— 3 —— 4 —— 5 —— 6 —— 7 —— 8 —— 9 —— 10

23. This power is superior because it exists on a higher plane. It has enabled you to discover laws that defy time and space.

    1 —— 2 —— 3 —— 4 —— 5 —— 6 —— 7 —— 8 —— 9 —— 10

24. The vital force of thought is producing massive changes within a 50-year span, and will continue to do so.

    1 —— 2 —— 3 —— 4 —— 5 —— 6 —— 7 —— 8 —— 9 —— 10

25. The wonders of nature constantly provide examples of how substance (ether or raw material) is universally present.

    1 —— 2 —— 3 —— 4 —— 5 —— 6 —— 7 —— 8 —— 9 —— 10

26. Substance manifests into form through polarity. To change the form, you change the polarity. This is the principle of causation.

    1 —— 2 —— 3 —— 4 —— 5 —— 6 —— 7 —— 8 —— 9 —— 10

27. It is important that you assimilate your mental food on that which you focus on this week, like you would nourish your body with food.

    1 —— 2 —— 3 —— 4 —— 5 —— 6 —— 7 —— 8 —— 9 —— 10

28. Appearances are deceptive, for many things in nature are not as they would appear.

    1 —— 2 —— 3 —— 4 —— 5 —— 6 —— 7 —— 8 —— 9 —— 10

29. Understand that the world is becoming more aware of the power that thought and action has on their ability to create.

    1 —— 2 —— 3 —— 4 —— 5 —— 6 —— 7 —— 8 —— 9 —— 10

Tally your total score by adding the number you allocated for yourself in each of the 31 principles above. Your score will range from 29 to 290.

If you scored between 203 and 290, you understand the power of your thoughts and how, through action, they manifest material into the world. Your thoughts require food, just like anything that is dynamic in this world requires fuel. You also understand how polarity plays a part in the dynamics of manifesting. Be sure to review the 29 principles in this segment and do the exercise daily.

If you scored between 116 and 202, while you have some understand of the principles of this chapter, you could expand your knowledge. Take some time to review each of the 29 statements, and do the exercise at least once each day, being sure to take the time to contemplate consciously and attentively.

If you scored between 29 and 115, you are struggling with fully integrating the concepts outlined in this chapter into your life. Take time to go through each of the 29 statements, along with the corresponding number in the survey above. Contemplate each of the statements, allowing them to permeate and ruminate within your heart and mind. Then do the exercise at least once each day and allow your body and mind to absorb them into your subconscious.

Introspection:

1. What did you learn about yourself after completing the Comprehension Survey?
2. Was your score what you expected it to be? Why or why not?
3. What areas of the segment of the book have you mastered?
4. What are the areas in this segment of the book that you need to focus on?
5. What three "takeaways" from this segment would you share with others and why?

Exercise

For your exercise this week, concentrate, and when I use the word concentrate, I mean all that the word implies; become so absorbed in the object of your thought that you are conscious of nothing else, and do this a few minutes every day. You take the necessary time to eat in order that the body may be nourished, why not take the time to assimilate your mental food?

NOTES IN RESPONSE TO PERFORMING THIS EXERCISE
Be sure to journal about any findings or experiences you have as you continue to do this exercise as outlined.

Part Twenty

INTRODUCTION

For many years there has been an endless discussion as to the origin of evil. Theologians have told us that God is Love, and that God is Omnipresent. If this be true, there is no place where God is not. Where, then, are Evil, Satan and Hell? Let us see:

God is Spirit.

Spirit is the Creative Principle of the Universe.

Man is made in the image and likeness of God.

Man is therefore a spiritual being.

The only activity which spirit possesses is the power to think.

Thinking is therefore a creative process.

All form is therefore the result of the thinking process.

The destruction of form must also be a result of the thinking process.

Fictitious representations of form are the result of the creative power of thought, as in Hypnotism.

Apparent representations of form are the result of the creative power of thought, as in Spiritualism.

Invention, organization and constructive work of all kinds are the result of the creative power of thought, as in concentration.

When the creative power of thought is manifested for the benefit of humanity, we call the result good.

When the creative power of thought is manifested in a destructive or evil manner, we call the result evil.

This indicates the origin of both good and evil; they are simply words which have been coined in order to indicate the nature of the result of the thinking or creative process.

Thought necessarily precedes and predetermines action; action precedes and predetermines condition.

Part Twenty will throw more light upon this important subject.

---

1. The spirit of a thing is that thing; it is necessarily fixed, changeless and eternal. The spirit of you is—you; without the spirit you would be nothing. It becomes active through your recognition of it and its possibilities.
2. You may have all the wealth in Christendom, but unless you recognize it and make use of it, it will have no value; so with your spiritual wealth: unless you recognize it and use it, it will have no value. The one and only condition of spiritual power is use or recognition.
3. All great things come through recognition; the scepter of power is consciousness, and thought is its messenger, and this messenger is constantly molding the realities of the invisible world into the conditions and environments of your objective world.
4. Thinking is the true business of life, power is the result. You are at all times dealing with the magical power of thought and consciousness. What results can you expect so long as you remain oblivious to the power which has been placed within your control?
5. So long as you do this you limit yourself to superficial conditions, and make of yourself a beast of burden for those who think; those who recognize their power; those who

know that unless we are willing to think we shall have to work, and the less we think the more we shall have to work, and the less we shall get for our work.

6. The secret of power is a perfect understanding of the principles, forces, methods and combinations of Mind, and a perfect understanding of our relationship to the Universal Mind. It is well to remember that this principle is unchangeable; if this were not so, it would not be reliable; all principles are changeless.

7. This stability is your opportunity; you are its active attribute, the channel for its activity; the Universal can act only through the individual.

8. When you begin to perceive that the essence of the Universal is within yourself—is you—you begin to do things; you begin to feel your power; it is the fuel which fires the imagination; which lights the torch of inspiration; which gives vitality to thought; which enables you to connect with all the invisible forces of the Universe. It is this power which will enable you to plan fearlessly, to execute masterfully.

9. But perception will come only in the Silence; this seems to be the condition re quired for all great purposes. You are a visualizing entity. Imagination is your workshop. It is here that your ideal is to be visualized.

10. As a perfect understanding of the nature of this power is a primary condition for its manifestation, visualize the entire method over and over again, so that you may use it whenever occasion requires. The Infinity of wisdom is to follow the method whereby we may have the inspiration of the omnipotent Universal Mind on demand at any time.

11. We can fail to recognize this world within, and so exclude it from our consciousness, but it will still be the basic fact of all existence; and when we learn to recognize it, not only in ourselves, but in all persons, events, things and circum-

stances we shall have found the "Kingdom of heaven" which we are told is "within" us.

12. Our failures are a result of the operation of exactly the same principle; the principle is unchangeable; its operation is exact, there is no deviation; if we think lack, limitation, discord, we shall find their fruits on every hand; if we think poverty, unhappiness or disease, the thought messengers will carry the summons as readily as any other kind of thought and the result will be just as certain. If we fear a coming calamity, we shall be able to say with Job, "the thing I feared has come upon me"; if we think unkindly or ignorantly we shall thus attract to ourselves the results of our ignorance.

13. This power of thought, if understood and correctly used, is the greatest labor-saving device ever dreamed of, but if not understood or improperly used, the result will in all probability be disastrous, as we have already seen; by the help of this power you can confidently undertake things that are seemingly impossible, because this power is the secret of all inspiration, all genius.

14. To become inspired means to get out of the beaten path, out of the rut, because extraordinary results require extraordinary means. When we come into a recognition of the Unity of all things and that the source of all power is within, we tap the source of inspiration.

15. Inspiration is the art of imbibing, the art of self-realization; the art of adjusting the individual mind to that of the Universal Mind; the art of attaching the proper mechanism to the source of all power; the art of differentiating the formless into form; the art of becoming a channel for the flow of Infinite Wisdom; the art of visualizing perfection; the art of realizing the omnipresence of Omnipotence.

16. An understanding and appreciation of the fact that the Infinite power is omnipresent and is therefore in the

infinitely small as well as the infinitely large will enable us to absorb its essence; a further understanding of the fact that this power is spirit and therefore indivisible will enable us to appreciate its presence at all points at the same time.

17. An understanding of these facts, first intellectually and then emotionally, will enable us to drink deeply from this ocean of Infinite power. An intellectual understanding will be of no assistance; the emotions must be brought into action; thought without feeling is cold. The required combination is thought and feeling,

18. Inspiration is from within. The Silence is necessary, the senses must be stilled, the muscles relaxed, repose cultivated. When you have thus come into possession of a sense of poise and power you will be ready to receive the information or inspiration or wisdom which may be necessary for the development of your purpose.

19. Do not confuse these methods with those of the clairvoyant; they have nothing in common. Inspiration is the art of receiving and makes for all that is best in life; your business in life is to understand and command these invisible forces instead of letting them command and rule you. Power implies service; inspiration implies power; to understand and apply the method, of inspiration is to become a superman

20. We can live more abundantly every time we breathe, if we consciously breathe with that intention. The IF is a very important condition in this case, as the intention governs the attention, and without the attention you can secure only the results which every one else secures. That is, a supply equal to the demand:

21. In order to secure the larger supply your demand must be increased, and as you consciously increase the demand the supply will follow, you will find yourself coming into a larger and larger supply of life, energy and vitality.

22. The reason for this is not difficult to understand, but it is another of the vital mysteries of life which does not seem to be generally appreciated. If you make it your own you will find it one of the great realities of life.
23. We are told that "In Him we live and move and have our being," and we are told that "He" is a Spirit, and again that "He" is Love, so that every time we breathe, we breathe this life, love and spirit. This is Pranic Energy, or Pranic Ether; we could not exist a moment with out it. It is the Cosmic Energy; it is the Life of the Solar Plexus.
24. Every time we breathe we fill our lungs with air and at the same time vitalize our body with this Pranic Ether which is Life itself, so that we have the opportunity of making a conscious connection with All Life, All Intelligence and All Substance.
25. A knowledge of your relation and oneness with this Principle that governs the Universe and the simple method whereby you can consciously identify yourself with it gives you a scientific understanding of a law whereby you may free yourself from disease, from lack or limitation of any kind; in fact, it enables you to breathe the "breath of life" into your own nostrils.
26. This "breath of life" is a super-conscious reality. It is the essence of the "I am." It is pure "Being" or Universal Substance and our conscious unity with it enables us to localize it, and thus exercise the powers of this creative energy.
27. Thought is creative vibration and the quality of the conditions created will depend upon the quality of our thought, because we cannot express powers which we do not possess. We must "be" before we can "do" and we can "do" only to the extent to which we "are," and so what we do will necessarily coincide with what we "are" and what we are depends upon what we "think."

28. Every time you think you start a train of causation which will create a condition in strict accordance with the quality of the thought which originated it. Thought which is in harmony with the Universal Mind will result in corresponding conditions. Thought which is destructive or discordant will produce corresponding results. You may use thought constructively or destructively, but the immutable law will not allow you to plant a thought of one kind and reap the fruit of another. You are free to use this marvelous creative power as you will, but you must take the consequences.

29. This is the danger from what is called Will Power. There are those who seem to think that by force of will they can coerce this law; that they can sow seed of one kind and by "Will Power" make it bear fruit of another, but the fundamental principle of creative power is in the Universal, and therefore the idea of forcing a compliance with our wishes by the power of the individual will is an inverted conception, which may appear to succeed for a while but is eventually doomed to failure, because it antagonizes the very power which it is seeking to use.

30. It is the individual attempting to coerce the Universal, the finite in conflict with the Infinite. Our permanent well being will be best conserved by a conscious co-operation with the continuous forward movement of the Great Whole.

31. For your exercise this week, go into the Silence and concentrate on the fact that "In Him we live and move and have our being" is literally and scientifically exact! That you ARE because He IS, that if He is Omnipresent He must be in you. That if He is all in all you must be in Him! That He is Spirit and you are made in "His image and likeness" and that the only difference between His spirit and your spirit is one of degree, that a part must be the same in kind and quality as the whole. When you can realize this clearly you will have

found the secret of the creative power of thought, you will have found the origin of both good and evil, you will have found the secret of the wonderful power of concentration, you will have found the key to the solution of every problem whether physical, financial or environmental.

*The power to think, consecutively and
deeply and clearly, is an avowed and deadly
enemy to mistakes and blunders, superstitions,
unscientific theories, irrational beliefs,
unbridled enthusiasm, fanaticism.*
—HADDOCK.

STUDY GUIDE

Part Twenty

Summary

This Part tells what the true business of life is and the result. It shows that we can obtain no results as long as we remain oblivious to the only power there is, an understanding of the principles, forces, methods and combinations of mind and its relation to the Universal mind. It explains that the Universal can act only through the Individual; it shows that we are the channel for its activity, that it is within us, that we are it. We can, of course, fail to recognize it and so exclude it from our consciousness, but it will nevertheless be the basic fact of all existence. It tells of inspiration, the art of adjusting the individual mind to that of the Universal, the art of becoming a channel for the flow of Infinite Wisdom.

1. If you believe that God or Source is Omnipresent, then where do you suppose evil exists?

2. Being in the likeness of God, you are a spiritual being. What evidence do you have of this fact?

3. Invention, organization and constructive work are all the result of the creative power of thought. What do you believe are some of the most powerful examples that are a result of thought. Explain why.

4. Provide three examples of what the creative power of thought has manifested to benefit humanity. Explain why.

5. Provide three examples of what the creative power of thought has manifested to in a destructive manner. Explain why.

Comprehension Survey

In this segment you will gain a greater understanding of how your thoughts precede and predetermines action, which precedes and predetermines condition. Once you have completed it, you will have even more understanding of The Master Key System and how it functions. For each of the principles below, choose the number that is most closely aligns to your beliefs (1 being "not at all" and 10 being "a great deal").

1. Your spirit is fixed, changeless and eternal. It becomes active through your recognition of it and the potential that it has.

    1 —— 2 —— 3 —— 4 —— 5 —— 6 —— 7 —— 8 —— 9 —— 10

2. Like material wealth, if you don't use and see the value of your spiritual wealth, it will have no value. Recognition is the one and only condition of spiritual power.

   1 —— 2 —— 3 —— 4 —— 5 —— 6 —— 7 —— 8 —— 9 —— 10

3. All greatest comes from recognition. Thought is the messenger of the power of consciousness and constantly molds the invisible world into the objective world around you.

   1 —— 2 —— 3 —— 4 —— 5 —— 6 —— 7 —— 8 —— 9 —— 10

4. Power is the result of your thinking. If you are unaware of it, how can you control results?

   1 —— 2 —— 3 —— 4 —— 5 —— 6 —— 7 —— 8 —— 9 —— 10

5. If you do not use your thought power, then you allow others who do to have power over you, and you merely become a worker as opposed to a creator.

   1 —— 2 —— 3 —— 4 —— 5 —— 6 —— 7 —— 8 —— 9 —— 10

6. The secret to gaining power is your understanding of the principles, forces, methods and combinations of your mind and its relationship to the Universal Mind. Like all principles, this principle is changeless.

   1 —— 2 —— 3 —— 4 —— 5 —— 6 —— 7 —— 8 —— 9 —— 10

7. The stability of this truth is your opportunity to be the individual through which the Universal acts.

   1 —— 2 —— 3 —— 4 —— 5 —— 6 —— 7 —— 8 —— 9 —— 10

8. This is the sequence of masterful and fearless manifestation: You know that Universal essence is within you . . . you feel your power . . . your imagination is fired up . . . that fire lights the torch of inspiration . . . that inspiration energizes thought..then thought connects you with all of the invisible forces of the Universe.

   1 —— 2 —— 3 —— 4 —— 5 —— 6 —— 7 —— 8 —— 9 —— 10

9. Perception, the power that enables you to plan fearlessly and execute masterfully, will only come when you are in the silence.

   1 —— 2 —— 3 —— 4 —— 5 —— 6 —— 7 —— 8 —— 9 —— 10

10. Visualize this method so that you can always make use of it at any time.

    1 —— 2 —— 3 —— 4 —— 5 —— 6 —— 7 —— 8 —— 9 —— 10

11. You will have found "The Kingdom of Heaven" once you recognize that it is in you, and in all persons, things events and circumstances.
1 — 2 — 3 — 4 — 5 — 6 — 7 — 8 — 9 — 10

12. This truth lies in the opposite as well. So if you deviate and focus on lack, limitation, disharmony, fear, unkindness or ignorance, you will attract more of that into your life.
1 — 2 — 3 — 4 — 5 — 6 — 7 — 8 — 9 — 10

13. Correctly understanding the power of your thoughts, is the greatest labor-saving device you will ever experience, as you can achieve the seemingly impossible.
1 — 2 — 3 — 4 — 5 — 6 — 7 — 8 — 9 — 10

14. When you recognize the unity of all things, you leave the ruts behind and tap into extraordinary means.
1 — 2 — 3 — 4 — 5 — 6 — 7 — 8 — 9 — 10

15. When you are inspired you are adjusting your individual mind to that of the Universal Mind. You are practicing the art of shifting the formless into form, channeling the flow of Infinite Wisdom, visualizing perfection and realizing the extraordinary spiritual power of Omnipotence.
1 — 2 — 3 — 4 — 5 — 6 — 7 — 8 — 9 — 10

16. You will always appreciate Infinite power when you realize that it is spiritual power that always exists and is in all things, big and small.
1 — 2 — 3 — 4 — 5 — 6 — 7 — 8 — 9 — 10

17. To bring Infinite power to action, you need both the mental and the emotional understanding of it.
1 — 2 — 3 — 4 — 5 — 6 — 7 — 8 — 9 — 10

18. Inspiration comes from within you, thus you must be relaxed and still to receive it.
1 — 2 — 3 — 4 — 5 — 6 — 7 — 8 — 9 — 10

19. Do not mistaken inspiration for clairvoyance. With inspiration, you command invisible forces. They do not command you.
1 — 2 — 3 — 4 — 5 — 6 — 7 — 8 — 9 — 10

20. You can live more abundantly with every breath you take only if you consciously breathe with that your attention on that intention.
1 — 2 — 3 — 4 — 5 — 6 — 7 — 8 — 9 — 10

21. As you consciously increase your demand, the supply will follow and you will find yourself having more powerful life experiences, and greater energy and vitality.
1 — 2 — 3 — 4 — 5 — 6 — 7 — 8 — 9 — 10

22. While this is not difficult to understand, it is often not appreciated. If you take advantage of it, you will find it one of life's most powerful realities.
1 — 2 — 3 — 4 — 5 — 6 — 7 — 8 — 9 — 10

23. Cosmic or Pranic Energy is the lifeforce that sustains us. It is the life of your Solar Plexus.
1 — 2 — 3 — 4 — 5 — 6 — 7 — 8 — 9 — 10

24. You have an opportunity to connect with All Life, All Intelligence and All Substance with every breath that you take.
1 — 2 — 3 — 4 — 5 — 6 — 7 — 8 — 9 — 10

25. Knowing that you are a part of oneness, gives you the scientific understanding of a law whereby you can free yourself from limitations of any kind.
1 — 2 — 3 — 4 — 5 — 6 — 7 — 8 — 9 — 10

26. Your conscious unity with the "breath of life" enables you to awaken the powers of its creative energy.
1 — 2 — 3 — 4 — 5 — 6 — 7 — 8 — 9 — 10

27. What you think affects who you are Who you are affects what you can do.
1 — 2 — 3 — 4 — 5 — 6 — 7 — 8 — 9 — 10

28. This unchangeable law only allows you to reap what you sew. That which you experience is in direct accordance with your thoughts.
1 — 2 — 3 — 4 — 5 — 6 — 7 — 8 — 9 — 10

29. You cannot force a different outcome through will power. It will fail as it upsets the very power that it is trying to use.
1 — 2 — 3 — 4 — 5 — 6 — 7 — 8 — 9 — 10

30. In such a case you, as the finite are in conflict with the Infinite, thus you cannot win.
1 — 2 — 3 — 4 — 5 — 6 — 7 — 8 — 9 — 10

31. You are a part of the Omnipresence, and if it exists in you, then you exist in it.

1 —— 2 —— 3 —— 4 —— 5 —— 6 —— 7 —— 8 —— 9 —— 10

Tally your total score by adding the number you allocated for yourself in each of the 31 principles above. Your score will range from 31 to 310.

If you scored between 219 and 310, you are really integrating the teachings of this book into your life. You are aware of the fact that little labor is required in your life as you attract that which you desire when you align yourself with Universal, Omnipotent Mind. Take time each day to do this exercise, focusing on the reality that you and Source energy are one.

If you scored between 125 and 218, you are doing a good joy of learning the lessons of this book. Review the 31 lessons in this chapter again, really allowing them to become a part of you. When you think of it, remember that you can manifest with every breath you take, knowing that each breath is evidence of the Infinite power of source at work within you. Be sure to do this exercise each day, focusing on the fact that you and source are one.

If you scored between 31 and 124, you have come a long way in your learning, and there is still room for integrating the wisdom of this book into your subconscious. If you haven't already done so, allow yourself to become passionate about learning and apply the Master Key System, knowing that your life will flow with greater joy and ease as you do. Be sure to do the exercise that ends this chapter, fully allowing yourself to feel into the realization that you and Source are one.

Introspection:

1. What did you learn about yourself after completing the Comprehension Survey?
2. Was your score what you expected it to be? Why or why not?
3. What areas of the segment of the book have you mastered?
4. What are the areas in this segment of the book that you need to focus on?
5. What three "takeaways" from this segment would you share with others and why?

Exercise

For your exercise this week, go into the Silence and concentrate on the fact that "In Him we live and move and have our being" is literally and scientifically exact! That you ARE because He IS, that if He is Omnipresent He must be in you. That if He is all in all you must be in Him! That He is Spirit and you are made in "His image and likeness" and that the only difference between His spirit and your spirit is one of degree, that a part must be the same in kind and quality as the whole. When you can realize this clearly you will have found the secret of the creative power of thought, you will have found the origin of both good and evil, you will have found the secret of the wonderful power of concentration, you will have found the key to the solution of every problem whether physical, financial or environmental.

NOTES IN RESPONSE TO PERFORMING THIS EXERCISE
Be sure to journal about any findings or experiences you have as you continue to do this exercise as outlined.

Part Twenty-One

INTRODUCTION

In paragraph seven of this Part you will find that one of the secrets of success, one of the methods of organizing victory, one of the accomplishments of the Master Mind is to think big thoughts.

In paragraph eight you will find that everything which we hold in our consciousness for any length of time becomes impressed upon our subconsciousness and so becomes a pattern which the creative energy will weave into our life and environment. This is the secret of the wonderful power of prayer.

We know that the universe is governed by law; that for every effect there must be a cause, and that the same cause, under the same conditions, will invariably produce the same effect. Consequently, if prayer has ever been answered, it will always be answered, if the proper conditions are complied with. This must necessarily be true; otherwise the Universe would be a chaos instead of a cosmos. The answer to prayer is therefore subject to law, and this law is definite, exact and scientific, just as are the laws governing gravitation and electricity. An understanding of this law takes the foundation of Christianity out of the realm of superstition and credulity and places it upon the firm rock of scientific understanding.

But, unfortunately, there are comparatively few persons who know how to pray. They understand that there are laws governing electricity, mathematics and chemistry, but, for some inexplicable reason, it never seems to occur to them that there are also spiritual laws, and that these laws are also definite, scientific, exact, and operate with immutable precision.

---

1. The real secret of power is consciousness of power. The Universal Mind is unconditional; therefore, the more conscious we become of our unity with this mind, the less conscious we shall become of conditions and limitations, and as we become emancipated or freed from conditions we come into a realization of the unconditional. We have become free!
2. As soon as we become conscious of the inexhaustible power in the world within, we begin to draw on this power and apply and develop the greater possibilities which this discernment has realized, because whatever we become conscious of, is invariably manifested in the objective world, is brought forth into tangible expression.
3. This is because the Infinite mind, which is the source from which all things proceed, is one and indivisible, and each individual is a channel whereby this Eternal Energy is being manifested. Our ability to think is our ability to act upon this Universal substance, and what we think is what is created or produced in the objective world.
4. The result of this discovery is nothing less than marvelous, and means that mind is extraordinary in quality, limitless in quantity and contains possibilities without number. To become conscious of this power is to become a "live wire"; it has the same effect as placing an ordinary wire in contact with a wire that is charged. The Universal is the live wire. It carries power sufficient to meet every situation which may arise in the life of every individual. When the individual

mind touches the Universal Mind it receives all the power it requires. This is the world within. All science recognizes the reality of this world, and all power is contingent upon our recognition of this world.

5. The ability to eliminate imperfect conditions depends upon mental action, and mental action depends upon consciousness of power; therefore, the more conscious we become of our unity with the source of all power, the greater will be our power to control and master every condition.

6. Large ideas have a tendency to eliminate all smaller ideas so that it is well to hold ideas large enough to counteract and destroy all small or undesirable tendencies. This will remove innumerable petty and annoying obstacles from your path. You also become conscious of a larger world of thought, thereby increasing your mental capacity as well as placing yourself in position to accomplish something of value.

7. This is one of the secrets of success, one of the methods of organizing victory, one of the accomplishments of the Master-mind. He thinks big thoughts. The creative energies of mind find no more difficulty in handling large situations, than small ones. Mind is just as much present in the Infinitely large as in the Infinitely small.

8. When we realize these facts concerning mind we understand how we may bring to ourselves any condition by creating the corresponding conditions in our consciousness, because everything which is held for any length of time in the consciousness, eventually becomes impressed upon the subconscious and thus becomes a pattern which the creative energy will weave into the life and environment of the individual.

9. In this way conditions are produced and we find that our lives are simply the reflection of our predominant thoughts, our mental attitude; we see then that the science

of correct thinking is the one science, that it includes all other sciences.

10. From this science we learn that every thought creates an impression on the brain, that these impressions create mental tendencies, and these tendencies create character, ability and purpose, and that the combined action of character, ability and purpose determines the experiences with which we shall meet in life.
11. These experiences come to us through the law of attraction; through the action of this law we meet in the world without the experiences which correspond to our world within.
12. The predominant thought or the mental attitude is the magnet, and the law is that like attracts like, consequently the mental attitude will invariably attract such conditions as correspond to its nature.
13. This mental attitude is our personality and is composed of the thoughts which we have been creating in our own mind; therefore, if we wish a change in conditions all that is necessary is to change our thought; this will in turn change our mental attitude, which will in turn change our personality, which will in turn change the persons, things and conditions, or, the experiences with which we meet in life.
14. It is, however, no easy matter to change the mental attitude, but by persistent effort it may be accomplished; the mental attitude is patterned after the mental pictures which have been photographed on the brain; if you do not like the pictures, destroy the negatives and create new pictures; this is the art of visualization.
15. As soon as you have done this you will begin to attract new things, and the new things will correspond to the new pictures. To do this: impress on the mind a perfect picture of the desire which you wish to have objectified and continue to hold the picture in mind until results are obtained.

16. If the desire is one which requires determination, ability, talent, courage, power or any other spiritual power, these are necessary essentials for your picture; build them in; they are the vital part of the picture; they are the feeling which combines with thought and creates the irresistible magnetic power which draws the things you require to you. They give your picture life, and life means growth, and as soon as it begins to grow, the result is practically assured.

17. Do not hesitate to aspire to the highest possible attainments in anything you may undertake, for the mind forces are ever ready to lend themselves to a purposeful will in the effort to crystallize its highest aspirations into acts, accomplishments and events.

18. An illustration of how these mind forces operate is suggested by the method in which all our habits are formed. We do a thing, then do it again; and again, and again, until it becomes easy and perhaps almost automatic; and the same rule applies in breaking any and all bad habits; we stop doing a thing, and then avoid it again, and again until we are entirely free from it; and if we do fail now and then, we should by no means lose hope, for the law is absolute and invincible and gives us credit for every effort and every success, even though our efforts and successes are perhaps intermittent.

19. There is no limit to what this law can do for you; dare to believe in your own ideal; remember that Nature is plastic to the ideal; think of the ideal as an already accomplished fact.

20. The real battle of life is one of ideas; it is being fought out by the few against the many; on the one side is the constructive and creative thought, on the other side the destructive and negative thought; the creative thought is dominated by an ideal, the passive thought is dominated by appearances. On both sides are men of science, men of letters and men of affairs.

21. On the creative side are men who spend their time in laboratories, or over microscopes and telescopes, side by side with the men who dominate the commercial, political and scientific world; on the negative side are men who spend their time investigating law and precedent, men who mistake theology for religion, statesmen who mistake might for right, and all the millions who seem to prefer precedent to progress, who are eternally looking backward instead of forward, who see only the world without, but know nothing of the world within.

22. In the last analysis there are but these two classes; all men will have to take their place on one side or the other; they will have to go forward, or go back; there is no standing still in a world where all is motion; it is this attempt to stand still that gives sanction and force to arbitrary and unequal codes of law.

23. That we are in a period of transition is evidenced by the unrest which is everywhere apparent. The complaint of humanity is as a roll of heaven's artillery, commencing with low and threatening notes and increasing until the sound is sent from cloud to cloud, and the lightning rends the air and earth.

24. The sentries who patrol the most advanced outposts of the Industrial, Political and Religious world are calling anxiously to each other. What of the night? The danger and insecurity of the position they occupy and attempt to hold is becoming more apparent every hour. The dawn of a new era necessarily declares that the existing order of things cannot much longer be.

25. The issue between the old regime and the new, the crux of the social problem, is entirely a question of conviction in the minds of the people as to the nature of the Universe. When they realize that the transcendent force of spirit or mind of the Cosmos is within each individual, it will be

possible to frame laws that shall consider the liberties and rights of the many instead of the privileges of the few.

26. As long as the people regard the Cosmic power as a power non-human and alien to humanity, so long will it be comparatively easy for a supposed privileged class to rule by Divine right in spite of every protest of social sentiment. The real interest of democracy is therefore to exalt, emancipate and recognize the divinity of the human spirit. To recognize that all power is from within. That no human being has any more power than any other human being, except such as may willingly be delegated to him. The old regime would have us believe that the law was superior to the law-makers; herein is the gist of the social crime of every form of privilege and personal inequality, the institutionalizing of the fatalistic doctrine of Divine election.

27. The Divine Mind is the Universal Mind; it makes no exceptions, it plays no favorites; it does not act through sheer caprice or from anger, jealousy or wrath; neither can it be flattered, cajoled or moved by sympathy or petition to supply man with some need which he thinks necessary for his happiness or even his existence. The Divine Mind makes no exceptions in favor of any individual; but when the individual understands and realizes his Unity with the Universal Principle he will appear to be favored because he will have found the source of all health, all wealth and all power.

28. For your exercise this week, concentrate on the Truth. Try to realize that the Truth shall make you free, that is, nothing can permanently stand in the way of your perfect success when you learn to apply the scientifically correct thought methods and principles. Realize that you are externalizing in your environment, your inherent soul potencies. Realize that the Silence offers an ever available and almost unlimited opportunity for awakening the highest concep-

tion of Truth. Try to comprehend that Omnipotence itself is absolute silence, all else is change, activity, limitation. Silent thought concentration is therefore the true method of reaching, awakening and then expressing the wonderful potential power of the world within.

*The possibilities of thought training are infinite,
its consequence eternal, and yet few take the pains
to direct their thinking into channels that will
do them good, but instead leave all to chance.*
—MARDEN.

STUDY GUIDE

Part Twenty-One

Summary

This Part explains how we may come into possession of power sufficient to meet every situation which may arise in life. It explains that the ability to eliminate imperfect conditions depends upon mental action. It explains that great ideas have a tendency to eliminate smaller ideas, so that it is well to hold ideas which are large enough to counteract and destroy all small or undesirable tendencies. This is one of the secrets of success, one of the accomplishments of the Master Mind. It explains that the creative energy finds no more difficulty in handling a large situation than a small one. It explains how conditions are produced in our lives by the predominant thoughts which we entertain. It explains how you may set causes in motion which will create an irresistible magnetic power which will bring the things you require to you. It explains the issue between the old regime and the new, it explains the crux of the social problem, it explains the true secret of health, wealth and power.

1. What do you consider big thoughts? Provide an example.
2. Do you consider yourself someone who is able to think big thoughts? Why or why not?
3. Do you believe in the power of prayer? Do you pray? Why or why not?
4. Do you believe all prayers are answered? Why or why not?
5. How do you account for situations in which it appears that one's prayers are not answered?
6. Do you believe prayer to be an exact science? Please explain.
7. What do you believe to be the right way to pray?

Comprehension Survey

In this segment you will better understand the power of thinking big. Once you have completed it, you will have a better understanding of significance and power of prayer. For each of the principles below, choose the number that is most closely aligns to your beliefs (1 being "not at all" and 10 being "a great deal").

1. Because the Universal Mind is unconditional, the more conscious you become of it, the less you will be encumbered by conditions and limitations. You will be free!

   1 —— 2 —— 3 —— 4 —— 5 —— 6 —— 7 —— 8 —— 9 —— 10

2. As you become fully conscious of the inexhaustible world within you, you will bring forth into the world that which you desire to manifest.

   1 —— 2 —— 3 —— 4 —— 5 —— 6 —— 7 —— 8 —— 9 —— 10

3. The Infinite Mind is one and indivisible, so it is in all things, including you. Your ability to see this and meet with it will bring your thoughts into the objective world.

   1 —— 2 —— 3 —— 4 —— 5 —— 6 —— 7 —— 8 —— 9 —— 10

4. You become a "live wire" when you are fully conscious of the limitless power of your mind when it connects to the limitless "power" of the Universal Mind.

   1 —— 2 —— 3 —— 4 —— 5 —— 6 —— 7 —— 8 —— 9 —— 10

5. The more conscious you are of your unity with Source, the greater your ability to eliminate imperfect conditions.

   1 —— 2 —— 3 —— 4 —— 5 —— 6 —— 7 —— 8 —— 9 —— 10

6. When you focus on large ideas, they eliminate smaller undesirable tendencies. They also place you in a position to experience things of greater value.

   1 —— 2 —— 3 —— 4 —— 5 —— 6 —— 7 —— 8 —— 9 —— 10

7. One of the secrets of success is that focusing on bigger thoughts takes no more energy than focusing smaller ones.

   1 —— 2 —— 3 —— 4 —— 5 —— 6 —— 7 —— 8 —— 9 —— 10

8. Anything you hold in your consciousness for any length of time, is impressed upon your subconsciousness and becomes a pattern which creative energy will bring into your life.

   1 —— 2 —— 3 —— 4 —— 5 —— 6 —— 7 —— 8 —— 9 —— 10

9. The science of your corrective thinking includes all of the other sciences.

   1 —— 2 —— 3 —— 4 —— 5 —— 6 —— 7 —— 8 —— 9 —— 10

10. Each of your thoughts creates an impression on your brain that create mental tendencies which build your experiences from the combined action of character, ability and purpose.
    1 — 2 — 3 — 4 — 5 — 6 — 7 — 8 — 9 — 10

11. These experiences come to you through the law of attraction as the outer world meets with your inner world.
    1 — 2 — 3 — 4 — 5 — 6 — 7 — 8 — 9 — 10

12. Your mental attitude is the magnet that attracts worldly conditions that correspond with its nature.
    1 — 2 — 3 — 4 — 5 — 6 — 7 — 8 — 9 — 10

13. Your personality is your mental attitude. Changing your thought will change your mental attitude, which will change your personality and in turn the persons, things, conditions or experiences that you will meet in your life,
    1 — 2 — 3 — 4 — 5 — 6 — 7 — 8 — 9 — 10

14. You can change your personality by destroying the negatives of the mental pictures you have created in your brain. This is the art of visualization.
    1 — 2 — 3 — 4 — 5 — 6 — 7 — 8 — 9 — 10

15. Once you have mastered visualization, hold the perfect picture of what you desire in your mind until you experience the desired results.
    1 — 2 — 3 — 4 — 5 — 6 — 7 — 8 — 9 — 10

16. If your desire requires determination, ability, talent, courage, power or any other spiritual power, then build those traits within you. For they are the feelings which, combined with thought creates the irresistible magnetic power to draw what you desire to you.
    1 — 2 — 3 — 4 — 5 — 6 — 7 — 8 — 9 — 10

17. Never hesitate to aspire to big things, for your mind is always ready and willing to lend themselves to higher purpose.
    1 — 2 — 3 — 4 — 5 — 6 — 7 — 8 — 9 — 10

18. When you form or break a habit, you may fail from time to time, but because the law of absolute, you will be energetically credited for every effort you make.
    1 — 2 — 3 — 4 — 5 — 6 — 7 — 8 — 9 — 10

19. Think of your ideal as already having been accomplished, for there is no limit to what the law can do for you.
1 —— 2 —— 3 —— 4 —— 5 —— 6 —— 7 —— 8 —— 9 —— 10

20. Focus your energy on your ideals. Constructive, creative thoughts are dominated by an ideal, and destructive, negative thoughts are passive and are dominated by appearances.
1 —— 2 —— 3 —— 4 —— 5 —— 6 —— 7 —— 8 —— 9 —— 10

21. Those on the creative side, are curious, investigating and evolving. Those on the negative side prefer existing patterns over progress and only see with their eyes, failing to see the potentiality that comes from inner vision.
1 —— 2 —— 3 —— 4 —— 5 —— 6 —— 7 —— 8 —— 9 —— 10

22. You only have two choices in a world where all is motion. Either you move forward and progress, or fall backwards.
1 —— 2 —— 3 —— 4 —— 5 —— 6 —— 7 —— 8 —— 9 —— 10

23. The unrest in this transition period starts with a murmur, and ends in the crashing sound of lighting.
1 —— 2 —— 3 —— 4 —— 5 —— 6 —— 7 —— 8 —— 9 —— 10

24. The dawn of this new era declares that the existing order of things can no longer be. Leaders of what was are calling anxiously upon one another.
1 —— 2 —— 3 —— 4 —— 5 —— 6 —— 7 —— 8 —— 9 —— 10

25. Once it is realized on a larger scale the relationship between the minds of mankind and the Universe, the laws shall consider the rights of many over the privileges of the few.
1 —— 2 —— 3 —— 4 —— 5 —— 6 —— 7 —— 8 —— 9 —— 10

26. The real interest of democracy is to lift up, free and recognize the divinity of the human spirit, knowing that all power is from within.
1 —— 2 —— 3 —— 4 —— 5 —— 6 —— 7 —— 8 —— 9 —— 10

27. When you understand your unity with Universal Principle, while not favored, you will appear to be because you have found source of all health, wealth and power.
1 —— 2 —— 3 —— 4 —— 5 —— 6 —— 7 —— 8 —— 9 —— 10

28. Know that you are externalizing your soul potencies on your environment. Silent thought concentration is the key to expressing the power of your potent inner world.

1 —— 2 —— 3 —— 4 —— 5 —— 6 —— 7 —— 8 —— 9 —— 1 0

Tally your total score by adding the number you allocated for yourself in each of the 28 principles above. Your score will range from 28 to 280.

If you scored between 197 and 280, you are freeing yourself of the limitations you previously placed upon yourself through continued study, concentration and commitment. Know that you are progressing as you complete every chapter of this book. Rest assured that the world is changing and that you are on the leading edge of True empowerment. Concentrate the Truth during the exercise this week and watch it continue to reveal itself to you.

If you scored between 112and 196, you are doing a wonderful job of progressing in your knowledge and application of these lessons. In this segment, you are encouraged to think big and to rest assured that great strides towards true power are being made in the world. Be sure to focus on your inner world, as you do the exercise daily. Concentrate on the truth, and as they say, it will set you free!

If you scored between 28 and 111, you are struggling somewhat with the tenets of this chapter. Know that your efforts have a profound effect on the outcome, for you are exerting energy from a positive place towards a deeper understanding. Be sure to review the 28 principles in this chapter and spend silent time each day, focusing on your inner world and connecting the benevolent Universal Source Mind.

Introspection:

1. What did you learn about yourself after completing the Comprehension Survey?
2. Was your score what you expected it to be? Why or why not?
3. What areas of the segment of the book have you mastered?
4. What are the areas in this segment of the book that you need to focus on?
5. What three "takeaways" from this segment would you share with others and why?

Exercise

For your exercise this week, concentrate on the Truth. Try to realize that the Truth shall make you free, that is, nothing can permanently stand in the way of your perfect success when you learn to apply the scientifically correct thought methods and principles. Realize that you are externalizing in your environment, your inherent soul potencies. Realize that the Silence offers an ever available and almost unlimited opportunity for awakening the highest conception of Truth. Try to comprehend that Omnipotence itself is absolute silence, all else is change, activity, limitation. Silent thought concentration is therefore the true method of reaching, awakening and then expressing the wonderful potential power of the world within.

NOTES IN RESPONSE TO PERFORMING THIS EXERCISE
Be sure to journal about any findings or experiences you have as you continue to do this exercise as outlined.

Part Twenty-Two

INTRODUCTION

In Part Twenty-Two you will find that thoughts are spiritual seeds, which, when planted in the subconscious mind, have a tendency to sprout and grow, but unfortunately the fruit is frequently not to our liking.

The various forms of inflammation, paralysis, nervousness and diseased conditions generally, are the manifestation of fear, worry, care, anxiety, jealousy, hatred and similar thought.

The life processes are carried on by two distinct methods; firstly, the taking up and making use of nutritive material necessary for constructing cells; secondly, the secretion and excretion of the waste material.

All life is based upon these constructive and destructive activities, and as food, water and air are the only requisites necessary for the construction of cells, it would seem that the problem of prolonging life indefinitely would not be a very difficult one.

However strange it may seem, it is the second or destructive activity that is, with rare exception, the cause of all disease. The waste material accumulates and saturates the tissues, which causes auto-intoxication. This may be partial or general. In the first case the disturbance will be local; in the second place it will affect the whole system.

The problem, then, before us in the healing of disease is to increase the inflow and distribution of vital energy throughout the system, and this can only be done by eliminating thoughts of fear, worry, care, anxiety, jealousy, hatred, and every other destructive thought, which tend to tear down and destroy the nerves and glands which control the excretion and elimination of poisonous and waste matter.

"Nourishing foods and strengthening tonics" cannot bestow life, because these are but secondary manifestations of life. The primary manifestation of life and how you may get in touch with it is explained in Part Twenty-Two.

---

1. Knowledge is of priceless value, because by applying knowledge we can make our future what we wish it to be. When we realize that our present character, our present environment, our present ability, our present physical condition are all the result of past methods of thinking, we shall begin to have some conception of the value of knowledge.
2. If the state of our health is not all that could be desired, let us examine our method of thinking; let us remember that every thought produces an impression on the mind; every impression is a seed which will sink into the subconscious and form a tendency; the tendency will be to attract other similar thoughts and before we know it we shall have a crop which must be harvested.
3. If these thoughts contain disease germs, the harvest will be sickness, decay, weakness and failure; the question is, what are we thinking, what are we creating, what is the harvest to be?
4. If there is any physical condition which it is necessary to change, the law governing visualization will be found effec-

tive. Make a mental image of physical perfection, hold it in the mind until it is absorbed by the consciousness. Many have eliminated chronic ailments in a few weeks by this method, and thousands have overcome and destroyed all manner of ordinary physical disturbances by this method in a few days, sometimes in a few minutes.

5. It is through the law of vibration that the mind exercises this control over the body. We know that every mental action is a vibration, and we know that all form is simply a mode of motion, a rate of vibration. Therefore, any given vibration immediately modifies every atom in the body, very life cell is affected and an entire chemical change is made in every group of life cells.

6. Everything in the Universe is what it is by virtue of its rate of vibration. Change the rate of vibration and you change the nature, quality and form. The vast panorama of nature, both visible and invisible, is being constantly changed by simply changing the rate of vibration; and as thought is a vibration we can also exercise this power. We can change the vibration and thus produce any condition which we desire to manifest in our bodies.

7. We are all using this power every minute. The trouble is most of us are using it unconsciously and thus producing undesirable results. The problem is to use it intelligently and produce only desirable results. This should not be difficult, because we all have had sufficient experience to know what produces pleasant vibration in the body, and we also know the causes which produce the unpleasant and disagreeable sensations.

8. All that is necessary is to consult our own experience. When our thought has been uplifted, progressive, constructive, courageous, noble, kind or in any other way desirable, we have set in motion vibrations which brought about certain results. When our thought has been filled

with envy, hatred, jealousy, criticism or any of the other thousand and one forms of discord, certain vibrations were set in motion which brought about certain other results of a different nature, and each of these rates of vibration, if kept up, crystallized in form. In the first case the result was mental, moral and physical health, and in the second case discord, inharmony and disease.

9. We can understand, then, something of the power which the mind possesses over the body.

10. The objective mind has certain effects on the body which are readily recognized. Some one says something to you which strikes you as ludicrous and you laugh, possibly until your whole body shakes, which shows that thought has control over the muscles of your body; or some one says something which excites your sympathy and your eyes fill with tears, which shows that thought controls the glands of your body; or some one says something which makes you angry and the blood mounts to your cheek, which shows that thought controls the circulation of your blood. But as these experiences are all the results of the action of your objective mind over the body, the results are of a temporary nature; they soon pass away and leave the situation as it was before.

11. Let us see how the action of the subconscious mind over the body differs. You receive a wound; thousands of cells begin the work of healing at once; in a few days or a few weeks the work is complete. You may even break a bone. No surgeon on earth can weld the parts together. He may set the bone for you, and the subjective mind will immediately begin the process of welding the parts together, and in a short time the bone is as solid as it ever was. You may swallow poison; the subjective mind will immediately discover the danger and make violent efforts to eliminate it. You may become infected with a dangerous germ; the subjective will

at once commence to build a wall around the infected area and destroy the infection by absorbing it in the white blood corpuscles which it supplies for the purpose.

12. These processes of the subconscious mind usually proceed without our personal knowledge or direction, and so long as we do not interfere the result is perfect, but, as these millions of repair cells are all intelligent and respond to our thought, they are often paralyzed and rendered impotent by our thoughts of fear, doubt and anxiety. They are like an army of workmen, ready to start an important piece of work, but every time they get fairly started on the undertaking a strike is called, or plans changed, until they finally get discouraged and give up.

13. The way to health is founded on the law of vibration, which is the basis of all science, and this law is brought into operation by the mind, the "world within." It is a matter of individual effort and practice. Our world of power is within; if we are wise we shall not waste time and effort in trying to deal with effects as we find them in the "world without," which is only an external, a reflection.

14. We shall always find the cause in the "world within"; by changing the cause, we change the effect.

15. Every cell in your body is intelligent and will respond to your direction. The cells are all creators and will create the exact pattern which you give them.

16. Therefore, when perfect images are placed before the subjective, the creative energies will build a perfect body.

17. Brain cells are constructed in the same way. The quality of the brain is governed by the state of mind, or mental attitude, so that if undesirable mental attitudes are conveyed to the subjective they will in turn be transferred to the body; we can therefore readily see that if we wish the body to manifest health, strength and vitality this must be the predominant thought.

18. We know then that every element of the human body is the result of a rate of vibration.
19. We know that mental action is a rate of vibration.
20. We know that a higher rate of vibration governs, modifies, controls, changes or destroys a lower rate of vibration.
21. We know that the rate of vibration is governed by the character of brain cells, and finally,
22. We know how to create these brain cells; therefore,
23. We know how to make any physical change in the body we desire, and having secured a working knowledge of the power of mind to this extent, we have come to know that there is practically no limitation which can be placed upon our ability to place ourselves in harmony with natural law, which is omnipotent.
24. This influence or control over the body by the mind is coming to be more and more generally understood, and many physicians are now giving the matter their earnest attention. Dr. Albert T. Shofield, who has written several important books on the subject, says: "The subject of mental therapeutics is still ignored in medical works generally. In our physiologies no reference is made to the central controlling power that rules the body for its good, and the power of the mind over the body is seldom spoken of.
25. No doubt many physicians treat nervous diseases of functional origin wisely and well, but what we contend is that the knowledge they display was taught at no school, was learned from no book, but it is intuitive and empirical.
26. This is not as it should be. The power of mental therapeutics should be the subject of careful, special and scientific teaching in every medical school. We might pursue the subject of maltreatment, or want of treatment, further in detail and describe the disastrous results of neglected cases; but the task is an invidious one.

27. There can be no doubt that few patients are aware how much they can do for themselves. What the patient can do for himself, the forces he can set in motion are as yet unknown. We are inclined to believe that they are far greater than most imagine, and will undoubtedly be used more and more. Mental therapeutics may be directed by the patient himself to calming the mind in excitement, by arousing feelings of joy, hope, faith and love; by suggesting motives for exertion, by regular mental work, by diverting the thoughts from the malady.

28. For your exercise this week concentrate on Tennyson's beautiful lines. "Speak to Him, thou, for He hears, and spirit with spirit can meet, Closer is He than breathing, and nearer than hands and feet." Then try to realize that when you do "Speak to Him" you are in touch with Omnipotence.

29. This realization and recognition of this Omnipresent power will quickly destroy any and every form of sickness or suffering and substitute harmony and perfection. Then remember there are those who seem to think that sickness and suffering are sent by God; if so, every physician, every surgeon and every Red Cross nurse is defying the will of God and hospitals and sanitariums are places of rebellion instead of houses of mercy. Of course, this quickly reasons itself into an absurdity, but there are many who still cherish the idea.

30. Then let the thought rest on the fact that until recently theology has been trying to teach an impossible Creator, one who created beings capable of sinning and then allowed them to be eternally punished for such sins. Of course the necessary outcome of such extraordinary ignorance was to create fear instead of love, and so, after two thousand years of this kind of propaganda, Theology is now busily engaged in apologizing for Christendom.

31. You will then the more readily appreciate the ideal man, the man made in the image and likeness of God, and you will the more readily appreciate the all originating Mind that forms, upholds, sustains, originates and creates all there is.

"All are but parts of one stupendous whole,
Whose body nature is, and God the soul."
—ALEXANDER POPE.

Opportunity follows perception, action follows inspiration, growth follows knowledge, eminence follows progress. Always the spiritual first, then the transformation into the infinite and illimitable possibilities of achievement.
—CHARLES F. HAANEL

STUDY GUIDE

Part Twenty-Two

Summary

This Part explains the cause of our present character, our present environment, our present ability, our present physical condition, and tells how we can make our future what we wish it to be. It explains how the vast panorama of Nature is being constantly changed by simply changing the rate of vibration. It tells how the rate of vibration is being constantly changed in our bodies, usually unconsciously and often with detrimental and disastrous results. It tells how we may effect this change consciously and thus bring about only harmonious and salutary conditions. It explains that the Law of Health is based on the law of vibration, and that with a proper knowledge of the law we may externalize health conditions. It explains the operation of this law and how it is being more generally understood and appreciated, and how many physicians are now giving the matter their earnest attention.

1. Charles Haanel opens this chapter stating that the fruits of your thoughts are frequently not to your liking. Provide examples of this from your life. What were your desires and what were the disappointing outcomes?

2. Various physical ailments or outward manifestations of your inner states of discord. What physical challenges are your facing? Can you connect them with any emotional disharmony you are experiencing? Please explain.

3. Life processes are based on two activities: consumption of nutrients in food, water and air, and the secretion and excretion of waste material. Proper processing of nutrients support the construction of cells, and improper destruction of waste material causes imbalance, disturbance and disease. Do you believe this theory to be true? Why or why not?

4. Have you seen evidence of this theory in your life, or in the lives of your loved ones? Please explain.

5. Healing requires the elimination of any thoughts of fear, worry, care, anxiety, jealousy, hatred, and every other destructive thought. Write a list of any destructive thoughts that you believe yourself to be harboring. Be honest, knowing that you cannot fool yourself.

Comprehension Survey

In this segment you will learn about the primary manifestation of life and how you can tap into it. Once you have completed it, you will have a better understanding of how creating emotional harmony in your life vastly affects your physical wellbeing. For each of the principles below, choose the number that is most closely aligns to your beliefs (1 being "not at all" and 10 being "a great deal").

1. Knowledge is priceless once you realize that your present experience is a result of your past methods of thinking.
   1 — 2 — 3 — 4 — 5 — 6 — 7 — 8 — 9 — 10

2. If you have physical challenges, examine your method of thinking. Every thought you have had has created a crop that must be harvested. In other words, your thoughts created energy, and that energy needs to respond.
   1 — 2 — 3 — 4 — 5 — 6 — 7 — 8 — 9 — 10

3. Are your thoughts creating disease germs? If so your harvest will be sickness.
   1 — 2 — 3 — 4 — 5 — 6 — 7 — 8 — 9 — 10

4. If you need to make physical changes, make a mental image of perfection in your mind until it is absorbed by the consciousness. This can take little time to accomplish.
   1 — 2 — 3 — 4 — 5 — 6 — 7 — 8 — 9 — 10

5. Your mind exercises its control over your body through the law of vibration. Any given vibration immediately modifies every life cell in the body.
   1 — 2 — 3 — 4 — 5 — 6 — 7 — 8 — 9 — 10

6. Thought is a vibration, thus with thought you can change the condition of your body.
   1 — 2 — 3 — 4 — 5 — 6 — 7 — 8 — 9 — 10

7. You are constantly using this power, whether consciously or unconsciously.
   Follow that which produces pleasant vibrations in the body, and know that it has an effect on your wellbeing.
   1 — 2 — 3 — 4 — 5 — 6 — 7 — 8 — 9 — 10

8. When your thoughts have been lifted, you have set in motion vibration which bring about results. When your thoughts are negative, they bring results of disharmony and disease.

   1 — 2 — 3 — 4 — 5 — 6 — 7 — 8 — 9 — 1 0

9. This makes clear the power that the mind possesses over your body.

   1 — 2 — 3 — 4 — 5 — 6 — 7 — 8 — 9 — 1 0

10. The results of your thoughts on your emotions is evident in your body. They are, however, results of your objective mind and temporary in nature.

    1 — 2 — 3 — 4 — 5 — 6 — 7 — 8 — 9 — 1 0

11. When your body is injured, your subconscious mind systematically and automatically heals.

    1 — 2 — 3 — 4 — 5 — 6 — 7 — 8 — 9 — 1 0

12. The subconscious mind heals our bodies perfectly and naturally, just as long as we don't interfere with our fearful, doubtful or anxious thoughts.

    1 — 2 — 3 — 4 — 5 — 6 — 7 — 8 — 9 — 1 0

13. If you are wise, you will focus on the world within and not waste time on the world without (which is only an external reflection).

    1 — 2 — 3 — 4 — 5 — 6 — 7 — 8 — 9 — 1 0

14. You will always find the "cause" from your inner world, and once you find it, you can change the effect.

    1 — 2 — 3 — 4 — 5 — 6 — 7 — 8 — 9 — 1 0

15. Every cell in your body is intelligent and responds to the exact patterns you give them.

    1 — 2 — 3 — 4 — 5 — 6 — 7 — 8 — 9 — 1 0

16. When you place perfect images before the subjective, the creative energies will build a perfect body.

    1 — 2 — 3 — 4 — 5 — 6 — 7 — 8 — 9 — 1 0

17. If you wish to manifest health, strength and vitality, your mental attitude conveys this and the message gets transferred to your body.

    1 — 2 — 3 — 4 — 5 — 6 — 7 — 8 — 9 — 1 0

18. Every element of your body is the result of a rate of vibration.
    1 — 2 — 3 — 4 — 5 — 6 — 7 — 8 — 9 — 10

19. Your mental action is a rate of vibration.
    1 — 2 — 3 — 4 — 5 — 6 — 7 — 8 — 9 — 10

20. Higher rates of vibration destroy lower rates.
    1 — 2 — 3 — 4 — 5 — 6 — 7 — 8 — 9 — 10

21. The rate of vibration you carry is controlled by the character of your braincells.
    1 — 2 — 3 — 4 — 5 — 6 — 7 — 8 — 9 — 10

22. You know how to create your brain cells.
    1 — 2 — 3 — 4 — 5 — 6 — 7 — 8 — 9 — 10

23. There is practically no limitation upon which you can place yourself in harmony with the omnipotent natural law.
    1 — 2 — 3 — 4 — 5 — 6 — 7 — 8 — 9 — 10

24. While the influence of the mind over the body is becoming more understood, the power of the mind over the body is seldom spoken of.
    1 — 2 — 3 — 4 — 5 — 6 — 7 — 8 — 9 — 10

25. The knowledge physicians display about nervous conditions is likely intuitive and empirical.
    1 — 2 — 3 — 4 — 5 — 6 — 7 — 8 — 9 — 10

26. The power of mental therapy should be studied in more detail, as results could be disastrous if neglected.
    1 — 2 — 3 — 4 — 5 — 6 — 7 — 8 — 9 — 10

27. You could direct your own mental therapy by learning how to calm your mind and arouse feelings of joy, hope, faith and love, along with redirecting your focus from sickness.
    1 — 2 — 3 — 4 — 5 — 6 — 7 — 8 — 9 — 10

28. For this week's exercise, contemplate on getting in touch with Omnipotence.
    1 — 2 — 3 — 4 — 5 — 6 — 7 — 8 — 9 — 10

29. Your awareness of Omnipresent power will destroy any form of sickness or suffering. While some believe suffering is sent by God, if that were the case, then every healthcare provided would be sacrilegious.

1 —— 2 —— 3 —— 4 —— 5 —— 6 —— 7 —— 8 —— 9 —— 10

30. For over two thousand years theology create a punishing fear-based God that they are now apologizing for.

1 —— 2 —— 3 —— 4 —— 5 —— 6 —— 7 —— 8 —— 9 —— 10

31. Because of this, you will more readily appreciate the ideal man made in the likeness of benevolent God that creates all there is.

1 —— 2 —— 3 —— 4 —— 5 —— 6 —— 7 —— 8 —— 9 —— 10

Tally your total score by adding the number you allocated for yourself in each of the 31 principles above. Your score will range from 31 to 310.

If you scored between 219 and 310, you have a great deal more clarity and understanding of how the mind and body function in tandem. You can further see how you can affect your body by calming your mind and focusing on constructive thoughts. Allow yourself to ruminate in the quote in the exercise, allowing it to sink into your subconscious.

If you scored between 125 and 218, you have a fair knowledge of the principles outlined in this chapter. To further explore how the mind works in relation to the body, re-read the 31 principles shared in this chapter. Allow yourself to fully explore the quote that is written in the exercise. Contemplate it, repeat it in your mind and allow it to seep into your subconscious.

If you scored between 31 and 124, spend some additional time researching the relationship between the mind and the body. Explore the ways in which mind body medicine has since been expanded upon in the world. Take time at least once a day to focus on the quote outlined in the exercise and allow it to echo in the inner recesses of your brain.

Introspection:

1. What did you learn about yourself after completing the Comprehension Survey?
2. Was your score what you expected it to be? Why or why not?
3. What areas of the segment of the book have you mastered?
4. What are the areas in this segment of the book that you need to focus on?
5. What three "takeaways" from this segment would you share with others and why?

Exercise

For your exercise this week concentrate on Tennyson's beautiful lines. "Speak to Him, thou, for He hears, and spirit with spirit can meet, Closer is He than breathing, and nearer than hands and feet." Then try to realize that when you do "Speak to Him" you are in touch with Omnipotence.

NOTES IN RESPONSE TO PERFORMING THIS EXERCISE

Be sure to journal about any findings or experiences you have as you continue to do this exercise as outlined.

Part Twenty-Three

INTRODUCTION

In this Part you will find that money weaves itself into the entire fabric of our very existence; that the law of success is service; that we get what we give, and for this reason we should consider it a great privilege to be able to give.

We have found that thought is the creative activity behind every constructive enterprise. We can therefore give nothing of more practical value than our thought.

Creative thought requires attention, and the power of attention is, as we have found, the weapon of the Super-man. Attention develops concentration, and concentration develops Spiritual Power, and Spiritual Power is the mightiest force in existence.

This is the science which embraces all sciences. It is the art which, above all arts, is relevant to human life. In the mastery of this science and this art there is opportunity for unending progression. Perfection in this is not acquired in six days, or in six weeks, or in six months. It is the labor of a life. Not to go forward is to go backward.

It is inevitable that the entertainment of positive, constructive and unselfish thoughts should have a far-reaching effect for good. Compensation is the key-note of the universe. Nature is constantly seeking to strike an equilibrium. Where something is sent out, something must be received; lest there should be a vacuum formed. By observance of this rule you cannot fail to profit in such measure as amply to justify your effort along this line.

---

1. The money consciousness is an attitude of mind; it is the open door to the arteries of commerce. It is the receptive attitude. Desire is the attractive force which sets the current in motion and fear is the great obstacle by which the current is stopped or completely reversed, turned away from us.
2. Fear is just the opposite from money consciousness; it is poverty consciousness, and as the law is unchangeable we get exactly what we give; if we fear we get what we feared. Money weaves itself into the entire fabric of our very existence; it engages the best thought of the best minds.
3. We make money by making friends, and we enlarge our circle of friends by making money for them, by helping them, by being of service to them. The first law of success then is service, and this in turn is built on integrity and justice. The man who at least is not fair in his intention is simply ignorant; he has missed the fundamental law of all exchange; he is impossible; he will lose surely and certainly; he may not know it; he may think he is winning, but he is doomed to certain defeat. He cannot cheat the Infinite. The law of compensation will demand of him an eye for an eye and a tooth for a tooth.
4. The forces of life are volatile; they are composed of our thoughts and ideals and these in turn are molded into form; our problem is to keep an open mind, to constantly reach out for the new, to recognize opportunity, to be interested in the race rather than the goal, for the pleasure is in the pursuit rather than the possession.

5. You can make a money magnet of yourself, but to do so you must first consider how you can make money for other people. If you have the necessary insight to perceive and utilize opportunities and propitious conditions and recognize values, you can put yourself in position to take advantage of them, but your greatest success will come as you are enabled to assist others. What benefits one must benefit all.
6. A generous thought is filled with strength and vitality, a selfish thought contains the germs of dissolution; it will disintegrate and pass away. Great financiers like Morgan and others are simply channels for the distribution of wealth; enormous amounts come and go, but it would be as dangerous to stop the outgo as the income; both ends must remain open; and so our greatest success will come as we recognize that it is just as essential to give as to get.
7. If we recognize the Omnipotent power that is the source of all supply we will adjust our consciousness to this supply in such a way that it will constantly attract all that is necessary to itself and we shall find that the more we give the more we get. Giving in this sense implies service. The banker gives his money, the merchant gives his goods, the author gives his thought, the workman gives his skill; all have something to give, but the more they can give, the more they get, and the more they get the more they are enabled to give.
8. The financier gets much because he gives much; he thinks; he is seldom a man that lets any one else do his thinking for him; he wants to know how results are to be secured; you must show him; when you can do this he will furnish the means by which hundreds or thousands may profit, and in proportion as they are successful will he be successful. Morgan, Rockefeller, Carnegie and others did not get rich because they lost money for other people; on the contrary,

it is because they made money for other people that they became the wealthiest men in the wealthiest country on the globe.

9. The average person is entirely innocent of any deep thinking; he accepts the ideas of others, and repeats them, in very much the same way as a parrot; this is readily seen when we understand the method which is used to form public opinion, and this docile attitude on the part of a large majority who seem perfectly willing to let a few persons do all their thinking for them is what enables a few men in a great many countries to usurp all the avenues of power and hold the millions in subjection. Creative thinking requires attention.

10. The power of attention is called concentration; this power is directed by the will; for this reason we must refuse to concentrate or think of anything except the things we desire. Many are constantly concentrating upon sorrow, loss and discord of every kind; as thought is creative it necessarily follows that this concentration inevitably leads to more loss, more sorrow and more discord. How could it be otherwise? On the other hand, when we meet with success, gain, or any other desirable condition, we naturally concentrate upon the effects of these things and thereby create more, and so it follows that much leads to more.

11. How an understanding of this principle can be utilized in the business world is well told by Mr. Atkinson in *Advanced Thought*. He says:

12. "Spirit, whatever else it may or may not be, must be considered as the Essence of Consciousness, the Substance of Mind, the reality underlying Thought. And as all Ideas are phases of the activity of Consciousness, Mind or Thought, it follows that in Spirit, and in it alone, is to be found the Ultimate Fact, the Real Thing, of Idea."

13. This being admitted, does it not seem reasonable to hold that a true understanding of Spirit, and its laws of manifestation, would be about the most "practical" thing that a "practical" person can hope to find? Does it not seem certain that if the "practical" men of the world could but realize this fact, they would "fall all over themselves" in getting to the place in which they might obtain such knowledge of spiritual things and laws? These men are not fools; they need only to grasp this fundamental fact in order to move in the direction of that which is the essence of all achievement.

14. Let me give you a concrete example. I know a man here in Chicago whom I had always considered to be quite materialistic. He had made several successes in life; and also several failures. The last time I had a talk with him he was practically "down and out," as compared with his former business condition. It looked as if he had indeed reached "the end of his rope," for he was well advanced into the stage of middle-age, and new ideas came more slowly, and less frequently to him than in former years.

15. He said to me, in substance: "I know that all things that 'work out' in business are the result of Thought; any fool knows that. Just now, I seem to be short on thoughts and good ideas. But, if this 'All-Mind' teaching is correct, there should be possible to the individual the attainment of 'direct connection' with Infinite Mind; and in Infinite Mind there must be the possibility of all kinds of good ideas which a man of my courage and experience could put to practical use in tho business world, and make a big success thereof. It looks good to me; and I am going to look into it."

16. This was about two years ago. The other day I heard of this man again. Talking to a friend, I said: "What has

come to our old friend X? Has he ever gotten on his feet again?" The friend looked at me in amazement. "Why," said he, "don't you know about X's great success? He is the Big Man in the '_____ Company' (naming a concern which has made a phenomenal success during the last eighteen months and is now well known, by reason of its advertisements, from one end of the country to another, and also abroad). He is the man who supplied the BIG IDEA for that concern. Why, he is about a half-million to the good and is moving rapidly toward the million mark; all in the space of eighteen months." I had not connected this man with the enterprise mentioned; although I knew of the wonderful success of the company in question. Investigation has shown that the story is true, and that the above stated facts are not exaggerated in the slightest.

17. Now, what do you think of that? To me, it means that this man actually made the "direct connection" with Infinite Mind—Spirit—and, having found it, he set it to work for him. He "used it in his business."

18. Does this sound sacrilegious or blasphemous? I hope not; I do not mean it to be so. Take away the implication of Personality, or Magnified Human Nature, from the conception of "The Infinite," and you have left the conception of an Infinite Presence Power, the Quintessence of which is Consciousness—in fact, at the last, Spirit. As this man, also, at the last, must be considered as a manifestation of Spirit; there is nothing sacrilegious in the idea that he, being Spirit, should so harmonize himself with his Origin and Source that he would be able to manifest at least a minor degree of its Power. All of us do this, more or less, when we use our minds in the direction of Creative Thought. This man did more, he went about it in an intensely "practical" manner.

19. I have not consulted him about his method of procedure, though I intend doing so at the first opportunity, but, he not only drew upon the Infinite Supply for the ideas which he needed (and which formed the seed of his success), but that he also used the Creative Power of Thought in building up for himself an Idealistic Pattern of that which he hoped to manifest in material form, adding thereto, changing, improving its detail, from time to time—proceeding from the general outline to the finished detail. I judge this to be the facts of the case, not alone from my recollection of the conversation two years ago, but also because I have found the same thing to be true in the cases of other prominent men who have made similar manifestation of Creative Thought.

20. Those who may shrink from this idea of employing the Infinite Power to aid one in his work in the material world, should remember that if the Infinite objected in the least to such a procedure the thing could never happen. The Infinite is quite able to take care of Itself.

21. "Spirituality" is quite "practical," very "practical," intensely "practical." It teaches that Spirit is the Real Thing, the Whole Thing, and that Matter is but plastic stuff, which Spirit is able to create, mold, manipulate, and fashion to its will. Spirituality is the most "practical" thing in the world—the only really and absolutely "practical" thing that there is!

22. This week concentrate on the fact that man is not a body with a Spirit, but a spirit with a body, and that it is for this reason that his desires are incapable of any permanent satisfaction in anything not spiritual. Money is therefore of no value except to bring about the conditions which we desire, and these conditions are necessarily harmonious. Harmonious conditions necessitate sufficient supply, so that if there appears to be any lack, we should realize that

the idea or soul of money is service, and as this thought takes form, channels of supply will be opened, and you will have the satisfaction of knowing that spiritual methods are entirely practical.

> *We have discovered that premeditated, orderly thinking for a purpose matures that purpose into fixed form, so that we may be absolutely sure of the result of our dynamic experiment*
> —FRANCIS LARIMER WARNER.

STUDY GUIDE

Part Twenty-Three

Summary

This Part tells of the money consciousness and the power which sets the current in motion which produces the attractive force which opens the doors to the arteries of commerce. It tells how the current is stopped or completely reversed and turned away from us. It tells how money is woven into the outer fabric of our existence. Why it engages the best thought of the best minds. How we make money. How to recognize opportunity. How to make a money magnet of yourself. How to get the necessary insight to perceive and utilize opportunities. How to recognize values. It tells how to convert an idea into an income, how to make a direct connection with the Universal Mind, how to secure practical results; in fact, it tells what the only really practical thing is.

1. The author opens this chapter with the statement, "the law of success is service." How much of our life have you focus your thoughts on service? Please explain.

2. According to Haanel, given that you get what you give, you should consider it a privilege to be able to give. What do you think he means by this?

3. "The power of attention is . . . the weapon of Superman." Attention develops concentration, which develops Spiritual Power, which is the mightiest force in existence. How strong is your power of attention? What do you tend to focus it upon?

4. Mastery of this science and this art is the labor of a lifetime. Not to move forward is to go backward. Do you believe that your passion to master it is strong enough to continue throughout your lifetime?

5. You cannot fail to profit if that which you focus on is constructive and unselfish. What are you most passionate about creating in your life? Does it serve the wellbeing of humankind in some way? Please explain.

Comprehension Survey

In Part Twenty-Three you will learn more about how the low of success applies to service and how money is weaved into the law of attraction.

Once you have completed it, you will get a better sense of how to acquire income in a way that supports others along with your higher state of consciousness. For each of the principles below, choose the number that is most closely aligns to your beliefs (1 being "not at all" and 10 being "a great deal").

1. In the case of money, your desire is the force, your attitude opens the door, and your fears are the great obstacles by which you stop or even reverse the flow of abundance.
   1 — 2 — 3 — 4 — 5 — 6 — 7 — 8 — 9 — 10

2. Fear is poverty consciousness and when you express it, you get what you feared.
   1 — 2 — 3 — 4 — 5 — 6 — 7 — 8 — 9 — 10

3. You make money by making friends, and you enlarge your circle of friends by being of service to them. The first law of success is service and it is built on integrity and justice.
   1 — 2 — 3 — 4 — 5 — 6 — 7 — 8 — 9 — 10

4. You must remain open, recognize opportunity and be interested in the race, as opposed to the goal.
   1 — 2 — 3 — 4 — 5 — 6 — 7 — 8 — 9 — 10

5. To be an effective money magnet, you must first consider how you can make money for others.
   1 — 2 — 3 — 4 — 5 — 6 — 7 — 8 — 9 — 10

6. Success will come to you when you realize that it is just as essential to give as to receive.
   1 — 2 — 3 — 4 — 5 — 6 — 7 — 8 — 9 — 10

7. Give in whatever way matches your skills. Doing so will naturally attract all that is necessary to itself.
   1 — 2 — 3 — 4 — 5 — 6 — 7 — 8 — 9 — 10

8. Highly successful financiers got wealthy because they made money for others.
   1 — 2 — 3 — 4 — 5 — 6 — 7 — 8 — 9 — 10

9. The average person does not put their attention on creative thinking. Thus they blindly follow the lead of the masses.
   1 — 2 — 3 — 4 — 5 — 6 — 7 — 8 — 9 — 10

10. What you focus your attention on amasses more. Thus, when you meet with any desirable condition, you naturally concentrate on its effects and create more.

    1 — 2 — 3 — 4 — 5 — 6 — 7 — 8 — 9 — 10

11. You have researched better understanding of this principle in Atkinson's book, Advanced Thought.

    1 — 2 — 3 — 4 — 5 — 6 — 7 — 8 — 9 — 10

12. In Spirit you will find the Ultimate Fact behind your Ideals or ideas.

    1 — 2 — 3 — 4 — 5 — 6 — 7 — 8 — 9 — 10

13. Understanding Spirit and its laws of manifestation is the most practical thing you can do to attract that which you desire into your life.

    1 — 2 — 3 — 4 — 5 — 6 — 7 — 8 — 9 — 10

14. Being materialistic will eventually slow new ideas down and impede upon your success.

    1 — 2 — 3 — 4 — 5 — 6 — 7 — 8 — 9 — 10

15. Like the man in Chicago (Mr. X) stated, business success starts with thought that is connected with "All-Mind" (or Universal Mind).

    1 — 2 — 3 — 4 — 5 — 6 — 7 — 8 — 9 — 10

16. Like Mr. X. experienced, once you apply this knowledge, innovative ideas and great success will follow.

    1 — 2 — 3 — 4 — 5 — 6 — 7 — 8 — 9 — 10

17. Making direct connection with Infinite Mind—Spirit—in business can work for you.

    1 — 2 — 3 — 4 — 5 — 6 — 7 — 8 — 9 — 10

18. There is no sacrilege in asserting that in harmonizing yourself with Source, you can manifest its Power, and you can do so in a practical way in your business endeavors.

    1 — 2 — 3 — 4 — 5 — 6 — 7 — 8 — 9 — 10

19. Harnessing the Creative Power of Thought, you can build for yourself an Idealistic Pattern that will manifest into form, which can later be changed or improved upon.

    1 — 2 — 3 — 4 — 5 — 6 — 7 — 8 — 9 — 10

20. If you shrink from the idea of using Infinite Power to aid you in your work, take note that manifestations could not happen if Source objected in any way.

1 —— 2 —— 3 —— 4 —— 5 —— 6 —— 7 —— 8 —— 9 —— 10

21. Spirit is the only practical thing there is, and matter is merely "plastic stuff" that it manipulates to its liking.

1 —— 2 —— 3 —— 4 —— 5 —— 6 —— 7 —— 8 —— 9 —— 10

22. The soul of money is service and it is the supply that feeds your harmonious conditions.

1 —— 2 —— 3 —— 4 —— 5 —— 6 —— 7 —— 8 —— 9 —— 10

Tally your total score by adding the number you allocated for yourself in each of the 31 principles above. Your score will range from 31 to 310.

If you scored between 219 and 310, you have a vast understanding of how "Spirituality" is practical. You know that when you focus on serving others, money and success naturally flows into your business. Give yourself time each day to contemplate the exercise, knowing that are you Spirit having a human experience.

If you scored between 125 and 218, you have a fair understanding of the principles outlined in this chapter. Continue researching how money and success have been amassed by the most powerful businesspeople in the world. Note those who were able to sustain wealth, and study those who were not able to do so. You will likely find that "service" was not the focal point for those who could not keep the wealth. Be sure to spend time in silence each day, contemplating the exercise and knowing that you Spirit incarnate, having a human experience.

If you scored between 31 and 124, you would be wise to take some time to study those business moguls who maintained success, focusing on serving others, as opposed to themselves. If you have any blocks around connecting with the divine Source as means of business development, look at your beliefs to better understand their origin, and how you might shift your perception. The answer lies in the teachings of this chapter. Be sure to do the exercise daily, and focus on the realization that you are, in fact, Spirit, having a human experience.

Introspection:

1. What did you learn about yourself after completing the Comprehension Survey?
2. Was your score what you expected it to be? Why or why not?
3. What areas of the segment of the book have you mastered?

4. What are the areas in this segment of the book that you need to focus on?
5. What three "takeaways" from this segment would you share with others and why?

Exercise

This week concentrate on the fact that man is not a body with a Spirit, but a spirit with a body, and that it is for this reason that his desires are incapable of any permanent satisfaction in anything not spiritual. Money is therefore of no value except to bring about the conditions which we desire, and these conditions are necessarily harmonious. Harmonious conditions necessitate sufficient supply, so that if there appears to be any lack, we should realize that the idea or soul of money is service, and as this thought takes form, channels of supply will be opened, and you will have the satisfaction of knowing that spiritual methods are entirely practical.

NOTES IN RESPONSE TO PERFORMING THIS EXERCISE
Be sure to journal about any findings or experiences you have as you continue to do this exercise as outlined.

Part Twenty-Four

INTRODUCTION

This is the final Part.

If you have practiced each of the exercises a few minutes every day, as suggested, you will have found that you can get out of life exactly what you wish by first putting into life that which you wish, and you will probably agree with the adept who said: "The Master Key thought is almost overwhelming; it is so vast, so available, so definite, so reasonable and so usable."

The fruit of this knowledge is, as it were, a gift of the Gods; it is the "Truth" that makes men free, not only free from every lack and limitation, but free from sorrow, worry and care. Is it not wonderful to realize that omnipotent law is no respecter of persons; that it makes no difference what your past habit of thought may have been, the way has been prepared.

If you are inclined to be religious, the greatest religious teacher the world has ever known made the way so plain that all may follow. If your mental bias is toward physical science, the law will operate with mathematical certainty. If you are inclined to be philosophical, Plato or Emerson may be your teacher; but, in each case, you may, by The Master Key, means reach degrees of power to which it is impossible to assign any limit.

An understanding of The Master Key, I believe, is the secret for which the ancient Alchemists vainly sought, because it explains how gold in the mind may be transmuted into gold in the heart and in the hand.

---

1. When the scientists first put the Sun in the center of the Solar System and sent the earth spinning around it, there was immense surprise and consternation. The whole idea was self-evidently false; nothing was more certain than the movement of the Sun across the sky, and anyone could see it descend behind the western hills and sink into the sea; scholars raged and scientists rejected the idea as absurd, yet the evidence has finally carried conviction in the minds of all.

2. We speak of a bell as a "sounding body," yet we know that all the bell can do is to produce vibrations in the air. When these vibrations come at the rate of sixteen a second they cause a sound to be heard in the mind. It is possible for the mind to hear vibrations at the rate of 38,000 a second. When the number increases beyond this all is silence again; so that we know that the sound is not in the bell, it is in our own mind.

3. We speak and even think of the Sun as "giving light." Yet we know it is simply giving forth energy which produces vibrations in the ether at the rate of four hundred trillion a second, causing what are termed light waves, so that we know that what we call light is simply a form of energy and that the only light there is, is the sensation caused in the mind by the motion of the waves. When the number increases, the light changes in color, each change in color being caused by shorter and more rapid vibrations; so that although we

speak of the rose as being red, the grass as being green, or the sky as being blue, we know that the colors exist only in our minds, and are the sensations experienced by us as the result of the vibrations of light waves. When the vibrations are reduced below four hundred trillion a second, they no longer affect us as light, but we experience the sensation of heat. It is evident, therefore, that we cannot depend upon the evidence of the senses for our information concerning the realities of things; if we did we should believe that the sun moved, that the world was flat instead of round, that the stars were bits of light instead of vast suns.

4. The whole range then of the theory and practice of any system of metaphysics consists in knowing the Truth concerning yourself and the world in which you live; in knowing that in order to express harmony, you must think harmony; in order to express health you must think health; and in order to express abundance you must think abundance; to do this you must reverse the evidence of the senses.

5. When you come to know that every form of disease, sickness, lack and limitation are simply the result of wrong thinking, you will have come to know "the Truth which shall make you free." You will see how mountains may be removed. If these mountains consist only of doubt, fear, distrust or other forms of discouragement, they are none the less real, and they need not only to be removed but to be "cast into the sea."

6. Your real work, consists in convincing yourself of the truth of these statements. When you have succeeded in doing this you will have no difficulty in thinking the truth, and as has been shown, the truth contains a vital principle and will manifest itself.

7. Those who heal diseases by mental methods have come to know this truth, they demonstrate it in their lives and the lives of others daily. They know that life, health and abun-

dance are Omnipresent, filling all space, and they know that those who allow disease or lack of any kind to manifest, have as yet not come into an understanding of this great law.

8. As all conditions are thought creations and therefore entirely mental, disease and lack are simply mental conditions in which the person fails to perceive the truth; as soon as the error is removed, the condition is removed.

9. The method for removing this error is to go into the Silence and know the Truth; as all mind is one mind, you can do this for yourself or anyone else. If you have learned to form mental images of the conditions desired, this will be the easiest and quickest way to secure results; if not, results can be accomplished by argument, by the process of convincing yourself absolutely of the truth of your statement.

10. Remember, and this is one of the most difficult as well as most wonderful statements to grasp. Remember that no matter what the difficulty is, no matter where it is, no matter who is affected, you have no patient but yourself; you have nothing to do but to convince yourself of the truth which you desire to see manifested.

11. This is an exact scientific statement in accordance with every system of Metaphysics in existence, and no permanent results are ever secured in any other way.

12. Every form of concentration, forming Mental Images, Argument, and AutoSuggestion are all simply methods by which you are enabled to realize the Truth.

13. If you desire to help some one, to destroy some form of lack, limitation or error, the correct method is not to think of the person whom you wish to help; the intention to help them is entirely sufficient, as this puts you in mental touch with the person. Then drive out of your own mind any belief of lack, limitation, disease, danger, difficulty or whatever the trouble might be. As soon as you have succeeded in doing this

the result will have been accomplished, and the person will be free.

14. But remember that thought is creative and consequently every time you allow your thought to rest on any inharmonious condition, you must realize that such conditions are apparent only, they have no reality, that spirit is the only reality and it can never be less than perfect.

15. All thought is a form of energy, a rate of vibration, but a thought of the Truth is the highest rate of vibration known and consequently destroys every form of error in exactly the same way that light destroys darkness; no form of error can exist when the "Truth" appears, so that your entire mental work consists in coming into an understanding of the Truth. This will enable you to overcome every form of lack, limitation or disease of any kind.

16. We can get no understanding of the truth from the world without; the world without is relative only; Truth is absolute. We must therefore find it in the "world within."

17. To train the mind to see Truth only is to express true conditions only, our ability to do this will be an indication as to the progress we are making.

18. The absolute truth is that the "I" is perfect and complete; the real "I" is spiritual and can therefore never be less than perfect; it can never have any lack, limitation, or disease. The flash of genius does not have origin in the molecular motion of the brain; it is inspired by the ego, the spiritual "I" which is one with the Universal Mind, and it is our ability to recognize this Unity which is the cause of all inspiration, all genius. These results are far-reaching and have effect upon generations yet to come; they are the pillars of fire which mark the path that millions follow.

19. Truth is not the result of logical training or of experimentation, or even of observation; it is the product of a developed consciousness. Truth within a Caesar, manifests in a

Caesar's deportment, in his life and his action; his influence upon social forms and progress. Your life and your actions and your influence in the world will depend upon the degree of truth which you are enabled to perceive, for truth will not manifest in creeds, but in conduct.

20. Truth manifests in character, and the character of a man should be the interpretation of his religion, or what to him is truth, and this will in turn be evidenced in the character of his possession. If a man complains of the drift of his fortune he is just as unjust to himself as if he should deny rational truth, though it stand patent and irrefutable.

21. Our environment and the innumerable circumstances and accidents of our lives already exist in the subconscious personality which attracts to itself the mental and physical material which is congenial to its nature. Thus is our future being determined from our present, and if there should be apparent injustice in any feature or phase of our personal life, we must look within for the cause, try to discover the mental fact which is responsible for the outward manifestation.

22. It is this truth which makes you "free" and it is the conscious knowledge of this truth which will enable you to overcome every difficulty.

23. The conditions with which you meet in the world without are invariably the result of the conditions obtaining in the world within, therefore it follows with scientific accuracy that by holding the perfect ideal in mind you can bring about ideal conditions in your environment.

24. If you see only the incomplete, the imperfect, the relative, the limited, these conditions will manifest in your life; but if you train your mind to see and realize the spiritual ego, the "I" which is forever perfect and complete, harmonious; wholesome and healthful conditions only will be manifested.

25. As thought is creative, and the truth is the highest and most perfect thought which anyone can think, it is self-evident that to think the truth is to create that which is true and it is again evident that when truth comes into being that which is false must cease to be.
26. The Universal Mind is the totality of all mind which is in existence. Spirit is Mind, because spirit is intelligent. The words are, therefore, synonymous.
27. The difficulty with which you have to contend is to realize that mind is not individual. It is omnipresent. It exists everywhere. In other words, there is no place where it is not. It is, therefore, Universal.
28. Men have, heretofore, generally used the word "God" to indicate this Universal, creative principle; but the word "God" does not convey the right meaning. Most people understand this word to mean something outside of themselves; while exactly the contrary is the fact. It is our very life. Without it we would be dead. We would cease to exist. The minute the spirit leaves the body, we are as nothing. Therefore, spirit is really, all there is of us.
29. Now, the only activity which the spirit possesses is the power to think. Therefore, thought must be creative, because spirit is creative. This creative power is impersonal and your ability to think is your ability to control it and make use of it for the benefit of yourself and others.
30. When the truth of this statement is realized, understood, and appreciated, you will have come into possession of the Master-Key, but remember that only those who are wise enough to understand, broad enough to weigh the evidence, firm enough to follow their own judgment, and strong enough to make the sacrifice exacted, may enter and partake.
31. This week, try to realize that this is truly a wonderful world in which we live, that you are a wonderful being, that many

are awakening to a knowledge of the Truth, and as fast as they awake and come into a knowledge of the "things which have been prepared for them" they, too, realize that "Eye hath not seen, nor ear heard, neither hath it entered into the heart of man," the splendors which exist for those who find themselves in the Promised Land. They have crossed the river of judgment and have arrived at the point of discrimination between the true and the false, and have found that all they ever willed or dreamed, was but a faint concept of the dazzling reality.

Though an inheritance of acres may be bequeathed, an inheritance of knowledge and wisdom cannot. The wealthy man may pay others for doing his work for him, but it is Impossible to get his thinking done for him by another, or to purchase any kind of self-culture.
—S. Smiles.

STUDY GUIDE

Part Twenty-Four

Summary

This Part explains the entire theory and practice of every system of Metaphysics; it tells how to express harmony, how to express health, how to express abundance. It explains the nature of all conditions, and how they may be changed or removed. It explains how every difficulty, no matter what it is or where it is, can be removed or dissolved, and it explains the only way in which this is ever done or can be done. It also tells of a Master Key by which those who are wise enough to understand, broad enough to weigh the evidence, firm enough to follow their own judgment, and strong enough to make the sacrifice exacted, may enter and partake.

1. "The Master Key thought is almost overwhelming: it is so vast, so available, so definite, so reasonable and so usable." Have you found this statement to be the case thus far in your exploration of this book?
2. How has exploring and applying this "Truth" freed you in your life?
3. How do you believe that applying this "Truth" will free you in the future?
4. "Omnipotent law is no respecter of persons" and "makes no difference what your past habit of thought may have been." Knowing this now, are you able to release any guilt of negative energy around choices you have made in your past? Please explain.
5. Whether you are religiously, scientifically, mathematically or philosophically inclined, by applying the wisdom and teachings of The Master Key, there is no limit to the power you can access. What powers do you wish to further develop in your life? Why?
6. Do you now believe in Alchemy? Why or why not?

Comprehension Survey

All that has previously been taught in this book has been encapsulated into this final chapter. Once you have completed it, you will have a greater sense of where your true power lies, and the spirit from which you came and are a part of. For each of the principles below, choose the number that is most closely aligns to your beliefs (1 being "not at all" and 10 being "a great deal").

1. When the concept of the sun as the center of the solar system was introduced, there was great skepticism, yet know evidence has changed the minds of the masses.
   1 — 2 — 3 — 4 — 5 — 6 — 7 — 8 — 9 — 10

2. A bell simply produces vibrations in the air, yet we call it a "sounding body." In the end, you know that the sound is not in the bell, but in your own mind.
   1 — 2 — 3 — 4 — 5 — 6 — 7 — 8 — 9 — 10

3. What you call light from the sun, is a star giving forth energy that produces vibrations, causing light waves. When the waves increase or decrease, the light changes in color. Thus the colors you see exist only in your mind. You cannot depend upon the evidence of your senses (or else the world would be flat and the sun would fall into the ocean every night).
   1 — 2 — 3 — 4 — 5 — 6 — 7 — 8 — 9 — 10

4. To express anything, you must first think it. Thus, the Truth is that you must reverse the evidence of your senses. To express harmony, health or abundance, you must first think each of them into being.
   1 — 2 — 3 — 4 — 5 — 6 — 7 — 8 — 9 — 10

5. You can now see how the "mountains" of doubt, fear, distrust or discouragement you feel need not only be removed, but be "cast into the sea."
   1 — 2 — 3 — 4 — 5 — 6 — 7 — 8 — 9 — 10

6. Your real work is convincing yourself of the truth the statements outlined in this book.
   1 — 2 — 3 — 4 — 5 — 6 — 7 — 8 — 9 — 10

7. Those who heal disease know that life, health and abundance are Omnipresent and are your birthright.
   1 — 2 — 3 — 4 — 5 — 6 — 7 — 8 — 9 — 10

8. Disease and lack are mental conditions in which you fail to perceive the truth. Once your erroneous thinking is removed, the condition is also removed.
   1 — 2 — 3 — 4 — 5 — 6 — 7 — 8 — 9 — 10

9. The fastest way to remove the error, go into Silence and experience the Truth. Allow new mental images of the conditions you desire to form.
   1 — 2 — 3 — 4 — 5 — 6 — 7 — 8 — 9 — 10

10. Whatever the circumstances, you have no patient but yourself. You need only convince yourself and that which you desire will manifest.
    1 — 2 — 3 — 4 — 5 — 6 — 7 — 8 — 9 — 10

11. This is in accordance with science and metaphysics. In fact, you can secure no permanent results in any other way.
    1 — 2 — 3 — 4 — 5 — 6 — 7 — 8 — 9 — 10

12. Forming mental images, argument and autosuggestion are all concentration methods that enable yourself to realize the truth.
    1 — 2 — 3 — 4 — 5 — 6 — 7 — 8 — 9 — 10

13. If you want to help someone, remove any form of lack or limitation from your thoughts about them. See them as happy, healthy and whole and they will be free.
    1 — 2 — 3 — 4 — 5 — 6 — 7 — 8 — 9 — 10

14. When your thoughts rest on any inharmonious condition, remember that it has no reality and that oneness with spirit or Universal Mind is the only reality.
    1 — 2 — 3 — 4 — 5 — 6 — 7 — 8 — 9 — 10

15. Just as light destroys darkness, your higher thoughts destroy every form of error.
    1 — 2 — 3 — 4 — 5 — 6 — 7 — 8 — 9 — 10

16. Truth is absolute and can only be found within you. The outer world is relative; a reflection of your inner world.
    1 — 2 — 3 — 4 — 5 — 6 — 7 — 8 — 9 — 10

17. Once your train your mind to only see Truth, the conditions you experience are the evidence that you are making progress.
    1 — 2 — 3 — 4 — 5 — 6 — 7 — 8 — 9 — 10

18. The real "I" is spiritual, thus it can be nothing less than perfect. The spiritual "I" recognizes that it is one with the Universal Mind, and in this recognition, genius is born.
    1 — 2 — 3 — 4 — 5 — 6 — 7 — 8 — 9 — 10

19. The degree to which you can influence the world depends upon the degree of truth that you are able to perceive. That truth will not manifest in what you say, but in what you do.
    1 — 2 — 3 — 4 — 5 — 6 — 7 — 8 — 9 — 10

20. Your character is a manifestation of your truth. If you complain, you are doing yourself and injustice. But know that truth, patient and indisputable, stands waiting for you.

    1 —— 2 —— 3 —— 4 —— 5 —— 6 —— 7 —— 8 —— 9 —— 10

21. If you are suffering from any apparent injustice, you must look within for the cause. Try to discover the mental fact within you that is responsible for the outward manifestation.

    1 —— 2 —— 3 —— 4 —— 5 —— 6 —— 7 —— 8 —— 9 —— 10

22. The truth sets you free, and your knowledge of it enables you to overcome any difficulty.

    1 —— 2 —— 3 —— 4 —— 5 —— 6 —— 7 —— 8 —— 9 —— 10

23. The way you face the outer world is a result of the conditions within you. Thus when you keep the perfect ideal in mind, you can bring ideal conditions into your environment.

    1 —— 2 —— 3 —— 4 —— 5 —— 6 —— 7 —— 8 —— 9 —— 10

24. If you train your mind to experience the spiritual "I" that is forever perfect and complete, then wonderful conditions will manifest in your life.

    1 —— 2 —— 3 —— 4 —— 5 —— 6 —— 7 —— 8 —— 9 —— 10

25. The truth the highest, most perfect thought you can think. If this is the case, then when you think it, anything that is false must no longer exist.

    1 —— 2 —— 3 —— 4 —— 5 —— 6 —— 7 —— 8 —— 9 —— 10

26. Spirit is mind because spirit is intelligent.

    1 —— 2 —— 3 —— 4 —— 5 —— 6 —— 7 —— 8 —— 9 —— 10

27. You understand that mind is not individual. Thus your mind, is not yours, for mind exists everywhere and is, therefore, Universal.

    1 —— 2 —— 3 —— 4 —— 5 —— 6 —— 7 —— 8 —— 9 —— 10

28. Man has used the word "God" to indicate the Universal. However, It is not a being outside of yourself. It is the very life, spirit without which you would be dead.

    1 —— 2 —— 3 —— 4 —— 5 —— 6 —— 7 —— 8 —— 9 —— 10

29. Being creative, the only activity spirit possesses is thought. Thus your ability to think, is your ability to control and make use of the impersonal creative power for yourself and others.

    1 —— 2 —— 3 —— 4 —— 5 —— 6 —— 7 —— 8 —— 9 —— 10

30. To fully integrate this into your life, you need to understand it, weight the evidence, follow your judgement and sacrifice your existing beliefs.
1 —— 2 —— 3 —— 4 —— 5 —— 6 —— 7 —— 8 —— 9 —— 10

31. You know that you understand this powerful Truth, and that are already are in the "Promised Land."
1 —— 2 —— 3 —— 4 —— 5 —— 6 —— 7 —— 8 —— 9 —— 10

Tally your total score by adding the number you allocated for yourself in each of the 31 principles above. Your score will range from 31 to 310.

If you scored between 219 and 310, you should congratulate yourself. You have taken to mind and heart the teachings of this book, and you are ready to see the evidence of your new wisdom take shape in your life. See your awakening to these insights as a new life that you can now shape for the betterment of both yourself and others. Take time each day to bask the in the wonders of the "Promised Land" that reigns within your heart. Then allow yourself to experience the highest of gratitude for the realization that you are an integral part of an extraordinary benevolent Universal Mind.

If you scored between 125 and 218, you have done a wonderful job of integrating a great deal of the wisdom shared with you in this book. Of most importance, take time to be silent and still, allowing yourself to align with the great connection with the Universal Mind. Know that every time you do, you will experience greater evidence of the power that rests within you. You may wish to re-read this book, noting that doing so will allow its messages to integrate further into your subconscious mind.

If you scored between 31 and 124, you should applaud yourself for taking the time to read this book and do these exercises. Know that you have opened the door to a vast portal of discovery that will ultimately lead you to fully understand the Truth. As you do, you will see evidence of it in the world around you. Take time each day to sit in silence, with the intention to connect to the Universal Mind and see the Truth of who you really are. As you practice this, and review the contents of this book, you can experience a life that is infinitely creative, joyful and connected.

Introspection:

1. What did you learn about yourself after completing the Comprehension Survey?
2. Was your score what you expected it to be? Why or why not?
3. What areas of the segment of the book have you mastered?
4. What are the areas in this segment of the book that you need to focus on?
5. What three "takeaways" from this segment would you share with others and why?

Exercise

This week, try to realize that this is truly a wonderful world in which we live, that you are a wonderful being, that many are awakening to a knowledge of the Truth, and as fast as they awake and come into a knowledge of the "things which have been prepared for them" they, too, realize that "Eye hath not seen, nor ear heard, neither hath it entered into the heart of man," the splendors which exist for those who find themselves in the Promised Land. They have crossed the river of judgment and have arrived at the point of discrimination between the true and the false, and have found that all they ever willed or dreamed, was but a faint concept of the dazzling reality.

NOTES IN RESPONSE TO PERFORMING THIS EXERCISE
Be sure to journal about any findings or experiences you have as you continue to do this exercise as outlined.

Afterword

A friend of mine in Thailand is a billionaire. He's only thirty-five years old.

When I asked him to tell me his story, I was shocked and inspired to hear him say that he was once homeless. He had nothing. He struggled and starved. When he begged for help from an old friend, that friend sent him a book. It was *The Secret*.

Reading that famous book put him on a quest to read more and learn more. He then told me the biggest secret of all to his success.

"It was *The Master Key* series that changed my life," he said. "I found a copy of the complete book and read it word for word, studying every idea, principle and method. I applied it all. It was one of the biggest reasons that I went from homeless to billionaire. That book changed my life forever."

My Thailand billionaire friend is Andres Pira. He is still growing and succeeding, at record breaking bounds, due to what he learned in *The Master Key*.

I, too, have been influenced by this great work. I, too, was once homeless, broke, starving and struggling. But it was long lost books like *The Master Key* that showed me the way out of the nightmare. I so loved the book that later, once I tasted fame and fortune, I found an entire original set of first editions and bought the treasure for my library.

The depth of wisdom in this masterwork and masterpiece is beyond description. If you just read the book, I encourage you to go back and reread it, take notes, and apply it to your life. And be sure to give copies to family and friends, clients and customers.

If this work of greatness can help Andres go from homeless to billionaire, and me go from homeless to bestselling author, what might it do for you and those you care about?

Read and share the book and, as I like to say, Expect Miracles.

Dr. Joe Vitale

www.MrFire.com

Glossary

ABSOLUTE—That which cannot be measured, determined, limited, expressed; the fundamentally and self-existently real from which all other reality springs.

ACCRETION—Growth or accumulation by external additions.

ALTRUISM—The instinct and emotion which prompts to effort on behalf of others.

ANALYTICAL—Proceeding by analysis; the separating of anything into first principles.

ANTHROPOMORPHIC—The ascription of human attributes, feelings and conduct to the Deity; the natural result of the limitation of human thought and language.

APPERCEPTION—The mental process which associates and brings to attention all the ideas and memories associated with the central thought to which the attention is directly given.

ARCANA—An inner secret or mystery; something hidden from the mass of men; one of the great secrets which the alchemists sought to discover.

ATTENTION—The act or process of giving especial clearness to one or more particulars in the complex content of consciousness. Thus the difference between an ordinary mind and the mind of a Newton consists principally in this, that the one is capable of a more continuous attention than the other.

Glossary 385

BELIEF—Confidence in the truth of a proposition which is felt to lack positive proof; acceptance without proof; that which is believed; a creed.

CELL—The smallest element of an organized body that manifests independent vital activities. The tissues of the human body are an aggregate of cells and their products; they are from 1-125 to 1-5000 of an inch in diameter.

CONCENTRATE—To draw or direct to or toward a common center.

CONCEPTION—The act of grasping two or more attributes into the unity of thought which we call a concept.

CONSCIOUSNESS—All forms of sensation, feeling, perception, planning and thought; a comprehensive tern for the complement of all our cognitive energies.

COSMIC—Pertaining to the universe as a harmonious and orderly system as opposed to chaotic.

COSMOLOGICAL—Relating to the nature and laws of the cosmos as an instituted and alterable order of things, as a cosmological argument.

DEDUCTION—Reasoning from the general to the particular; deduction proceeds from a general principle, through an admitted instance to a conclusion.

DIFFERENTIATION—The process of making or becoming different, as the hypothesis that the characteristic cell growth and divergent particularization of all organisms are due to environment and local conditions as opposed to inherited differentiation by which the characteristics are inherent in the composition of the embryo.

EGO—The "I" which thinks, feels and acts; the conscious individual or the thinking self as distinguished from all objects of thought and from its own states or powers; the pure principle of personal identity.

ELECTRICITY—A material agency which, when in motion, exhibits magnetic, chemical and thermal effects.

ELOHIM—The Hebrew title of most frequent occurrence in the Old Testament, expressing absolute Divine power.

EVOLUTION—The unity of action exhibited in the operations of nature; the act or process of evolving; the succession of changes by which a germ passes from a simple to a complex condition. "With each succeeding Kingdom, evolution has changed its direction upward from the physical to the psychical."—Funk.

ELECTRON—The smallest known component of matter; always associated with an unvarying unit charge of negative electricity.

FAITH—Active belief; belief which amounts to a basis for action upon the accepted premises.

GERMINATE—The first act of growth, in a seed, spore or ovum.

GLOSSARY—An explanatory vocabulary dealing with a class of words, as of those of a dialect or a science.

GOD—The embodiment or some aspect of reality or of some being regarded as the ultimate principle of the universe.

GRAVITATION—The tendency of every particle of matter in the universe toward every other particle; also the law which expresses this force which is; the accelerating tendency of bodies toward the center of the earth is equal to the earth's attraction minus the centrifugal force arising from the rotation of the earth on its axis.

HARMONY—Completeness and perfection resulting from diversity in unity; agreement in relation; orderliness.

IDEA—A thought which is conceived to be in a measure independent of the thinker, and, in a sense, self existent, "Thought" is used to name the presentation which is the direct product of the active mind and which would not and could not exist apart from the acting mind, while "idea" is used to name the presentation of the mind which is no longer considered as acting; a presentation which might even exist apart from, and independently of, a mind or its activities. A thought is felt to be peculiar to the one thinking it, while the idea is felt to be, in a measure, self-determined or due to the nature of that with which it is associated so that all minds would foam it the same; the term still feels the influence of Plato's conception of the ideas as the forms of fundamental reality.

IDEALIZE—To render ideal, to conform to some mental standard as of perfection.

INHIBIT—To restrict by prohibition; to check; to suppress.

IMAGINATION—The act or power of combining products of past experiences in new, modified or ideal forms. The creative or constructive power of the mind. The act of constructive intellect in grouping knowledge or thought into new, original or rational systems. "Science, Invention and Philosophy have little use for fancy, but the creative, penetrative power of imagination is to them the breath of life, and the condition of all advance and success."

IMMUTABLE—Not capable of change, either by increase or decrease, by development or self evolution; unchangeable; invariable and permanent.

INDUCTION—The scientific method that proceeds by 1, exact operation; 2, correct interpretation; 3, rational explanation; 4, scientific construction. Reasoning from the particular to the general; induction proceeds from a number of collated instances, through some attribute common to them all, to a general principle.

INDIVIDUAL—A complete independent single being; incapable of division without loss of identity.

INEXORABLE—Not to be moved by entreaty; unyielding; unrelenting; implacable; inflexible.

INFINITE—Self-existent and all-inclusive reality; unmeasured, undetermined, unlimited; independent of expression, yet including all expressions, or actualized things; the absolute.

INSIGHT—A perception of the inner nature of a thing.

INSPIRATION—The inbreathing or imparting of an idea, emotion or mental or spiritual influence; the elevating and creative influence of genius.

INTANGIBLE—Incapable of being touched; not perceptible to the senses, having no clear foundation in fact.

INTUITION—A conclusion which was arrived at without the conscious use of reason and not directly traceable to ordinary understandings of sensory experiences; the faculty of (unconscious). mind by which we arrive at intuitions, or know things without being taught; direct, or immediate knowledge of physical or moral values.

KEY—Anything which discloses or opens something to the understanding, as a key to a subject or problem; that which opens the way to other projects or renders further progress possible.

KINETIC—Producing motion; active as opposed to latent; the kinetic theory has been found capable of explaining nearly all the phenomena of gases and is now generally accepted.

LEAVEN—Anything that by exerting a secret or silent influence gradually brings about a change in character or conditions.

LOGIC—The science or doctrine of correct thinking; the principles governing the reasoning faculties in the pursuit and exposition of truth.

LOVE—The outgoing or yearning of the soul for what is good or excellent.

MASTER—One who controls or has authority; a superior, a ruler or governor; one who gains the victory as "I am the master of my fate."

MASTER KEY—A key which controls a number of locks, the separate keys of which are not interchangeable.

MATTER—That fours of being or substance that is characterized by extension, inertia, weight, etc.; or, in general, by the properties cognized by the senses.

MECHANISM—The structure or means of action of any mechanical contrivance. "A human organism with all its parts in harmonious action is a splendid mechanism."—Winchell.

METAPHYSICS—The science of the first principles of being and of knowledge; the reasoned doctrine of the essential nature and fundamental relations of all that is real.

MIND—An abstract, collective form for all forms of conscious intelligence.

NATURAL LAW—That which is normal or in accordance with the ordinary course of things; as opposed to the supernatural.

NEGATIVE—Absence or obscurity of anything affirmative or definite; emptiness; voidness; nullity. Thus, "You can never overthrow falsehood by negative, but by establishing the antagonistic truth."—Robertson.

OBJECTIVE—Having the nature of an object or being that is thought of or perceived; as opposed to that which thinks or perceives.

OMNISCIENCE—Knowledge of all things; infinite or unlimited knowledge.

OMNIPOTENT—Possessing unlimited or universal power, applicable to the Deity alone.

OMNIPRESENCE—Essentially present everywhere at the same time.

PERCEPTION—Any insight or intuitive judgment that implies unusual discernment of fact or truth.

PERSONAL—Pertaining to, or characteristic of a human being.

PHILOSOPHY—Knowledge, in a scientific system, of the ultimate principles, elements, cause and laws that underlie and explain all knowledge and existence, and their application in the explanation of these.

PHYSICS—That science or group of sciences which treats of the phenomena associated with matter in general, especially in its relation to energy and the laws governing these phenomena.

PHYSIOLOGY—The branch of biology which treats of the vital phenomena manifested by animals and plants.

PLASTIC—Capable of being molded into form; as the plastic mind of Truth; or the inner mind of man as having a plastic power over his material body.

POLARITY—That quality of a body by which its smallest parts have certain properties related to a line of direction through its mass, the properties at one end of the line being opposite to the properties at the other end of it, as in a magnet.

POSITIVE—Inherent in a thing, by and of itself; not related to other things, or to human judgment or feeling; absolute; inherent; not admitting of doubt; final; undeniable and incontestable.

POTENTIAL—Possible, but not actual; possessing inherent qualities for development; inherent power, capability, efficiency, as opposed to actuality.

PRANA—The breath of life.

PRECEDENT—Something antecedent in matter, manner or form; which may be cited as an example, model, authority or justification.

PREDOMINANT—Superior in power, influence, effectiveness; having ascendency or control.

PREMISE—A proposition laid down, proved, supposed or assumed that serves as a ground for an argument or conclusion.

PRINCIPLE—The ultimate essential element that enters into the composition of all being. The moving cause, power or force by which being manifests. The Universal truth expressing the law of this manifestation; that which determines the nature, character and essence of anything.

PROPHYLACTIC—Any measure efficacious in protecting from disease.

PSYCHICAL—Pertaining to the mind or soul; mental as distinguished from the physical of physiological.
PSYCHOLOGY—The science which treats of the mind, its functions, condition of activity and development, its essential nature and place in nature at large.
RADIANT—Emitting rays of light or brightness; figuratively, beaming with joy, kindness and love.
RADICAL—Proceeding from the root, source or foundation. Hence, thorough-going, extreme, fundamental.
REALITY—That which is believed to exist independently of thoughts or opinions; the independently existent; the genuine; opposed to the imaginary or fanciful. That appears reality which receives a major share of the attention.
REASON—(1) The faculty of mind by which experiences are compared and inference drawn; (2) The process of arriving at conclusions by means of comparisons; (3) A proposition from which another is validly inferred.
RELAX—To make less vigorous or stringent; abate in strictness or severity; mitigate; to relieve from strain or effort; abate in attention or assiduity, as to relax the mind.
SAGACITY—The power of ready, far-reaching and accurate inference from slight facts; or readiness to see the result of any action; especially upon human actions or conduct.
SAMENESS—The least degree of diversity.
SCIENCE—Knowledge gained and verified by exact observations and correct thinking, methodically formulated and arranged in a rational system.
SERVICE—The act of helping another or promoting his interests in any way.
SOLAR PLEXUS—The largest sympathetic plexus in the body found behind the stomach in front of the aorta and the pillars of the diaphragm. It is composed of branches of the pneumogastric and great splanchnic nerves; the most important ganglia connected with its cords are the right

and left similunar. A number of smaller plexus are derived from it.

SPIRIT—The Invisible and incorporeal principle in man; the principle of self-consciousness, self-activity and of rational power in general; that which signifies a likeness in man to the Divine Being.

SUBCONSCIOUS—That which pertains to the real nature or essence of a person or thing; proceeding from or taking place within the subject, as opposed to the objective. Thus sensation is subconscious, while perception is an objective experience.

SUBJECTIVE—Such processes as seem to have psychical characteristics, but are not attended by consciousness.

SYLLABUS—A concise statement of a subject; an epitome, abstract statement or summary.

SYLLOGISM—A logical formula or analysis of a formal argument, consisting of three propositions, the first two of which are called the premises and the third the conclusion.

SYSTEM—The orderly combination or arrangement into a whole; especially such combinations according to some rational principle or organic idea giving it unity and completeness.

TELEPATHY—(Greek, tele, at a distance, pathos, to experience.) The communication of thoughts between minds without any material medium, ordinary expression or the use of the senses.

THEOLOGY—The science that treats of the being of God, the attributes of God, the doctrine of the Trinity and creation and providence.

THERAPEUTIC—The art and science of curing disease.

TRANSCENDENTAL—Rising above the ordinary notions of men; transcending all ordinary specified bounds or powers; surpassing the limits of individual experiences, but forming the universal and necessary conditions of experiences in general.

TRUTH—A statement or belief which represents or conforms to the reality; a law or principle established by correct reasoning.

UNIVERSAL—Relating to the entire universe; all-embracing; unlimited; regarded or existing as a whole; entire.

UNIVERSAL MIND—The life principle of every atom in existence.

VIBRATION—A rapid motion back and forth; a vibration is completely determined by its amplitude, frequency and period; thus the lowest vibrations appreciated in a musical note are sixteen per second and those which produce the highest tone 41,000 per second.

VISUALIZE—To give pictorial vividness to a mental representation; to construct a visual image in the mind.

VOLATILE—Not lasting or permanent; fleeting; transient; changeable; evaporating.

WILL—The mental power to choose; the power to mold the expressions of the mind; the realization of desires; volition.

> *"I hold it true that thoughts are things*
> *Endowed with being, breath and wings*
> *And that we send them forth to fill*
> *The world with good results, or ill."*
> —Ella Wheeler Wilcox

Questions and Answers

Some Questions asked by Correspondents, with the Answers given by Mr. Charles F. Haanel Author and Exponent of *The Master Key*.

1. In referring to the subconscious and conscious minds, or the objective and subjective, which is the technically correct expression, "We have two minds which, although related, are distinct," or, "We have one mind with two distinct functions?" The correct expression is, "We have one mind with two distinct functions." There are not two minds.

2. Are the Devil in religion, the Negative in Science, and the Bad in Philosophy merely imaginary manifestations of thought energy, or shall we class them as wrong yet real manifestations? If all that we have and are, all of our powers come from one eternal source, to what must we attribute these imaginary entities?
These are not imaginary entities. They are simply perversions. If you use electricity for light, you call it good. If you grasp a wire which has not been properly insulated and it kills you, it is not for that reason bad or evil. You were simply careless or ignorant of the laws governing electricity. For the same reason,

the one Infinite Power, which is the source of all Power, manifests in your life either as good or as evil, as you make use of it constructively or destructively.

3. Is not the Master Key Idea of "God" Pantheistic?
This depends entirely upon your idea of Pantheism. Pantheism is a loose term and may be interpreted in various ways, for instance, Pantheism conceives the Universe to be one eternal, involuntary evolution of an Infinite Being, as contrasted with Atheism, which is a positive denial of the Divine Immanence, and Agnosticism, which is a dogmatic doubt of the existence of God.

4. Is this right? Truth is absolute, but conception of truth varies with the individual consciousness. Therefore, no one can say when the ultimate truth has been reached, because no one can say when the individual consciousness has been developed to the point where further development is impossible.
Yes, truth is absolute, but the conception of truth varies with the individual consciousness. On the other hand, truth is not a matter of belief. It is a matter of demonstration. It is not a question of authority, but a question of perception.

5. Since the real "I" is spiritual and therefore perfect, and since it "controls and directs both the body and mind," how is it that we see such imperfect results?
We see no imperfect results. We see nothing but perfection. Perfection means that the Law operates with immutable precision. Spiritual law always operates perfectly. If the individual thinks constructively, results are constructive, harmonious. If he thinks destructively, he reaps exactly what he sows. The Law works perfectly. We see no imperfect results whatever. We may freely choose what we think, but the result of our thought is governed by an immutable law.

6. "What is Life?"

Life is that quality or principle of the Universal Energy which manifests in so-called organic objects as growth and voluntary activity, and which is usually co-existent in some degree, with some manifestation of that same Universal Energy as the quality or principle termed intelligence. You must understand that there is only one Supreme Principle, evading all comprehension of its essential nature. It is the Absolute. Man can think only in terms of the relative. Therefore, he sometimes defines It as the Universal Intelligence, the Universal Substance, as Ether, Life, Mind, Spirit, Energy, Truth, Love, etc. His particular definition at any moment is governed by the particular relationship of the phenomena of Being in which he thinks of this Principle at that moment.

7. How is the law governing success or prosperity placed in operation?

The human brain is the finest and most vibrant mechanism in existence. Every time you think you send a message into the formless energy from which and by which all things are created. This starts a train of causation which relates with the things that correspond with the image of your thought. If your thought is sufficiently refined and concentrated you will be placed in harmony with the object of your thought quickly; if not, more time will be required. Most persons are busily engaged in concentrating upon lack, limitation, loss and inharmony of every kind, and they are therefore attracting these conditions, a few are busily engaged in concentrating upon success, prosperity and harmonious conditions generally, and find that their environment reflects the quality of their thought.

8. How is prayer answered?

The Universal Mind, the Omnipotent Power, the Supreme Being, does not change the modus operandi of the Universe, in order to comply with our requests, nor does it make exception, but it does act through well-known laws, and these laws can be placed into operation, consciously or unconsciously, by accident or design. It is the operation of this marvelous law of attraction which has caused men in all ages and in all times to believe that there must be a personal Being who responded to their petitions and manipulated events in order to meet their demands.

9. You correctly state that "Possession depends on use." How can this fact be best explained to show that this is the only way in which to acquire a "reservoir of power, possession, etc.," to draw on in time of emergency, etc.?
By illustration: A man desires to strengthen his arm. He wishes it to become powerful. He does not conserve what strength he has in the arm by binding it to his side. If he did this, he would soon lose what strength he already had. On the contrary, he begins to use it, he begins to exercise it, and he finds that the more he uses it, the more strength is secured.

The more he gives of his strength, the more he gets. The same rule applies in regard to mental and spiritual strength.

10. "Unless we are willing to think we shall have to work, and the less we think the more we shall work, and the less we shall get for our work." Is it possible to conceive of a world in which there are no "hewers of wood"?
Thought has taken much drudgery out of work, but much so-called "scientific management" and "efficiency and engineering systems" look upon millions of human beings as mere machines capable of making so many motions less or more per hour.

To labor is to serve and all service is honorable. But a "hewer of wood" contemplates blind service instead of intelligent service. Labor is the creative instinct in manifestation. Owing to the changes which have taken place in the industrial world, the creative instinct no longer finds expression. A man cannot build his own house, he cannot even make his own garden, he can by no means direct his own labor; he is, therefore, deprived of the greatest joy which can come to man, the joy of achieving, of creating, of accomplishing, and so this great power is perverted and turned into destructive channels. He can construct nothing for himself, so he begins to destroy the works of his more fortunate fellows. Labor is, however, finding that the Universe is not a chaos but a cosmos, that it is governed by immutable laws, that every condition is the result of a cause and that the same cause invariably produces the same effect. It is finding that these causes are mental, that thought predetermines action. It is finding that constructive thought brings about constructive conditions, and destructive thought brings about destructive conditions.

11. **You say that "Life is an unfoldment, not accretion; what comes to us in the world without is what we already possess in the world within." Do you not take into consideration knowledge a person acquires from books, experiences, etc.?** You can derive absolutely no benefit from books, experiences, environment or anything else until you have created brain cells capable of receiving the thought. Your world within is an exact correspondence of your world without. Suppose for the moment that you are unfamiliar with the Hebrew language. A book might be given to you with the most beautiful thoughts written in the most wonderful language, but it would mean nothing to you until you had made yourself acquainted with the Hebrew language, and so with everything else. No thought, no idea, no experience has any value for us until we are capable of receiving it. For this reason the same thought would make absolutely no impression upon one man, while it would be received with amazement and delight by another. The first man has formed no brain cells capable of receiving it.

The second man is ready for it. He understands the beauties contained in the idea.

12. Is it correct to say that true religion and true science are "twins" and that the death of one death the means the death of the other? Why?

True science and true religion are certainly twins. There can be no death for either, because what is true cannot die. "The essential characteristic of truth is steadfast fidelity to order and Law. The mind takes offence at every phenomenon of both inner and outer experience which appears to contradict that steadiness and constancy which it regards as the very essence of truth." You will see that this applies to both science and religion. What is true in science must be true in religion. There cannot be a scientific truth and a religious truth, all truth is one and indivisible.

13. How do Materialism and Spiritualism find harmony in the Master Key System?

The Master Key System teaches that there is but one Principle—One Power. That everything which exists is a materialization of this One Power. The power itself is Spiritual, but the manifestation of the Power is material. One is subjective and the other objective. Two phases of one being. We find this everywhere in Nature, Man is a spiritual being, but he also has a material body. Spirit must manifest upon the objective plane in an objective manner. The Spiritual in this sense has nothing whatever to do with what are usually considered spiritualistic phenomena.

14. What explanation is to be given of the fact that although a great majority of the people not only throughout Europe but in the United States are sick of war and want only peace and a return to prosperous normal conditions, that the return of the desired normal prosperous conditions is such a slow hard process?

There is, of course, as you say, no desire on the part of anyone for more war, just as there is no desire for poverty, crime or for any other destructive condition, but there is, on the other hand, a conscious and a subconscious desire for the things which bring about war, destruction, poverty and crime, and this lust of power or separation is the old question of "who is to be the greatest in the kingdom?"

The law is not a respecter of persons. This is true concerning nations as well as individuals. Nations as well as individuals will eventually learn that force can always be met with equal if not superior force, and for this reason can never be the determining factor of any situation.

Objective harmony can come only as a result of subjective harmony, and subjective harmony can come only as a result of vision, understanding and perception.

15. In the "Acme of Achievement" aimed at by The Master Key, how is it possible to ignore Theology?

A few centuries ago it was thought that we must choose between the Bible and Galileo. Fifty years ago it was thought that we must choose between the Bible and Darwin, but as Dean Inge, of St. Paul's Cathedral, says: "Every educated man knows that the main facts of organic evolution are firmly established, and that they are quite different from the legends borrowed by the ancient Hebrews from the Babylonians. We are not required to do violence to our reason by rejecting the assured results of modern research. Traditional Christianity must be simplified and spiritualized. It is at present encumbered by bad science and caricatured by bad economics and the more convinced we are of this, the less disposed we shall be to stake the existence of our faith on superstitions which are the religion of the irreligious and the science of the unscientific."

16. What is the meaning of the statement, "Only five percent have the vision to annex the strategic position, to see and feel a thing before it happens?"
Ninety-five percent of the people are busy attempting to change effects. Something happens which they do not like and they try to change the situation. They soon find that they are simply changing one form of distress for another. The other five percent are busily engaged with causes. They know that in order to make any permanent change it is the cause which they must seek. They soon find that the cause is within their control. It is the five percent who do the thinking, and the ninety-five percent who merely accept the thought of others. It is those only who think who can see and feel a thing before it happens.

17. What, more explicitly, is to be understood by the term "polarity" as applied to the mental process?
Polarity is the tendency or inclination of a thought or feeling in a particular direction. When we think along certain lines continuously the thought becomes polarized, we can see other and different points of view with difficulty or not at all.

18. What is Truth?
Truth is the imperative condition of all wellbeing. To be sure, to know the truth and to stand confidently on it is a satisfaction beside which no other is comparable. Truth is the underlying verity, the condition precedent to every business or social relation. Truth is the only solid ground in a world of conflict and doubt and danger.

Every act not in harmony with Truth, whether through ignorance or design, cuts the ground from under our feet, leads to discord, inevitable loss and confusion, for while the humblest mind can accurately foretell the result of every correct action, the greatest, most profound and penetrating mind loses its way hopelessly and can form no conception of the results due to a departure from correct principles.

19. How are Germs created?

Creation consists in the art of combining forces which have an affinity for each other, in the proper proportion. Thus oxygen and hydrogen combined in the proper proportions produce water. Oxygen and hydrogen are both invisible gases, but water is visible.

Germs, however, have life; they must therefore be the product of something which has life or intelligence. Spirit is the only Creative Principle in the Universe, and Thought is the only activity which spirit possesses. Therefore, germs must be the result of a mental process.

A thought goes forth from the thinker, it meets other thoughts for which it has an affinity, they coalesce and form a nucleus for other similar thoughts: this nucleus sends out calls into the formless energy, wherein all thoughts and all things are held in solution, and soon the thought is closed in a form in accordance with the character given to it by the thinker.

A million men in the agony of death and torture on the battlefield send out thoughts of hatred and distress; soon another million men die from the effect of a germ called "influenza." None but the experienced metaphysician knows when and how the deadly germ came into existence.

As there are an infinite variety of thoughts, so there are an infinite variety of germs, constructive as well as destructive, but neither the constructive nor the destructive germ will germinate and flourish until it finds congenial soil in which to take root.

20. What has given rise to the idea of Reincarnation?

The germ plasma in each generation always contains the sum of all that has passed before it. The nucleus of every cell contains the chromosomes and these reproduce the species of nature and condition according to definite law. Each chromosome, microscopically small as it is, contains the elements of every other cell in a matured body, plus characteristics of species, plus characteristics of form and appearance, plus family resemblance, plus nature, plus mind, plus matured tendencies, plus everything that makes personality and individuality. We are then physically exactly what our forefathers were, plus environment and education. It is this persistency of the identity of the individual chromosome from generation to generation which has given rise to the idea of reincarnation.

21. What is Black Magic?

The idea that there is a phenomenon called Black Magic is attributable to credulity, superstition and a lack of understanding of the laws governing in the mental world. All thoughts and all things are held in solution in the Universal Mind. The individual may open his mental gates and thereby become receptive to thoughts of any kind or description. If he thinks that there are magicians, witches or wizards who are desirous of injuring him, he is thereby opening the door for the entrance of such thoughts, and he will be able to say with Job, "The things I feared have come upon me." If, on the contrary, he thinks that there are those who are desirous of helping him, he thereby opens the door for such help, and he will find that "as thy faith is, so be it unto thee" is as true to-day as it was two thousand years ago.

22. I do not seem to grasp fully the application of the law of vibration to the thought world. How, for instance, are we to change the rate of vibration here? In what direction shall it be changed to produce best results?

Every thought changes the rate of vibration. As you are enabled to think greater, deeper, higher and more forceful thoughts, the brain cells are refined, they become more powerful, and they are enabled to receive finer vibrations.

This is not only true in the mental and spiritual world, but in the physical world. As the ear becomes trained in music, it is enabled to receive finer vibrations, until the trained musician can hear harmonies of sound of which the ordinary person is entirely unaware.

23. Amid the seeming chaos of present day conditions is it not easy to discern the coming of that dawn which all the great ones of earth have foretold, the second coming of the Millennium?

One of the characteristic signs of a general awakening is the optimism shining through the mist of doubt and unrest, this optimism is taking the form of illumination, and as the illumination becomes general, fear, anger, doubt, selfishness and greed pass away. We are not looking for the Christ child, but the Christ consciousness. We are anticipating a more general realization of the Truth which is to make men free. That there may be one man or one woman who shall first realize this Truth in the new era is barely possible, but the preponderance of evidence points to a more general awakening to the Light of Illumination.

24. You speak about the originating mind that forms, upholds, sustains and creates all there is. Does this explain the source from which comes man's ability to think lack, to think war and crime, etc.?

Yes, this includes man's ability to think lack, war and crime. If he can think constructive thought he can also think destructive thought; but as soon as man learns that thinking is a creative process, that we are creators, not creatures, he will discontinue the process of thinking destruction for himself and his fellows.

25. You are, without doubt, correct in stating that Carlyle's attitude of hatred of the bad was not conducive toward his own best development; on the other hand, what should be the attitude toward the giant evils of the day, such as war, corruption, murder, vice, theft and the like? Is it not often true that a tearing down, a clearing away of the brushwood, so to speak, must precede constructive work?

No, it is not true, the tearing down process is not at all necessary. We do not need to laboriously shovel the darkness out of a room before letting in the light; on the contrary, all that is necessary is to turn on the light and the darkness vanishes; likewise, if but one-tenth of one percent of the money and effort were spent in constructive work that is now being spent in destructive work, the giant evils of the day to which you refer would disappear as if by magic.

The unit of the Nation is the individual. The Government represents only the average intelligence of the units comprising the Nation. Therefore, our work is with the unit. When the thought of the individual has been changed the collective thought will take care of itself, but we try to reverse the process. We try to change governments instead of individuals, which cannot be done. But with a little intelligent organized effort the present destructive thought could be readily changed into constructive thought.

Temples have their sacred images, and we see what influence they have always had over a great part of mankind; but in truth, the ideas and images in men's minds are the invisible powers that constantly govern them; and to these they all pay universally a ready submission.
—JONATHAN EDWARDS.

CPSIA information can be obtained
at www.ICGtesting.com
Printed in the USA
JSHW051710220522
26021JS00002B/2